Healing

—

Honestly

Healing

—

Honestly

The Messy and Magnificent
Path to Overcoming
Self-Blame and Self-Shame

Alisa Zipursky

Berrett–Koehler Publishers, Inc

Berrett-Koehler Publishers, Inc.
1333 Broadway, Suite 1000
Oakland, CA 94612-1921
Tel: (510) 817-2277 | Fax: (510) 817-2278
www.bkconnection.com

ORDERING INFORMATION
Quantity sales. Special discounts are available on quantity purchases by corporations, associations, and others. For details, contact the "Special Sales Department" at the Berrett-Koehler address above.

Individual sales. Berrett-Koehler publications are available through most bookstores. They can also be ordered directly from Berrett-Koehler: Tel: (800) 929-2929; Fax: (802) 864-7626; www.bkconnection.com.

Orders for college textbook/course adoption use. Please contact Berrett-Koehler:
Tel: (800) 929-2929; Fax: (802) 864-7626.

Distributed to the U.S. trade and internationally by Penguin Random House Publisher Services.

Berrett-Koehler and the BK logo are registered trademarks of Berrett-Koehler Publishers, Inc.

Printed in the United States of America

Berrett-Koehler books are printed on long-lasting acid-free paper. When it is available, we choose paper that has been manufactured by environmentally responsible processes. These may include using trees grown in sustainable forests, incorporating recycled paper, minimizing chlorine in bleaching, or recycling the energy produced at the paper mill.

Library of Congress Cataloging-in-Publication Data
Name: Zipursky, Alisa, author.
Title: Healing honestly : the messy and magnificent path to overcoming
    self-blame and self-shame / Alisa Zipursky.
Description: First Edition. | Oakland, CA : Berrett-Koehler Publishers,
    [2023] | Includes bibliographical references and index.
Identifiers: LCCN 2022055252 (print) | LCCN 2022055253 (ebook) | ISBN
    9781523001408 (paperback) | ISBN 9781523001415 (pdf) | ISBN
    9781523001422 (epub) | ISBN 9781523001439 (audio)
Subjects: LCSH: Self-actualization (Psychology) | Mind and body. |
    Self-talk. | Sexual abuse victims—Psychology.
Classification: LCC BF637.S4 Z57 2023 (print) | LCC BF637.S4 (eboosk) |
    DDC 158.1—dc23/eng/20230222
LC record available at https://lccn.loc.gov/2022055252
LC ebook record available at https://lccn.loc.gov/2022055253

First Edition
30 29 28 27 26 25 24 23   10 9 8 7 6 5 4 3 2 1

Book production: Linda Jupiter Productions   *Edit:* Elissa Rabellino
Text design: Lewelin Polanco, The Cosmic Lion   *Proofread:* Mary Kanable
Cover design: Ashley Ingram   *Index:* Lieser Indexing

In loving memory of my favorite writer,
my grandmother, Charlotte Chazie Zipursky.

We wrote a book; isn't that just the nuts?

This book is dedicated to all of us.

We deserve to laugh together, rage together, grieve together,
rest together, celebrate together, and so much more.

Contents

Preface

Welcome, enthusiastic friends and understandably skeptical readers— let's get comfy

W ow, I am so thrilled you are here. I get that you might not be as jazzed as I am: I will be enthused for the both of us.

A few years ago, I began writing on the internet about what it meant for me to try to live a full and vibrant life while contending with the countless ways that child sexual abuse (CSA) impacts me. I was so tired of the intense isolation and shame that wasn't mine to hold. What I found was hundreds of thousands of people from all around the world who were also asking the same questions about how to hold two truths at the same time: we are not defined by our trauma, and also, our trauma affects every single aspect of our lives.

Through my writing, workshops, and coaching programs, I have gotten to surround myself with the transformative power of survivor-to-survivor friendships. Friendships where we can validate one another, laugh about the absurdity of living with trauma, and share strategies for learning how to put down misplaced shame and tap into deep wells of self-compassion. These friendships have fundamentally changed me. They've helped me call out all the ways survivors are taught our pain isn't real and we are to blame for how we survived. These friendships have shown me that we are all capable and worthy of living full and vibrant lives.

My goal for this book is to offer you all that I have received from my survivor-to-survivor friendships. I am here to talk with you as someone who has also been deep in the shit, who remembers what the isolation and self-blame feels like and knows that we are entitled to so much more. I am not a doctor, a therapist, or licensed in any professional capacity. I am here to be the friend who can help you identify and call bullshit on the factors that surround us, all telling us we are to blame for shit that is never our fault.

I am here to be the friend who encourages you over and over again to honor your own inner expert that tells you what you need for your own healing journey. And, perhaps the best part, I am here to be the friend who introduces you to my other dope survivor friends who have taught me so much wisdom.

I know you may be reading this with a lot of nerves. I've read many books on trauma, and each and every time I pick one up, I still feel super worried that it will be extremely triggering for me or I will read something that makes me feel like my survivorship doesn't count. It is hot garbage that we have to worry that the things meant to help us may make us feel much, much worse. As I love to say ironically: trauma is such a fun and sexy time.

So I want to tell you first thing, I have taken every step I could think of to try to make this the *least* retraumatizing book about healing from CSA that I possibly could. As a part of that effort, there will be no descriptions of any sexual abuse from me or any other survivor in the book. I also use humor, where I can, to help offer moments of levity while navigating heavy shit. We will spend less time focusing on what happened to us and much more on the *what the fuck am I supposed to do now?* of it all.

While I wish I could give you some outlandish promises about this book magically transforming you from a survivor to a thriver (which is just rhyming nonsense), that, unfortunately, is not a thing that exists. But I hope this book will make you feel less alone and more validated in your pain and experiences, and will offer clarity on why we feel the ways we feel.

With all that said, when you are ready (and hydrated!), we can move on to the next pages. Let's go at our own pace, give ourselves what we need, and take things one step at a time.

I am so glad you are here.

While I center CSA survivors, I happily welcome everyone here

All people living with trauma or supporting someone living with trauma are welcome here! I center CSA because of my experiences, and also because CSA survivors are overlooked in conversations of sexual violence and survivorship. Yet, child sexual abuse is extremely common and exists in every single community across the world. Approximately one in four girls and one in six boys experience sexual violence before their 18th birthday.[1] It's almost like people in power are actively trying to avoid talking about it! Hmm! Looks like we will be getting into all that too.

Often when I talk about child sexual abuse, people ask me if the specifics of what they experienced "count." I'm not here to offer a definition. Everyone belongs here, regardless of whether their experiences align with a particular definition of abuse. I know so many people who have found healing and support through my work who may have experienced sexual violence as adults or people who experienced nonsexual abuse as children. Everyone is welcome.

A quick word about words

I use the term *survivor* to refer to someone who has experienced child sexual abuse. I understand it's a term that lots of you may feel is not reflective of your experiences, and that is totally cool. I use it to get the idea across, not because I am interested in strict definitions. Even if it isn't a term you use to describe yourself, I hope you know that you are seen and very much welcome here.

I also use language on racial, sexual, and gender identity; social justice; and violence that is reflective of where language is in this moment in time. As adrienne maree brown wrote in *Pleasure Activism*, "If this is being read in the future in which this language has evolved, then please know I would be evolving right along with you."[2]

How to use this gorgeous, brilliant, endlessly clever book

Each chapter focuses on a different aspect of our lives that is impacted by our trauma, like friendships, sex, and family, contrasting untrue stories about survivorship with the stories that help us heal honestly.

Untrue stories

Untrue stories are inner narratives taught by society, telling us that we should feel shame and self-blame for the ways we endure and heal. They tell harmful lies: we are damaged goods, not "real" survivors; we are not worthy or capable of love and friendship. When we look this bullshit in the eye, we can understand it isn't our fault that we feel so much shame and self-blame for things that aren't our fault. We can turn the volume down on harmful bullshit and hear our own truth louder.

So how are we going to do that? In each chapter, we will explore where our untrue stories come from, asking the following questions:

- ► Who are the people, especially people I trusted, who repeated these untrue harmful stories to me?
    - Examples include: family members, friends, therapists, doctors, teachers.
- ► What cultural, institutional, and structural forces are reinforcing these untrue harmful stories?
    - Examples include: pop culture, movies/TV shows, the criminal justice system, the medical system, white supremacy, the patriarchy.

It isn't our fault that these shitty untrue stories are in our thoughts. There are so many people and systems that benefit from us feeling like we are to blame for our own abuse and that the way we live with trauma is "wrong." The truth is, our abusers benefit tremendously from making us believe we are to blame for our own trauma.

In each chapter, I will invite you to reflect on what your true stories may be. True stories remind us that we deserve not shame or judgment, but rather all the love, understanding, and support in the world.

Strategies

In this book, we'll also experience survivor-led wisdom that builds our tool kit for self-compassion and self-care. This isn't about solving a specific problem. It's about getting curious together around new ways to reduce self-blame and self-shame.

Some strategies may be right up our alley, and others might not be the right fit. Some strategies might be relevant right now, while others we may want to come back to in the future. My hope is that, in hearing different survivor perspectives, you'll be inspired to expand your own practices of self-compassion and understanding.

It'll be a better time than a root canal, but not quite as good of a time as watching *Mamma Mia!* drunk with your favorite people.

We get to embrace the mess together

As we go on this journey, you may notice that I am not sharing every detail of my story with you. You may have questions about the who/what/when/where of my timeline. I invite you to let go of those questions for now. Because the point of this book is not what happened to me then, it's about what's happening to *us* now. It's about the questions we can explore together, the wisdom we can share with one another, and the community we can cultivate right here.

Trauma is messy and nonlinear. We do not need to recount, nor may we be able to recount, all the details of our abuse in order to share our stories with each other. If people ask this of us, they are likely struggling to make sense of something that doesn't really make sense to us, either. As survivors, we may feel pressured to present our stories with color-coordinated documents of evidence and trifold diagrams depicting the timeline of our various traumas, like the world's most miserable science fair entry. It is wrong and harmful for people to demand that of us.

And so here I am to remind you, as often as you need, that our stories are our own to tell, however the hell we please. I hope that by sharing this with you, it may encourage you to see that your truth does not have to wrap up in a neat little bow for it to matter. Our stories do not have to be nice and tidy in order for other survivors to find support and healing in them.

My story is messy and incomplete, but it is all mine, and I'm grateful to get to share it with you.

Finally, I encourage you to listen to your inner expert while reading

Our healing is so specific to each of us; what I have needed in my healing will necessarily be different than what you need. I encourage you to take what is useful to you from this book and leave what isn't. You are the expert in your own safety and healing, and you know what you need, including things I may not mention in these pages. If you do not see your own experiences reflected in my words, know that it is only because of my own limitations, not a reflection of the validity of your experiences.

Whatever your emotional responses are, it is okay. You may, in one moment, feel immense relief from receiving validation you may have desired for so long and then the next moment feel grief and anger that you had to spend so many years without receiving the support you deserved. Healing, like living with trauma, is nonlinear.

The only "right way" to read this book is to listen to our inner expert about what we need and honor what it tells us. It may tell us that we want to read one chapter, then put the book down and pick it up again six months later. That's totally cool. It may tell us that we only want to read this book when we are in a certain frame of mind or physical place that makes us feel safe and good. It may tell us that after we read some, we do something self-soothing afterward.

For my fellow overachievers: you do not get a prize for powering through! There is no gold star for reading the whole book quickly! Anything involving our healing takes time: as much as we may desire it, there is no fast-forward button for our healing. So I encourage you to move at the pace your mind and body tell you is aligned with your safety and well-being. Also, I promise my jokes are funnier if you take your time.

1

You Are a Real Survivor

UNTRUE STORY
There is a "real" survivor out there, and I am not it

BUT TRUTHFULLY
Our pain is real and worthy of healing

In *The Sound of Music,* a film that had me explaining to my gentile friends way too young what Nazis were, Julie Andrews sang, "Let's start at the very beginning, a very good place to start." The best place to start is the untrue story that prevents so many of us from getting the support that we deserve. Perhaps it is even coming up for you at this moment, making you think this book isn't for you.

That untrue story sounds like this: "I am not a 'real' survivor because _____." At that underlined part right there, you can insert any of the hundreds of reasons that may be coming up for you. Maybe it's because you were harmed by a woman, or perhaps the person harmed others with greater frequency than they did you. Maybe you don't know what to call what you've been through, or you don't remember clearly what happened, or you've never told anyone about it, or perhaps your mind can think of a way of blaming yourself for the abuse. Or maybe it's for the countless other reasons I've come across.

Before we go any further, even if you swear to me that, for some reason, you are not a real survivor: your trauma is very real. Your pain is real, and it matters, no matter what you call it—I promise.

I also promise that whatever you fill in the blank with in "Mad Libs™: Rape Culture Edition! Game," you are in the best company, and it's very likely that I've heard your reason many times before. I can emphatically assure you that no matter what comes up for you, this is not your fault. You did not "invent" your untrue story. We live in a world that implicitly and explicitly tells them. Please be gentle with yourself!

I've been publicly writing about my survivorship for six years now, traveled around the country talking about CSA, and supported thousands of survivors in their healing, and yet when things feel triggering, new, scary, or challenging, this untrue story pops back in. It sounds like a record of a song that gets stuck in my head ad nauseam (think '90s dance classic "Cotton-Eyed Joe") that tells me I am not a real survivor, and maybe I'm just crazy and making this all up.

Oh, how I would love to shatter that record into a thousand little shards on the floor, but it isn't that simple. This shit runs deep. That song comes from decades of being told by our culture and people close to me that my pain wasn't real and it didn't count. The good news is, with loads of practice and strategies that I'll be sharing with you, I am able to turn the volume down on that record with increasing ease and swiftness. In these pages, we will turn the volume down together. Remember: there is no way to be good or bad at exploring our untrue stories. We are just thinking, reflecting, and practicing together.

I'm in this with you, and I didn't feel like a "real" survivor either

Since you and I just met, I want to give you a quick overview of my fun little trauma history, so you can understand where I'm coming from, while hopefully avoiding any triggers for you. Okay, I'm going to inhale deeply and try to do this all in one breath, like I'm running a live auction:

Although I spent every other weekend with my biological father ever since my parents divorced when I was a baby, I spent the vast majority of my time with my mom and loving stepfather, whom I will call Jack. My mom married Jack when I was just three years old, and he was a wonderful, supportive man who cared for me as his own child. He and my mother gave us a beautiful home in the suburbs of Washington, DC, filled with laughter, wisdom, and deep-in-the-bones kind of love.

This privileged upbringing they provided has impacted my life and healing in countless ways. Growing up around that kind of love, respect, and admiration fueled my childhood resilience. But when I was 20 years old, all of that changed. In between my sophomore and junior years of college, Jack died of cancer. His death shook every thread of safety and stability I had. In the midst of my grief, the floodgates of my dormant childhood trauma blew wide open.

In the weeks after Jack's death, I began having sporadic nightmares of my biological father sexually abusing me but wouldn't tell even my therapist about them for another two years. I was diagnosed with PTSD, founded in the trauma of Jack dying, but in retrospect I understand that the trauma I was reliving extended beyond him and was tapping into a childhood full of abuse.

Phew—okay, I'm out of breath.

I didn't talk about my trauma because I was sure that people would think I was crazy

It took two years of experiencing nightmares and other severe symptoms to tell my therapist about them. I was afraid to tell my therapist because, like so many survivors, I didn't think I was telling her my father had sexually abused me. No, I was sure I was telling her I was a sick human, because the nightmares made me fear I was complicit or cooperative. I was confident that she'd tell me I was a broken, delusional person.

Luckily, my therapist was hella trauma-informed (Thanks, Connie! You're a gem!) and immediately took what I was saying to her as an indication not that something was wrong *with* me but rather that something wrong happened *to* me. I started learning about the relationship between CSA and memory, and how it is normal for survivors to not remember clearly what happened to them but to remember via body memories.

But I still struggled with the label of *survivor*. I wanted to claim it, but it didn't feel like mine to hold. In my version of the untrue story, that word was reserved for the people who clearly remembered their abuse.

Even as I was preparing to launch HealingHonestly.com to talk openly about what it meant to be a young person healing from CSA, I feared connecting with other survivors. I'd dip my toe into Facebook groups and find myself convinced that everyone else was a "real" survivor and I didn't belong. When connecting with other public survivors, I would brace myself for the inevitable rush of internal voices that would come roaring at me that called me a fraud, a liar, and a drama queen.

Then I had a life-changing conversation over burgers with an old friend

A few months after launching the website, an old friend from college, Chris, asked me out for drinks. We hadn't seen each other in years, and over beers at a local bar in DC, he told me that he had asked to meet because he was also a survivor and had been quietly following my writing.

I was floored. While he and I had always been friendly, I had mostly seen him as a local celebrity I was lucky to know, who rose to prominence as a civil rights leader within our community while I was also busy running a large nonprofit on campus. We had both spent college admiring one another in all our overachieving tendencies, having no idea we were struggling with the same immense shit.

As Chris shared the details of his abuse, I found the familiar harmful voices swirling in my head. I was trying so hard to stay present with him but could only think of myself. I remember hearing in my head, "Now that's a *real* survivor. He knows exactly when/where/what happened to him. Not like you, you fraud."

Then Chris said something that truly changed my life. As he began to conclude the story of his abuse that he had shared with such clarity and honesty, his voice shifted into a dismissive tone as he said, "But you know, it only happened once. Not like you. Yours has happened more times." As if to say, once didn't count. Once? NBD.

Here we were, sitting inches apart in a booth across half-eaten burgers, sharing harrowing details of our experiences as children going through the worst shit, simultaneously thinking to ourselves, "Yeah, it wasn't good, but that person across from me is the *real* survivor, not me."

I nearly cried when I recognized that he was minimizing his trauma the same way as I did. When I told him I had been feeling the exact same way, we both laughed, a mixture of relief and a realization of how fucking ridiculous it is to exist in the world as CSA survivors.

Thinking I wasn't a real survivor wasn't about me and my story. If Chris could feel this way, then any of us could. That night began my journey to explore why so many of us feel like this, what forces in the world are creating this invalidating hell for survivors, and how we can hear our own truth more clearly.

I invite you to gently consider your own version of this untrue story

Do you also hear voices that say you aren't a real survivor? What do those voices sound like; what do you find them saying? Those voices can make us feel the most invalidating feelings: our pain doesn't count, we are overreacting, others won't honor our truth.

Sometimes reflecting on this untrue story can bring up old feelings that we are being overly dramatic or too sensitive, internalized messages from our childhood. "The voices in my head that tell me I'm not a 'real survivor' say that I'm just trying to get attention, that I'm looking for something that will make me 'special' or that I can use to excuse bad behavior," shared Carla, a survivor.

What is important to remember as you reflect on your own version of this untrue story is that it isn't your fault you hear this inner narrative, even if it sounds eerily like your own voice. You are not being too sensitive. You are not exaggerating. Your pain is real and it matters.

This is usually the point in reading a book about trauma that my anxiety poops start coming on. So if that's happening for you, please, for the love of God, take a break, go to the bathroom, hit up the Imodium or a ginger tea, and take your time continuing on. We will still be here post–bubble gut.

What are the origins of the bullshit?

There are people I trusted who reinforced my untrue story

The people closest to us can have the greatest impact on our thinking. The super bummer is that these people often have repeated our untrue stories and may cause us to feel more shame and blame.

My people who added to my feeling that I wasn't a real survivor were my family members (now extremely supportive, but not then). When I first told them what I was going through when I was 23, I felt comfortable disclosing that I suspected my father had sexually abused me. I hoped they would take my words and rally around me and support my decision to cut him out of my life. It seemed simple, especially because my parents hadn't been married since I was a baby, and it was no secret to my mom's family that my dad hadn't been a good parent.

But what I received for the next four years was a series of invalidating questions like, "Well, how do you really know this happened?" and actions that showed me that my family didn't think of me as a survivor, including not respecting my need to have zero contact with my father.

Knowing what I know now, from supporting thousands of other survivors dealing with CSA within their families, is that our family's resistance has to do with them, not us. In the case of my family, they were invalidating my survivorship because it was too painful for them to process that they had failed to protect me from this pain. During those years, they denied my abuse because of the shame they felt over not having stopped this from happening to a child they loved. Unfortunately for me, their shame was contagious and caught onto me, even though it wasn't mine to hold.

I know I am not alone in having experiences with family members that leave us feeling like maybe our trauma wasn't real. Bryanna, a CSA survivor, shared with me, "When I told my mom for the first time that I thought I was sexually abused, she called me a liar and said that my therapist was feeding me this information. She then went on to tell my family lies about my experience and created her own narrative. This negative experience in sharing my story makes me doubt whether I am a real survivor."

It is important that we can recognize with whom our need for validation lies. Is there a person, or people, in your life who you think hold the key to making you feel like you're a real survivor? In what ways do you think their response was about you, and in what ways was their response motivated by their own shame, ignorance, or other feelings? By thinking critically about the role that people close to us have played in our self-doubt, we can begin to see that the self-doubting narrative isn't actually ours and that their words are not rooted in our truth.

We can move that validation inward onto ourselves (yes, it is really hard!), regardless of other people's feelings. It's okay if that doesn't feel like a possibility for you right now—remember, we have nine-and-a-half more chapters together. So don't worry, my friend, we have lots of time to get into these really complicated feelings—I know, what a fun time to look forward to!

The myth of the perfect survivor is everywhere

Across popular culture, the legal system, and even some survivor advocacy spaces, we see the myth of the perfect victim, which says that there is a "good" survivor worthy of attention, justice, support, and healing, and then there's everyone else. The privileges we hold directly correspond to the impact of the myth. Because I'm a cisgender hetero college-educated white woman from money, my privileges mean that I am punished less for my departures from the myth.

Still, the myth of the perfect survivor is relevant to everyone. There isn't a single survivor whose story holds up under these pop culture standards of who is a real victim.

HERE'S WHAT THE MYTHICAL PERFECT VICTIM LOOKS LIKE

The mythical, nonexistent perfect victim is a white cisgender heterosexual woman. She remembers exactly what happened and has irrefutable evidence. She is well-educated, can perfectly articulate her harm with the *right* kind of emotion to demonstrate that she is upset and was harmed, but is not so emotional that she appears unstable and hysterical.

She immediately reported what happened to the police, using the correct tones to tug at heartstrings but seem like she was really injured, with the evidence neat and organized but not too organized, or else, like, that's not realistic, right? She would like her abuser to be in prison for the rest of his life. She has never gotten into any "trouble" before or spoken a negative word about any living thing in her life. She also has never expressed any interest in her sexuality and doesn't even have knowledge about sex other than being vigilant about the risk of sexual violence.

She goes to talk therapy and does yoga and doesn't self-medicate with alcohol, plant-based medicine, or any other drugs. She talks about what happened to her not too much, but just enough to seem palatable and safe for people. She does not challenge any systems of power: family, workplace, criminal justice system, or patriarchy. She publicly forgives the person who harmed her and doesn't seem too angry (but also not too indifferent and cold!) and leaves her trauma "in the past." She's no longer a survivor; she's a thriver! Also, she shits rainbows and pees liquid gold and recently cured cancer. Mazel tov to her!

Every single one of us deviates in some, or many, ways from this description. If it weren't one aspect of our survivorship, then it would be something else. The world would point and say, okay, but for *this* reason you are not worthy of support, validation, and justice. Deviating from this mythic victim isn't a bad thing, even though the world tries to tell us it is!

As well as the myth of the perfect victim, we also have the myth of the boogeyman abuser. These two myths uphold one another.

HERE'S WHAT THE MYTHICAL BOOGEYMAN ABUSER LOOKS LIKE

The mythical boogeyman abuser is a cisgender man who is a stranger to the victim. The man who harmed her is generally considered to be a bad person with zero redeemable qualities, with a long proven rap sheet of harming people. No one loves him; no one even thinks of him in a neutral way. He is not in any meaningful positions of power or a valued member of any communities. He is low-income and uneducated. The myth of the boogeyman abuser is a tool of white supremacy, and therefore the mythical boogeyman abuser is a man of color, specifically a Black man. When he goes to prison, no one will weep for him or have any compassion for the inhumane treatment he may find while incarcerated.

These two myths are a binary

In this myth, someone is either a victim or an abuser and cannot have both been victimized and also caused harm. Which, as you may have already guessed, is absolute hot garbage bullshit.

The myth of this victim/abuser binary means that we, as survivors, are not supposed to see the humanity in the person who harmed us and should only see them as a monster. This can make us feel guilty if we have feelings of compassion or positive memories of the person who harmed us. The idea that we are supposed to feel a certain way about the people who harmed us is nonsense! However you feel, no matter how conflicting it may be inside you, is never, ever wrong.

We do not need to be perfectly good, nor our abuser perfectly evil, for our pain to be real and matter.

Many people who sexually abuse children were themselves sexually abused as kids. It's super hard to talk about, which of course means we'll talk about it much more! This isn't to say that having been sexually abused justifies our abusing someone else or makes us fated to repeat abuse. No, never! But the binary of victim/abuser makes it impossible for us to have honest conversations about abuse, and it can feel so silencing when we reckon with the fact that victims aren't perfect humans and abusers may themselves also have been victims.

Why does the perfect-victim/boogeyman-abuser myth exist?

This myth makes it easier for people and systems of power to ignore the violence we experience at epidemic rates and not have to face the role they've played in allowing the violence to continue. If people and institutions can find a way to say, "Well, maybe this person isn't very believable or credible" or "That abuser isn't a person, he's a monster," then they don't have to face the reality that (1) child sexual abuse exists in every community and is common in families, and (2) we live in a culture that allows for it to continue.

This myth is all around us. It comes up when a male survivor publicly shares his story and people say that because of his gender, he can't actually be a victim. It comes up when people dismiss and joke about the sexual violence that occurs in prisons. It comes up when people adamantly resist finding out that some beloved celebrity or politician sexually harmed someone else. What's an example of where you've seen this myth played out?

How do race, gender identity, and sexual orientation intersect with the myth of the perfect victim?

While all of us are negatively impacted by this myth, we are not all equally impacted. Forms of oppression, including homophobia, transphobia, white supremacy, classism, and ableism, all come into play within the myth.

Countless stories of perfect white women victimhood were made up to justify lynching Black people, as in the case of Emmett Till, a Black boy lynched because white people claimed he spoke to a white woman. In many cases, the white woman victim story was also created to deny the truth of consenting interracial relationships. Victimhood was co-opted to uphold white supremacy and patriarchy. This history is still very much alive today, where survivors of color are even more ruthlessly invalidated, and the abstract idea of victimized white women is used as a talking point to defend a racist incarceration system.

Society erases survivors who were harmed by women, survivors who are trans, survivors who are nonbinary, and survivors who are men. To quote the musical *Spring Awakening*: It's totally fucked. This is particularly wild when talking about child sexual abuse because it is nearly as likely to happen to boys as to girls. Again, approximately one in four girls and one in six boys experience sexual violence before their 18th birthday.[1] My website's readership is slightly more than half men.

This narrow way of thinking of gender and who gets to be a victim leaves huge swaths of CSA survivors invalidated and without sufficient healing resources. Parker, a male CSA survivor, put it this way: "There are very few groups and places to talk about CSA, but ones geared specifically towards male-identified folks just simply don't exist. So we're stuck in a cycle of wanting help but being unable to find it." Robby describes this dynamic leaving him hardly ever feeling understood. "I constantly feel guilty when I share my experience with others—I feel like others will only see it as attention- seeking, or selfish, or dramatic, and so I rarely share. I have never met another adult male survivor of child abuse in person, or at least one that I know of, because we don't talk about it."

Jaden Fields, the codirector of Mirror Memoirs, a national abolitionist organization intervening in rape culture by uplifting the narratives, healing, and leadership of BIPOC LGBTQIA child sexual abuse survivors, explained to me, "Gender nonconformity is a risk factor for sexual abuse." In accordance with a 2012 study conducted by the American Academy of Pediatrics, specifically male-assigned children between ages 7 and 11 who are gender nonconforming are six times more likely to be sexually abused than their gender-conforming peers.[2]

Transphobia and homophobia tell a lie that people who are queer and/ or trans are somehow more likely to be predatory and sexually abuse children. This lie was created and is perpetuated to justify the oppression of queer and trans people. The reality is that people who are queer and/or trans are at greater risk of being victims.

"If we follow that number that they are six times more likely, then that means likely most male-assigned people who were gender nonconforming as kids, most trans women, and most nonbinary male-assigned people were sexually abused as children. Yet, so much of the survivor-led work centers the idea that the most vulnerable are cis gender white girls," shared Jaden.

Jaden explained that not only does the myth of the perfect survivor fail and harm anyone who deviates from it, but also the myth completely erases the history of the movement to end sexual violence. "In 1866, Frances Thompson, a formerly enslaved Black trans woman, was the first person on record who ever testified about her rape before a congressional committee in the United States," he said. LGBTQIA survivors of color have always been on the forefront of advocating for the rights of survivors and an end to sexual violence.

The myth also completely ignores the fact that children with disabilities are three times more likely to be sexually abused than their peers without disabilities. (That rate is even higher among children with intellectual or mental health disabilities.³) "Ableism is a system that creates this idea of what is a good, right kind of body and mind and 'other,' and the other is made to be seen as bad, unhealthy, difficult, something to fix, something to dismiss," Jaden said. "So many disabled children are targeted because, due to ableism, children with disabilities are seen as the kinds of kids adults aren't going to listen to or believe."

What does it feel like for you to consider your own story in the context of the myth of the perfect victim? Beyond the myth of the perfect victim and perfectly villainous abuser, what are other cultural or institutional forces that you see at play in your untrue story?

Elizabeth, a survivor in New Zealand, shared how those feelings have come up for her: "I have a sensitive claim with ACC, the government-funded accident compensation system in New Zealand, because of an event that I can remember involving a man taking advantage of me as an adult. The terrible thing is that I've come to feel grateful for that event because if it hadn't happened, I probably wouldn't have received financial support. But all along, the bit that really hurts me is the harm that happened in the hazy mess of my childhood. It is the abuse that I can feel but cannot remember. I know the ACC would not have recognized that pain. So, how can I?"

Of course we feel invalidated when people and systems that we rely on for our healing and well-being do not recognize our pain. It is important that you know the blame is squarely on the failure of those systems, and not because any part of what you've been through isn't real and important. The system is fucked up, not you!

Strategies

Let's get into some strategies; but trust your instincts about what feels helpful and what doesn't feel right. Maybe you'll think of a creative new way of dealing with this untrue story that never would've dawned on me, and that's totally wonderful.

STRATEGY: If you're asking if it was "bad enough," the answer is yes, I promise

The first strategy is a simple one, but its beauty is in its simplicity: If you find yourself asking if it was "bad enough," the answer is yes, I promise.

These feelings of minimization can run deep. KP told me, "I feel terrible even feeling affected by it when I am aware that so many survivors have experienced so much more distressing and ongoing abuse than me." Jude described it in this way: "I often feel like I am not a real survivor and feel like the abuse I suffered wasn't bad enough to be classed as a survivor," these feelings having made her uncomfortable accessing healing resources, adding, "I have felt guilty about seeking help because I thought there were other people who needed more than me."

Nearly every survivor I know has some version of these feelings. I encourage each of us to push back on the scarcity mindset that tells us there is a limited amount of compassion, understanding, and support out there. All of us are deserving. We are conditioned to believe that asking for anything is too much, but that just isn't true. There is no finite amount of compassion in this world, and there's no limit on how much of it you deserve.

If you are wondering often if it was "bad enough," I find it can help to complete the sentence. For example, "Was my experience bad enough to _____ [insert here: justify creating and maintaining boundaries / warrant

the traumatic responses my body is having / devote energy to healing, etc.].
In coaching, when people worry that what happened to them wasn't bad
enough, I ask, "Bad enough to what?" That often helps us get to the root of
some of the ways they're feeling shamed for surviving and healing.

However you are feeling, if you find yourself asking whether it was bad
enough, the answer is yes. It was bad enough to justify needing to prioritize
your own safety. It was bad enough for you not to feel like you're overreacting or being dramatic in the traumatized ways your body is responding.
It was bad enough for you to be worthy of healing and all that healing can
bring you. You no longer need to minimize your feelings and your body's
response to what you've been through.

STRATEGY: We can use whatever language feels right to us today

Your trauma is just as real whether you feel comfortable using the term *victim* or not. So use the words that feel right to you at any particular moment
in time. Terms like *survivor, victim,* and *CSA* can mean different things to
different people. The key thing is that your pain is real, and it matters, no
matter what you call it.

If you're struggling with what words to use, remember that you aren't
alone! Eleni described her own struggles with the terms: "I don't feel like my
experiences fit into the boxes of 'child sexual abuse' or 'rape,' and I feel like
a liar when I say I was sexually assaulted. I know what people assume happened to me when I use that term, and my reality doesn't fit into the narrow
definition most people think of."

I've found in my own journey that there were years when I felt comfortable saying something traumatic and abusive happened to me, but I wasn't
comfortable calling myself a survivor or even using the term *CSA*. My resistance to those terms came from a lot of places, including that minimizing
my own abuse was a coping strategy that I relied on my entire childhood in
order to get through it and keep the peace in my family, as well as fearing that
my story didn't count, since I couldn't remember clearly what happened. I
also resisted the term *CSA* because I feared it meant being fated to a certain
terrible life. The stigma of survivorship was scary to me.

"If you would have asked me two years ago if I was sexually abused as a
child, I would have definitely said not. For the past year and a half, I would

have a different answer for you depending on the day: 'Yes,' 'Maybe,' 'A little,' 'Probably,' 'I'm not sure' . . . Overall, I have a hard time calling myself a survivor," Stephanie shared with me.

I don't care what words you use! Whether any particular words fit you or not, please validate your own truth.

STRATEGY: Let's all tap into some much-needed self-compassion

The last strategy is to tap into self-compassion when you notice that the untrue story is coming up loud in your mind. I know from myself and also from the survivor community that we often have an uncanny ability to blame ourselves for shit that isn't our fault, which stems from experiencing a lot of misplaced blame for our trauma.

When you hear the inner narrative say you aren't a real survivor, I encourage you to not get frustrated. Healing is nonlinear. Maybe you go through whole months feeling confident in your survivorship, and then something happens and you feel like you are back to questioning the validity of your own experience. While being extremely frustrating, it is also a totally normal experience!

As I mentioned earlier, I can still hear that inner narrative in myself. Instead of feeling bad that after all my years of working on my healing I still hear a voice saying, "Hey bitch, maybe you're making this all up," or seeing that voice as a sign that I haven't healed "enough," can I see it as an indication that I'm doing something difficult and triggering? If yes, then can I teach myself to associate that voice with needing to be extra loving, gentle, and affirming to myself? Remember, there is nothing wrong *with* us. Instead, something wrong happened to us, and that's why we are hearing these crappy voices.

If you need help tapping into that self-compassion, think about how, even if you don't know other publicly out survivors, you are surrounded in this world by other people feeling the exact same way as you. Perhaps you are a data person—that's cool! Here's some data for you:

I put out a Google Forms survey in 2019 that I kept open for a few months and asked anyone who identified as a CSA survivor to fill it out. In the survey, 949 people checked off whether the untrue stories I listed were ones they heard in their own heads. Here are some stats for my number-loving friends:

- ▶ "Maybe I'm just crazy."—75 percent
- ▶ "It wasn't that bad, and it could've been worse."—69 percent
- ▶ "There's a real survivor out there, and I am not it."—55 percent

My hope is that you can look at these numbers and see them as just a snapshot indication of how you're not alone. In my little Healing Honestly CSA survivor world, worrying that we aren't "real" survivors is one of the most unifying challenges we experience! I want you to know that you are in the best company—there are so many people you don't know who've got your back. We know you aren't crazy. We know your pain is real and it matters, and you are worthy of support and healing. And hopefully, reading this over whenever you need it can be a strategy that helps you tap into that compassion and kindness toward yourself that I wish so deeply for you.

As you continue to process your own untrue story, it may feel discouraging to consider how much bullshit we have directed toward us that makes it so difficult for us to stand in our truth. Simply put, we shouldn't have to go through all of this. Remember, no matter what, you aren't alone in your feelings, and it is not your fault that this is so hard.

It is natural to wish for affirmation from people close to us and the world around us: we deserve it. But I want you to know that no matter how loud that record that says you aren't a real survivor is playing in your head, you are worthy and capable of support and healing.

Who here could use a nap?

Take a breather. Get a bite to eat, lie down, go get some fresh air, and do whatever feels soothing and good to you, because reading this chapter, asking these questions of yourself, is genuinely hard work. If you're feeling exhausted or your brain is swirling, take a break! These words will still be here, I promise—the other nine chapters aren't going anywhere. When you're ready, whether it's in an hour or a year, turn the page and we will continue on together.

2

Our Brains Are
Protecting Us

UNTRUE STORY
We have to remember our abuse clearly in order to heal from it

BUT TRUTHFULLY
Whatever we remember right now is enough for us to heal

Welcome back, friend! You've made it through the first chapter (or you're skipping around—shhh, I won't tell anyone), and you've come back to dive into one of my most favorite sexiest and flirtiest topics: traumatic memory. I promised you fun, and I dare you to identify anything more fun than the intersection of neuroscience and trauma.

Along with *Golden Girls* trivia and women's soccer, learning about traumatic memory has become a hobby for me. Sadly, there is so much pseudoscience garbage on the internet about traumatic memory, and for many years I was triggered by what I googled. But when I started sharing my fears about my lack of memory with other survivors, I became passionate about the topic.

It is a normal, scientifically explained response to CSA to not clearly remember our abuse. There are so many of us out there whose bodies remember our abuse, but our conscious minds may not recall clearly what happened to us.

We've lived lives where we've been systematically told to distrust ourselves and our bodies. But when we peel back the layers, at our core we have all the information we need. In my experience, healing doesn't come from discovering new information about abuse, but rather from learning how to give ourselves permission to trust in ourselves and the memories stored in our bones. I invite you to consider the idea of cultivating and strengthening our self-trust, along with the radical but simple idea that we may have all the knowledge we need in order to accept our truth.

I'm in this with you, and I used to think I had to remember more in order to heal

Let's start by going back to 2017, which was about a year after I launched HealingHonestly.com. I had been publishing my stories out on the internet about being in my 20s and struggling to heal from CSA while also dating, having friends, and generally trying to have a full life. I started to receive messages from other survivors around the world who were connecting with my writing and sharing their stories with me.

It felt so incredible to know that by simply telling the truth in my own words, I was able to make someone else feel less alone. But that awesome realization was always followed by a dose of some stone-cold bummer feelings that, despite the name of the website, I wasn't being totally honest. I worried that I was gaining readers who, if they knew my truth, would recognize me as the fraud I feared I was deep down, because I had not yet shared with them the fact that I didn't have any clear memories of my abuse.

Now you may (understandably) be thinking, "What the fuck is she talking about—how does she know she's a survivor if she doesn't remember what happened?" It's okay, because it's a question I'm quite familiar with myself!

As I mentioned in the last chapter, when I was 20 years old, my stepfather, Jack, died. My trauma over his death also triggered a previously repressed trauma of my biological father abusing me.

With Jack no longer alive to offer me emotional safety and stability, my trauma floodgates burst wide open.

These symptoms and experiences are super unpleasant, so I am going to, for everyone's sake, rush through them a bit so that you can understand what I am trying to communicate without my bumming you the hell out or triggering you. Feel free to skip the next paragraph, which has a content warning for traumatic symptoms.

I had constant nightmares of my father sexually abusing me, and what was particularly excruciating about them was that often I wasn't fighting back in the dreams, which made me feel deep shame, like I was sick and perverse (self-victim-blaming knows no bounds!). Those nightmares grew in such frequency that they were no longer limited to when I was asleep, and while I was awake I continued to see flashes of my father sexually abusing me. It got so bad that not only could I not safely have any sort of sexual contact with another person without being triggered, but I couldn't masturbate or even nonsexually touch myself, like when showering, or wipe my goddamn ass on the toilet without being triggered. I was walking around with a trauma bomb inside me that exploded at any moment, from any trigger, all the fucking time.

If you've experienced this sort of resurgence of your trauma, you know this shit is miserable, and I am so sorry you had to go through that. It may have left you wanting to scream, "What the hell? Why now?!"

It took me a year of struggling from my nightmares in silence to confide in my therapist. I was so sure she was going to tell me I was sick and broken and needed intense reprogramming. Instead, she met me with deep compassion and a message that my mind and body didn't make up these trauma symptoms, but rather, they were trying to communicate some critical information to me.

When I found it hard to discuss my father with my therapist, I realized, to my horror, that there were huge multiyear gaps in my memory of my childhood. With remembering so little, I learned, over time and with lots of practice, to focus on what I did remember and know:

I remember, as a child, crying for days before and after I'd visit my father. I remember daydreaming about running away when I was with him. I remember being 10 years old and telling a child psychologist that I fantasized about him peacefully, painlessly dying. Equally important for me was to learn to pay attention to all I had no memory of—not just the sexual violence, but also that I did not have a single memory of ever feeling safe when I was near my father.

Even though I had all the knowledge I needed, I had such a difficult time believing that he could've sexually abused me without my having a memory of it. I knew all the trauma math added up, in that truly the only logical conclusion from what I had experienced mentally, emotionally, and physically was that my father had sexually abused me, but I felt I couldn't stand firmly in that truth without any real memory of any particular incident. I didn't know, like I do now, that this was a completely normal traumatic memory response to CSA.

I felt so isolated by my untrue story that I couldn't be open about my CSA without having clear memories of it. I wanted to share with friends about what I was going through but was so afraid they'd think I was a liar or making it up. I wanted to try connecting with other survivors but found myself constantly comparing my own story with theirs. I was still holding on to the lie of the perfect survivor and was so concerned about how my story didn't hold up to that mythic idea.

Then, one day in March 2017, I decided that I was done tiptoeing around the discomfort I felt about memory and my own story of abuse, and I published a story I had written, called, "What It's Like to Remember What You Can't Remember." In it, I described my journey to accepting the undeniable truth that I had been sexually abused, and parts of my brain might never remember it clearly, but my body perfectly remembered what happened. I explained that my body had been reenacting and reliving my abuse over and over again. I compared the experience to knowing all the moves to the '90s dance craze the Macarena, yet having no memory of ever learning the steps, and my body was obligated to perform the dance whenever the music played. I had no control over when the song played and no control over my body's movements when I heard it. My body had a mind of its own and had to relive the dance over and over again. I described the time-traveling nature of traumatic memory—how you aren't really remembering something in the past but rather reliving it as though it's happening in real time, as a truly terrible party trick that nobody wants.

I never expected the thousands of supportive messages that I received from around the world of people just like me who were struggling with knowing they had been sexually abused while not having a clear narrative memory. I read countless emails that started with "I've never told anyone this, but . . . " as they described their traumatic memories and fears that they were losing their minds. They shared with me their overwhelming relief to learn that they weren't crazy and they weren't alone. Many people have told me that reading the article saved their life.

Then the wildest fucking thing happened! Truly wild, fucking crazy. Six months after I posted that story, the contemporary iteration of Tarana Burke's #MeToo Movement blew the fuck up, and the traffic on my memory story went completely bananas. In the following months, as conversations around sexual violence were inescapable and it seemed like a whole swath of the world was in a perpetual state of being triggered (through no fault of their own!), a lot of people, for the first time, were processing the reality that they had experienced sexual violence that their bodies were reliving, even if their minds didn't remember it clearly. My inbox was flooded with messages from survivors around the world—teenagers and, more surprising to me, people in their 60s and 70s who, for the first time, were sharing with someone (me!) that they believed they had been sexually abused but felt crazy, since they didn't remember it clearly. It was the perfect example of how doing something that was aligned with my healing ended up supporting other people in their healing, too, and being this bomb-ass cycle of validation.

Whether you want to put your business all over the internet, like this messy bitch right here, or you want to keep your truth to the privacy of your own mind and body, every survivor deserves to feel the solidarity and peace that come from knowing that other survivors also have bodies that remember more than their minds, and still trust themselves.

I invite you to consider your own untrue stories about memory and CSA

There are a lot of ways traumatic memory can look for each of us. I asked a few survivors to share with you the different ways memory has worked for them:

"I don't have clear or complete visual memories of my abuse, both because the abuse occurred at a young age and because I disassociated. It took me a long time to understand that this didn't mean the abuse never occurred. Through body memories, flashbacks, and nightmares, I have come to learn more about the extent of the abuse, although doubt still lingers. Sometimes, even right after a flashback, I would start to question the validity of the flashback and wonder if I was just losing my mind," Nell recalled.

"My memory of the events is very unclear, and it doesn't all add up. However, I have very clear body memories and can remember bizarre details about the most random things in that moment. For example, the exact way the sun was coming through the curtains," said KP.

"I have also had periods of time when I was so set on remembering everything and could not, then I would get frustrated and doubt myself, as I couldn't remember exactly every detail and I felt I needed to," Sarah Joy told me. "The fact that I have a great memory when it comes to everything for my entire life was truly hard for me to deal with before counseling and learning the process of healing."

Whether your traumatic memory looks like any of these examples, or it manifests in a completely different way, know that your traumatic memory is real! You did nothing to "cause" the way your mind and body are and are not remembering your trauma. You are capable and deserving of healing, no matter how much you remember.

What are the origins of the bullshit?

Therapists who made things worse for us by failing to properly understand traumatic memory

When I think about the people I trusted who repeated my untrue story to me, the first people who come to mind are shitty therapists and psychiatrists. A few years back, I went through a nightmare experience of searching for a new therapist after my previous one retired.

Over the course of a couple of weeks, I found myself in the offices of no fewer than three potential new therapists who approached my survivorship in a way that triggered the shit out of me. The first asked me to try to place childhood experiences in chronological order, and I felt like a fraud when I couldn't recall any of the things she was asking me. She kept asking how I knew I was abused, and I left feeling like she thought I was a liar and an object of fascination. The visit with the second therapist went similarly. By the time the third therapist asked me how I could know I was abused without clear memory, I replied, "Because I know. And if that isn't enough for you, then we aren't going to work well together."

The damage of meeting with all those trauma-ill-informed therapists fucked me up for a while. They were in positions of power and authority and deemed my understanding of my survivorship insufficient. They acted as though they were entitled to details of my abuse, and as if those details are remotely relevant to my healing all these years later (to be clear, they aren't).

Since that experience, I've met so many other survivors who have found themselves in the offices of therapists, psychiatrists, and other doctors who are still spewing outdated, scientifically invalidated ideas about memory and abuse.

"I had one therapist who didn't really understand trauma and body memories, and unfortunately, at the time, neither did I," Elizabeth shared with me. "She would look for other ways to explain my physical sensations, including suggesting I go to the doctor to talk about fibromyalgia and going off hormonal contraception. It made me quite panicky about my health because I started to turn all of my sensations of the body memories into something physically wrong with me."

Carla recalled, "When I started looking for EMDR practitioners, I had only recently begun to acknowledge my history and didn't feel comfortable telling my story with the certainty I do now. At the beginning of a consultation with a potential therapist, I told her I 'thought' I had been abused as a child. Later in the appointment, she used that one word to cast doubt on the evidence I brought forward to support my very strong feelings that I had experienced abuse, and listed off all the other reasons I might be feeling this way. I walked out of that appointment and almost stopped looking for a therapist. Thankfully I didn't, and now I have a practitioner who never questions my experience even on the occasions when I do."

It's important that you know this: if you've found yourself in one of these therapy sessions from hell, it just means your therapist literally does not know what the fuck they're doing, and get your ass out of there! If a therapist is making you feel like a fraud or like you are a fascinating science experiment, get the fuck out!

It's so fucked up how hard it is to find (or afford) any therapist, let alone a decently trauma-informed one. But you deserve to feel seen, validated, and understood in your therapeutic partnership.

The False Memory Syndrome Foundation—the worst, most nightmare bananas organization to fuel our untrue stories about CSA and memory

Now is the time when I tell you the story of the False Memory Syndrome Foundation (FMSF), and my blood boils with a righteous rage. This is a tale full of hot garbage.

The FMSF was a nonprofit established in 1992 by Pamela and Peter Freyd, a married couple, in response to their adult daughter privately telling them that she had recovered memories of her father, Peter, sexually abusing her as a child.[1] That daughter is Jennifer Freyd, PhD, the founder of the Center for Institutional Courage and a renowned expert on the psychology of sexual violence and CSA.

Pamela Freyd, a schoolteacher, and Peter Freyd, a mathematician, founded the FMSF specifically to invalidate their daughter's private accusations. Peter was sexually abused as a boy and appears to have weaponized his survivorship to invalidate that of his daughter, Jennifer. They recruited other accused parents along with psychologists and scientists to join their efforts. The FMSF created the diagnosis of "false memory syndrome." "False memory syndrome is mostly rhetorical and political, and is not a scientifically validated syndrome," Jennifer Freyd explained to me. "You are not going to find it in any established diagnostic guidelines."

Let's take a beat to process the infuriating information I just laid before you. Parents, in response to their adult child confronting them about her CSA, decide not just to deny the harm they caused her, but also to make up a fake diagnosis in order to say that medically, scientifically, their daughter and other survivors are liars! This is some next-level gaslighting and a steaming-hot pile of shit.

I KNOW, THIS SHIT IS WILD, AND IT BAFFLES MANY OF US

If you're wondering right now how on earth there were providers that took FMSF seriously and didn't just immediately call bullshit on this completely transparent attempt of parents to deny their own history of sexually abusing children, then you are not alone.

In 1992, Judith Herman, MD, a psychiatrist and sexual violence expert, first published the groundbreaking book *Trauma and Recovery*, in which she discussed traumatic memory, especially within the context of CSA. In it she explained, "Traumatic events may sever these normally integrated functions from one another. The traumatized person may experience intense emotion but without clear memory of the event, or may remember everything in detail but without emotion. She may find herself in a constant state of vigilance and irritability without knowing why."[2]

Five years later, Dr. Herman wrote an afterword for the 1997 edition of her book, where she reflected how her work around traumatic memory had become deeply controversial, due, in large part, to the FMSF bullshit. She wrote,

> Advocates of accused perpetrators have argued that complaints based on delayed recall should be dismissed out of hand, because recovered memories cannot possibly be true. . . . When these arguments were first proposed several years ago, I found them almost ludicrously implausible, and thought that their frank appeal to prejudice would be transparent at once. The women's movement had just spent twenty years deconstructing the presumption that women and children are prone to lie, fantasize, or fabricate stories of sexual violation. . . . Yet once again, here were eminent authorities proclaiming that victims are too weak and foolish to know their own minds. Hadn't we just gone through all of this? Did we really need to go through it again? Apparently the answer was yes.[3]

I don't know about you, but it helps me when reading about this stuff to know that there were experts out there, like Dr. Herman, who were calling out the absurdity of a fake diagnosis developed so that people who sexually abused children could deny that they ever had. This shit is crazy and infuriating.

UNFORTUNATELY, THE FMSF WAS
VERY GOOD AT BEING VERY BAD

While the FMSF wasn't the first organization established by accused parents to try to discredit CSA survivors, it certainly was the most effective. As reporter Mike Stanton explained in a 1997 article on the organization in the *Columbia Journalism Review*, "As controversial memory cases arose around the country, FMSF boosters contacted journalists to pitch the false-memory argument, more and more reporters picked up on the issue, and the foundation became an overnight media darling."[4] Members of the FMSF would call up journalists who were writing stories on CSA to encourage them to include their nonscientific "false memory syndrome" diagnosis in their articles. "The press seemed to be tired of hearing about victims and eager to take the side of those who insisted that they had been wrongly accused," Dr. Herman wrote in her 1997 afterword.[5]

The PR worked: One study published by University of Michigan (not the time but, Go Blue!) sociologist Katherine Beckett, PhD, found a sharp shift in how the four leading newsmagazines treated CSA. In 1991, more than 80 percent of the coverage was weighted toward supporting survivors, and recovered memory was respected and not invalidated. By 1994, more than 80 percent of the coverage of CSA focused on false allegations and "false memory." Beckett credits the FMSF with that shift.[6] This fills me with the fire of a thousand suns.

When I see Dr. Beckett's numbers, on the one hand, I feel a sense of clarity that this suspicion I had of the harm of the FMSF is real and tangible, but on the other hand, I feel so furious and heartbroken knowing how harmful this work has been to millions of survivors just like me. Because while we may be able to see metrics on how the media landscape shifted against CSA survivors, the pain that shift has caused survivors is incalculable.

The FMSF was dissolved in 2019. My understanding is that the organization called it quits due to the aging of its founders and because donations dried up. At the time of the FMSF's dissolution, they publicly stated that they stood by their work. Peter and Pamela Freyd have never publicly acknowledged their lies, their fake science, nor the tremendous harm they've caused their daughter and millions of others.

While the organization is donezo, its terrible impact will continue to reverberate throughout society for many years to come. Recently, I received a concerned text from a survivor friend who, while watching a network medical drama, had to endure a story line in which "false memory syndrome" in the context of CSA was actually a thing, not a made-up, scientifically unfounded diagnosis.

"Between 1992, when the foundation was launched, and December 2019, when it abruptly shuttered, it bolstered the defense strategy employed by countless sex offenders, from Michael Jackson to Bill Cosby and Harvey Weinstein. Today, the notion that one's own memories of sexual violence are unreliable is owed, in large part, to how the Freyds responded to their daughter," explained *New York Magazine* writer Katie Heaney in her 2021 article "The Memory War."[7]

The legacy of the FMSF is why it's hard to find an informed health care professional. Despite the lack of scientific evidence, the concept of false memory is all over psychology textbooks and is still taught in many universities. It's a fucking enraging mess.

WE ARE LEFT TO DEAL WITH THE LEGACY OF THIS TOTAL NONSENSE GARBAGE

I know far too many survivors who came forward about their CSA, and then family members brought up the possibility that they had false memory syndrome, unaware of where that rhetorical, political, and unscientific diagnosis came from. Fear of the fake diagnosis leads survivors to isolate and stay silent about their experiences.

As Max put it, "I remember when things first started to emerge for me, my first line of denial was, 'Well, I know that false memory is vastly more common than true recovered memory, so it's much more logical that . . . ,' and when my therapist very gently asked, 'Where do you know that from?' I couldn't answer. I'm a feminist who has a PhD in psychiatric genetics, but

I didn't even think that there was a source to scrutinize. That's how much power there was. That's how much some people wanted survivors' voices to be silenced." I don't blame any survivor for being triggered or silenced by the lie of the false memory syndrome: experiences like Max's are all too common.

The psychology field is reckoning with its own past around what some have coined "The Memory Wars," especially with the overwhelming popularity of Bessel van der Kolk's *The Body Keeps the Score*, which describes how memory is stored in the body, even when the conscious mind appears to not recall the trauma.[8] Yet a lot of those advances haven't trickled down to the general population's understanding of traumatic memory.

What does it feel like for you to consider the legacy of the FMSF? What is it like for you to connect the ways your untrue story has made you feel to a known, multidecade concerted effort by accused parents to make us feel this way? If it angers you, know that it is a righteous anger!

The dreaded Dick Wolf effect

A cultural influence that has contributed to the harmful thinking around traumatic memory is something I'm calling "the Dick Wolf effect," named after the creator of *Law & Order*, whose name appears in bold lettering at the end of every episode. The impact of *Law & Order* and the many other copaganda shows cannot be overstated. It informs the way that we, and the people around us, think about violence.

The Dick Wolf effect leads us to think about violence in terms of "proof" and what is provable. This leads to a horribly invalidating litmus test where we wonder if the criminal legal system would deem our survivorship to be credible. While I knew I had neither any interest nor any reason to engage with the criminal legal system when it came to my trauma, I realized that the idea of how my story would hold up in a court of law was impacting how I was thinking about my abuse. In the early years of processing my trauma, I imagined that I was sitting in a dank police station with cops questioning me at a cold metal table, laughing at the impossibility of my story.

Our whole lives, we've seen the way that survivors get torn apart in the news and in the courts for being deemed not credible, and this is especially true if there is a blurry memory or an unclear detail. It was so retraumatizing for me to watch the national treatment of Christine Blasey Ford, PhD, when she testified against Brett Kavanaugh during his Supreme Court confirmation hearing. The way Dr. Blasey Ford was perpetually deemed not credible because of the details that she couldn't remember from the night Brett Kavanaugh allegedly sexually assaulted her, as opposed to being deemed credible for what she could remember, burned within me.

It's normal to feel shitty about how our stories would be treated in the legal system, but we cannot allow that to define the validity of our survivorship.

Strategies

As we delve into strategies, you'll notice an undercurrent that ties them all together, and it's this:

You do not need to "remember" your abuse the same way you recall other things in your life in order to heal from it. It's okay if you don't believe me or feel some resistance to that idea—I get it! The key underlying truth is: you do not need to remember more than you already have in order to heal from your CSA.

STRATEGY: Let's learn together
about traumatic memory in a safe way

Our first strategy is to learn about traumatic memory in a safe, trauma-informed way, to help us fortify our trust in ourselves. It can be so validating to understand more about how the brain under trauma works. At the same time, seeking out that information can lead us into a minefield of triggers, especially when there is so much harmful literature out there, much of which is heavily influenced by the work of such organizations as the FMSF.

So let me do the work for you, let me earn the good money you paid for this book, by sharing with you this information in a way that is survivor-centric and prioritizes our safety and well-being, so you hopefully can be spared reading the bullshit I've read.

I have two caveats. The first is from what I've learned from my own reading as well as from talking to one of my besties who has a PhD in neuroscience from Northwestern (flex flex): there is still so much we do not know about the brain. As a layperson, I'm struck by how scientists talk about the brain versus other parts of our body, as if it is a big black box sitting atop our shoulders. As with any continuously developing field of research and study, there are a lot of conflicting and opposing ideas. I am writing this with the best knowledge I've got in the year of some people's lord 2021.

The second caveat is that I will be referring to *The Body Keeps the Score: Brain, Mind, and Body in the Healing of Trauma*, by Bessel van der Kolk, MD.[9] His 2015 book, in which he explains his theory on the way the body stores and remembers trauma, is a useful and imperfect tool (as are all tools, including this here book) in these conversations. Dr. van der Kolk has helped millions of people better understand the way trauma impacts the mind and body, and I admire that. However, according to the *Boston Globe*, in 2018 Dr. van der Kolk was fired from the Trauma Center in Brookline, Massachusetts, which he had founded 35 years earlier, due to alleged mistreatment of his employees, and I cannot help but think about the harm he may have caused those who worked with him.[10] I am also critical of *The Body Keeps the Score* because it contains content that I, and many CSA survivors I know, found super triggering, including very graphic descriptions of sexual violence that center the abuser and not the victims. If you do choose to read it, please take good care of yourself while doing so.

With all that said, let's talk about the science of memory and trauma! Fun and sexy times ahead, my friends!

The idea that memory of traumatic events may be repressed or never encoded into memories to begin with is well-documented, despite the way people have made it a controversial concept. "Advances in neurobiology have documented the effects of trauma on the brain that cause 'repressed memories.' Additional studies have also shown that recovered and continuous memories are equally likely to be accurate," Judith Herman explained in her 2015 epilogue to *Trauma and Recovery*.[11]

While psychologists have observed for decades that people can repress trauma, only for it to resurface years later, including a mention of this in the Diagnostic and Statistical Manual of Mental Disorders (DSM) in 1980, modern-day functional brain-imaging studies that show scans of how brains on trauma work offer even clearer evidence of how trauma fucks with our memory.[12]

THE SCIENCE TRANSLATED INTO NONSCIENTIFIC TERMS

As for the science of what is happening in our brains during trauma, I am going to offer you an explanation that Dr. van der Kolk provides in *The Body Keeps the Score* and then do a fun translation for those of us who don't speak science fluently. I once interviewed for a job at NASA (true story!) and, while in the lobby of their DC headquarters, nervously googled how many planets there were. So I'm not exactly one of society's greatest scientific minds. For anyone wondering, in my limited experience, one is not asked how many planets there are when one interviews for a job at NASA.

This, I promise, is the only block of scientific jargon I will throw at you in this entire book, so hang in there with me through Dr. van der Kolk's explanation:

> When memory traces of the original sounds, images, and sensations are reactivated, the frontal lobe shuts down, including, as we've seen, the region necessary to put feelings into words, the region that creates our sense of location in time, and the thalamus, which integrates the raw data of incoming sensations. At this point the emotional brain, which is not under conscious control and cannot communicate in words, takes over.[13]

In Alisa-friendly English, I'll translate: When we are traumatized, the parts of our brain that put feelings into words and give us a sense of place and time shut down (the frontal lobe and thalamus). The "emotional brain" (the limbic area and brain stem, also where the fight/flight response lives) takes over. Without the balance between these two areas of our brain, our brain cannot properly store new memories.

For some people, their memories of the abuse may become deeply repressed in an inaccessible part of the brain, and for others, those memories were never created to begin with. For all the ill-informed pressure there may be on survivors to "try to remember" their abuse, we could be torturing ourselves trying to "uncover" memories that never existed in the first place, through no fault of our own.

In the moment of trauma, you do not get to make a conscious decision about how your brain is and isn't making memories about what's going down. This shit is going on in such a deep level that you cannot consciously control. I am so adamant about this point because it isn't your fault, nor was it your decision to have limited memories of your trauma. There's nothing you could have done to change what your brain did in those times of trauma and abuse as it worked overtime to try to keep you safe and alive.

THERE ARE SOME BIG DIFFERENCES BETWEEN HEALTHY MEMORIES AND TRAUMATIC MEMORIES

Not only do our brains store, or fail to store, memory differently during trauma, but the memories that are stored are different from healthy nontraumatic memories. Dr. van der Kolk explains that there are two major differences between healthy and traumatic memories. The first difference is how the memories are organized. Healthy, nontraumatic memories are stored in a narrative way, with a beginning, middle, and end; traumatic memories are more sensory and disorganized—we may not be able to identify the details of when, where, how, but rather, remember within the sensations of how something smelled, how our bodies felt, or how something sounded.

The second difference is how we physically react to the memories. When we remember a healthy memory, it may make us smile or offer a nice exhalation, but for the most part, we are not physically responsive to memory—rather, it is just chilling in our minds. When we remember a traumatic memory, our bodies are physically reliving and reenacting how they were at the moment of initial trauma.

I'll illustrate this healthy memory versus traumatic memory difference with an example from my life:

When I think of a happy memory, like my wedding day (awww shucks yes cute very sweet love is forever yada yada), even though it was a very overwhelming day, I remember it as a beginning, middle, and end. Can I recall all the details of the day? Absolutely not. But I generally remember having three different breakfasts that day, I remember my sister beautifully doing my makeup even though I was moving around in my chair too much, I remember what it felt like during the ceremony, I remember the toasts, I remember dancing to a band floating in the middle of an indoor pool at my favorite tiki bar, and I remember the night ending with eating french fries in bed.

When it comes to my wedding day, I remember everything in order, but I don't really remember what it smelled like, tasted like, sounded like. When I think of Charlie, my husband, and me exchanging rings, I don't feel a sensation on my ring finger. When I think about us kissing at the end, I don't feel any sensation on my lips. I have no physical reaction to the memory, except a smile. In other words, I am reflecting on an organized narrative story memory, not reliving a past experience.

I invite you to do this exercise for yourself with a positive memory from your life. Some things for you to observe:

- ► Is there broadly a beginning, middle, and end to it?
- ► Do you feel like, if you had to, you could tell someone about it as though it were a story?
- ► Do you feel like your body is involved when remembering, or is it something that feels more like it lives in your head?

Now I'll take a traumatic memory. When trying to think of an example, my mind, predictably, is completely disorganized and chaotic, which is in and of itself textbook for traumatic memory. There are huge gaps of my childhood missing from my memory, and the little I see, images and sounds, have no story that goes along with them. I see it all without any real context, like time and place, to make sense of it. The flashes I do see, and sensations of what I feel and snippets of sounds, cause me to have enormous physical reactions, including nausea, hunching my body, a curling feeling in my stomach, sweaty palms, and a general full-body ickiness (technical term).

It varies by person. You could have the total opposite, where you remember your entire childhood but are blanking on a very specific time. You may know time and place but can't remember another element. Your traumatic memory may show up as depersonalization, which, from the outside, can appear like you're frozen or completely shut down. We may dissociate and feel nothing or be numb. All of this is normal.

Just like there are different ways of not remembering, there are different ways that survivors recover memories. While some people may recover memories that are clear and that offer missing pieces to the narrative of their abuse, for others, their recovered memories may continue to live more in the body and as sensations. Everyone's brain is different, and I know sets of twins who were both abused by the same person, and one twin remembers it happening to them and their twin, and the other has absolutely no memory of it. Brains are complicated, remember? And different brains do different things to help us cope and survive.

THE EXTREMELY USEFUL THEORY OF BETRAYAL TRAUMA HELPS US BETTER UNDERSTAND CSA AND MEMORY

I want us now to look at trauma and memory specifically as it relates to CSA, and there's no better source than our friend Dr. Jennifer Freyd, whom you read about earlier (her parents founded the FMSF).

In 1996, almost 20 years before *The Body Keeps the Score* was published, Dr. Freyd published *Betrayal Trauma: The Logic of Forgetting Childhood Abuse*.[14] In it, Dr. Freyd introduces us to her well-researched theory of betrayal trauma, which "proposes that the traumas that are most likely to be forgotten are not necessarily the most painful, terrifying, or overwhelming ones (although they may have those qualities), but the trauma in which betrayal is a fundamental component." This theory centers our relationship to the people who've harmed us as it relates to how much we remember. "The more the victim is dependent on the perpetrator—the most power the perpetrator has over the victim in a trusted and intimate relationship—the more the crime is one of betrayal. This betrayal by a trusted caregiver is the core factor in determining amnesia for trauma," Dr. Freyd theorizes.

To put it in simpler terms, Dr. Freyd's theory of betrayal trauma suggests that the level of betrayal a child experiences within their abuse impacts how much that child can then remember about said abuse. She explains how, as children, leaving or fighting back may not be an option for us, and we are often reliant on our abusers and those complicit in our abuse for fundamental survival: "In the case of betrayal, those situations occur when the person doing the betraying is someone the victim cannot afford *not* to trust."

Dr. Freyd isn't suggesting that we consciously make a decision to repress memories of our abuse, but rather, that a deep survival mechanism kicks in that makes us unable to remember the abuse in order to keep us safe in impossible situations. She notes that a child may be abused by someone whom they are very dependent on and remember it clearly, as memory repression isn't the only survival mechanism available to kids. Again, we don't get to choose how our brains respond to keep us alive and as safe as possible during the deepest betrayal. In *Trauma and Recovery*, Judith Herman offers an understanding in a similar vein to Dr. Freyd's theory of betrayal trauma.[15]

The same concept of not remembering abuse in order to maintain our primary relationships can be true for us as adults too. We block out traumas (even as adults) because to process them fully would lead us to isolate ourselves from potentially abusive people we may rely on for basic survival: housing, financial, and social support.

I wish we could each trust that our brain has been trying to do what's best for us to keep us safe and alive. It may not be how we wished it all had gone down, but our brain was dealing with a kind of fear and pain no human should have to endure, and the end result isn't cute and is super messy. But our brain got us here. It did what needed to be done. And now we get to shift from that survival mode to more of a healing mode. Over time, we recognize that we did what we needed to survive, and now there's an option for our mind and body to better cooperate.

How does it feel for you to consider what we know about how trauma in our brains works? Whether you want to learn more or feel you have learned enough, it's okay.

STRATEGY: We gotta focus on what we *do* know

It's the most natural thing in the world for us to harp on ourselves about what we can't recall about our abuse, but the more time I've spent validating the knowledge I already have, the more I've come to trust my own inner expert.

Carla has been on that journey herself: "I constantly waver back and forth about whether I'd like to remember my abuse or not. At first, I thought it would help me heal faster or better. Now I know that narrative memories are only one part of the puzzle. I have enough information to heal even without knowing the details of what exactly happened or even who abused me."

Sometimes, this is easier said than done. A couple of years back, I interviewed Dr. Freyd for HealingHonestly.com and asked her advice. She shared,

> It is important for you to pay attention to what you know. You may not be able to know some things with full certainty, but you can know how the person [who harmed you] is behaving right now. You can know if they are supporting you or attacking you. Are they being honest and fair with you at this moment?
>
> You can know how you feel being around that person. You may not be able to prove it to anyone else, but you know how you feel. It's much easier to know how you feel than the absolute accuracy of your memory because feeling is in the moment. Focus on what you can know and see what it tells you. Is this the behavior of a loving parent [or whomever harmed you] that they are treating you this way right now? You may not know exactly everything that happened in the past, but you can know what's happening right now.

You all see why I am such a fan of this extraordinary researcher? I found this advice to be immensely helpful. It inspired me to ask myself these kinds of questions:

- ► How does it feel when I am around the person who harmed me?
- ► How does it feel when I think of the person who harmed me?
- ► How does it feel when I engage in any sort of sexual activity?
- ► What offers me a sense of safety?
- ► What things make me feel unsafe? When do I feel unsafe?
- ► What things make me feel guilt and shame? What things reduce my feelings of guilt and shame?

When I explore these questions, I realize there's a ton of information that lives inside of me. I know that when I think about my father, my body starts to feel sick, and I experience a burning feeling through my body, with sweaty palms and nausea. I know that when I have to think about him a lot, my nightmares increase dramatically, and when I have distance from him, my nightmares reduce. I recognize that all my triggers have to do with him, whether it's songs he used to play or places he would take me.

By asking these questions, I began to understand that while I'm not necessarily "recovering" any smoking-gun memories that could tell me when/where the abuse happened, my body is reenacting what happened to me on a pretty regular basis. More regular than I'd like, if yaknowwhatimean. It's not accurate emotionally, or scientifically, for me to say I don't remember my abuse. My body remembers it perfectly every time it performs my trauma Macarena when I am triggered.

Dr. van der Kolk once wrote, "Traumatized people simultaneously remember too little and too much."[16] On one hand, we do not have the narrative memories that could help us answer important questions or help other people understand our truths more easily. On the other hand, our bodies remember our trauma so perfectly that we relive our trauma over and over again.

What is it like for you to consider how much you do remember? What are some ways we can reframe the value we put on our body's wisdom? Nell has been working through those questions: "Working with a somatic therapist, I have learned to trust my body memories and flashbacks and understand that my brain will never comprehend the full picture of my abuse. Although doubt still arises at times, my body and my heart feels and knows the truth."

IMAGINING OUR PERSONAL HEALING RETREAT

One way I've been able to reframe the value I put on the memories I have is by visualizing my dream healing retreat during vulnerable times. What could your personal healing retreat look like? Who would be there, and what affirming things would they say? What comforts would be around you; what would help you stay connected to your body and its wisdom?

DATA COLLECTION FOR MY DATA-LOVING FRIENDS

Here is another way for us to honor our body's wisdom—with an opportunity to make a gorgeous color-coordinated spreadsheet. Use those fancy pens! Create a system involving stickers! Soothe your organizing soul.

How I approach my data collection is as follows: I begin by tracking my triggers. As Dr. van der Kolk explains, "Traumatic memories are precipitated by specific triggers."[17] One of the reasons we all have different triggers is that triggers are so specific to each of our memories of what was going on when we were being abused. Paying attention to the nature of our triggers can provide a wealth of valuable data for us.

In order to track my triggers, I look for patterns over time with myself. Not all triggers feel the same—they can change and ebb and flow over time. For me, signs of triggers look like sweaty palms, nausea, really dry lips and throat that clue me in that I may be hyperventilating, migraines, heart racing, head spinning, and feelings of dissociation as though I'm no longer in my body. Your trigger signs may look totally different from mine.

What are some of your own signs that show you're experiencing a trigger? There's no wrong way to answer this. It's okay if it doesn't feel easy to list! Build this awareness in whatever way feels right for you.

Once I feel aware of what constitutes a trigger sign for me, I then make a list of all the specific triggers I've experienced. Triggers change over time—some things that used to be triggering for me no longer are, and new things become triggering all the time. This list doesn't need to be all-encompassing; it is just a place for us to begin collecting data.

To highlight how personal this is, I'll list some of my past and current triggers: goatee facial hair, so many classic rock songs, the sound of gold chain bracelets hitting a hard surface, every time I see a child trying to speak up and being silenced or not believed, any depiction of someone being trapped, the smell of certain foods, the sound of men giving off a deep belch, literally entire cities on the Eastern seaboard, some older movies, and sweet dear God the sound of Neil Young's voice kill me now.

Please don't feel shame or self-blame when looking at triggers. Your list is reflective of having a brain on trauma, and we aren't going to impose any ableist bullshit that tells us we should feel bad for the ways our brains are wired!

Now that I have my working list through my data-collection phase, next comes my analysis (This is how science works, right? Omg what if I had actually worked at NASA?). For the analysis phase, I look for patterns. To do this, I gently ask myself questions like these:

- What does this particular trigger remind me of?
- Do any of these triggers have anything in common to me?
- Are any people, or places, or periods of my life being reflected back to me throughout this list?

It's okay if none of these questions spark anything for you. I encourage you to come up with your own questions too. This doesn't need to be a one-stop-shop exploration—it's just me encouraging you to deepen your relationship with your inner wisdom in whatever way feels safe and useful.

Once I do the analysis, I see the information my body has about my childhood. It's clear from the analysis that my body is remembering a specific person. My body associates danger with a person rather than a moment in time. It may be totally different for you, and that's cool too—remember, it's a good thing that human brains are different from one another! Also pay attention to what can reduce the frequency of the triggers. Reflect on times, whether it's people, places, or moments in life, that haven't been triggering for you. You have so much helpful data inside you. All of that knowledge is real, important, and worthy of honoring.

STRATEGY: It's fun to talk about ourselves in the third person

I've found it helpful to tell myself my own story, but in the third person, as though it happened to someone else. This is a strategy I learned from my survivor friend Brooke, who once said to me, "I tell myself all the facts, including the flashes of memory I have, all the things I can't remember, and the way being around my abuser makes me feel. I list out all my trauma symptoms, including how much my trauma shows up in my sex life. And I ask myself, if someone was telling me about my own life, rationally, I can see the only logical conclusion is that this person sexually abused me. The less rational, more outlandish, difficult-to-believe conclusion would be that I am delusional and somehow made all this up and manifested all these classic symptoms of CSA."

Brooke's words floored me. When it comes to conversations of CSA and traumatic memory, harm-doers and the world around us (thanks, rape culture!) weaponize the concepts of logic and reason to say that we must be crazy and delusional, and that the rational conclusions are that we are "unwell" or "attention-seeking" or "overly dramatic."

But Brooke, in all her brilliance, showed me that not only is that total bullshit, but it's completely ass-backwards. Logic and reason actually are on our side, regardless of the crap that people try to impose on us. Why would we feel the way we feel, have the triggers we have, if not for the abuse?

You can dispassionately tell yourself your own story in the third person, as though someone else is saying it, and ask yourself what you'd think about hearing the story from someone else. You can also ask a trusted safe person in your life to practice this with you. Ask them to help you talk back to yourself and recognize that logic and reason are on your side.

STRATEGY: Learning to live with some doubts

Our next strategy can be a trickier one, and it's totally okay if you feel some resistance around it. Not all strategies are for everyone. The strategy is to work toward accepting that we may always live with some doubts and tapping into self-compassion.

One of the most common questions that fellow CSA survivors ask me is, "Do you still have moments of self-doubt?" To which I always want to reply, "Ummm . . . of fucking course." When I've been triggered or retraumatized, the first place my mind goes is a flood of self-doubt and invalidation. I would love to think there is some point in my healing where I never have those voices of self-doubt again, but I know that's not how trauma works.

When I interviewed Dr. Freyd, she gave me this life-changing advice: Sometimes we have to live with a certain degree of uncertainty. When we are dealing with something for which there is no physical evidence and the people around us are denying it happened, that will necessarily cause us some uncertainty. It doesn't mean we've done anything wrong.

It's the most natural thing in the world to have feelings of doubt when dealing with something as misunderstood as traumatic memory, and we have the people denying what happened. Dr. Freyd reminded me, "You have to also question if there is a big motivation the person [who harmed you] might have to deny something that really did happen. Maybe they are denying it not because it didn't happen, but because they don't want to be held accountable or they don't want to believe it.

"Learning to live with a level of uncertainty and being compassionate towards yourself about the situation is an important part of dealing with this,"[18] she shared with me. It was healing and validating: here I had an expert who has been studying child sexual abuse, memory, and trauma for decades, saying that it's okay for us to live with uncertainty.

Her words made me reflect on all the ways we are gaslit and conditioned to deny our reality. For those of you unfamiliar with the term, gaslighting is when someone manipulates you to make you question your own sanity. For me, it looked like the person harming me was trying to convince me that my trauma was my own fault and that I was delusional.

I found this really dope passage from Jody Messler Davies and Mary Gail Frawley's 1994 book, *Treating the Adult Survivor of Childhood Sexual Abuse: A Psychoanalytic Perspective*, which they wrote to help other clinicians treat CSA survivors. It also shows me that people who have spent a lot of time with CSA survivors know that this doubt is a part of the whole shebang:

> A sense of chronic doubting and questions about the accuracy of these recollections almost inevitably plague the therapeutic process. Chronic doubts about what did and did not happen, along with a persistent inability to trust one's perceptions of reality, are perhaps the most permanent and ultimately damaging long-term effects of childhood sexual abuse. Such doubts make it extremely difficult for the patient to arrive at a point where she can come to believe in her own history.[19]

It may seem impossible, but perhaps coming to acceptance with some level of doubt will help us to not feel so devastated each time a wave of self-questioning comes over us.

Jocelyn shared with me, "I guess I have no choice other than to live with the doubt, but it doesn't mean it isn't difficult to live with the doubt. I wonder, 'How could someone who is supposed to love me and take care of me do such a horrible thing?' Doubt creeps in with questions like, 'But did he really do that to you? He was a nice father from your good memories.'"

I agree with Jocelyn that living with doubt can be really challenging. I've lately tried to create some distance between myself and self-doubt, by just saying things like, "Oh, hello, devilish old friend. Of course you've returned right now during my vulnerable moments. You are right on time." It helps me remember that the doubt isn't something I need to believe, but rather is more of a trauma nuisance.

Having these moments of doubt actually is evidence that I've been traumatized and abused. Doubting myself, finding ways to blame myself for my abuse, and looking for ways to diminish my pain are such unifying survivor experiences. What does it feel like for you to consider that our doubts aren't evidence of a lack of abuse, but rather that doubt is a natural and logical outcome to the abuse we experienced and the gaslighting we continue to endure?

However you are feeling, I encourage you to make space for all your feelings, including those that may be conflicting with one another. You are the expert in yourself and what you need. Prioritize your well-being and your healing over other people's expectations based on their ignorance of how traumatic memory works.

STRATEGY: Remembering that we aren't alone, like, ever

One of the most important strategies I can offer you is to remember how not alone you are in these feelings. Dealing with traumatic memories can leave us feeling so misunderstood and like we are the problem. The most powerful tool we have to fight against stigma is to connect with other people who are dealing with the same shit.

If other survivors in the proverbial room have clearer memories than you, don't worry! Remember from the previous chapter, no one is more or less of a "real" survivor than anyone else! Incomplete memory is a common enough challenge that there will definitely be survivors like you. I have a group coaching program for CSA survivors who've struggled around memory, so that everyone in the virtual room has that shared understanding. If you can't access a peer support group that works, I hope this chapter can help the same way.

First, for my quantitative friends, I have some numbers for you. When I polled 949 CSA survivors, this is what I found:

- ► 83 percent said they hear the untrue story "I can't be a real survivor if I don't remember clearly what happened to me."
- ► 75 percent said they hear the untrue story "Maybe I'm just crazy."

For my qualitative friends, I want you to hear from some survivors whose friendship and connection have supported me so much. Elizabeth shared this practice: "I did something really brave one day. I wrote in my journal that I believe myself. It felt rebellious, even dangerous. I wrote over and over that I believe myself and my feelings and my experience. I thought I needed my concrete memories to come back. But I realized I didn't need to treat myself like I was in a court case. I could believe myself without that 'evidence.'"

And we have this powerful reminder of self-trust from Carla: "Turning to my gut and inner voice has helped me find healing and acceptance in the face of not remembering my abuse. Every time I catch myself thinking 'What if I'm making it all up?' I tune in to my gut and it reminds me of all the times I've been sure. If I can tap into that gut memory, I don't need to rely on brain memories to validate what I know to be unequivocally true."

You are in the best company of other survivors working hard alongside you to trust themselves and their own inner wisdom.

Is it snack o'clock yet?

Wow, friends. You just went on a real traumatic-memory nerd journey with me, and I for one think we've all collectively gotten a lot smarter. Smart enough to work at NASA. Smart enough to google, and remember what Google tells us about how many planets there are.

Advocate for your own safety and well-being. People have different definitions of what healing means to them, as they should! Healing should mean something unique and specific to each of us, and our definitions may even change for ourselves from day to day. But for rhetorical ease, I'm going to broadly offer a working definition I have for myself: healing doesn't mean my trauma disappears, but rather that I feel affirmed in my own truth, no longer feeling misplaced self-blame and shame for my abuse and the impact of the trauma on me, and that I am able to live a full and vibrant life capable of feeling the full spectrum of emotion.

While your definition may be different from mine, remember that healing doesn't necessarily require remembering or understanding more about your abuse than you know today. To me, the key to healing is that piece about no longer feeling any misplaced shame. To let go of shame, I honor my own body's wisdom and understand that my traumatic memory is a typical neuroscientific response to abuse: not my fault, not under my control.

What does healing mean to you? It's okay if you don't have an answer for that question right now—we have so many more chapters together to work through all this and more. For now, know that I know your pain is real and valid, just like you know mine is too, and for right now, that is enough. Now let's go get some nosh.

3

No One Should Dismiss Our Health Needs

UNTRUE STORY
Our health and trauma are totally separate

BUT TRUTHFULLY
Our health and our trauma are inextricably tied together

Now it is time for us to dive into the ways CSA can impact our health in the long term. If I were you, I'd read that last sentence and groan. I say that because I have spent so many hours deep in the Google abyss looking for healing resources and have run headfirst into so much information about the health impacts of CSA that has made me feel like absolute garbage. Oh, the hair-pulling impulse that comes from article after article describing to me all the ways that my friends and I are destined to a lifetime of health fuckery!

Call me crazy, but I don't find it helpful to read about how much more statistically likely I am to get cancer, have diabetes, or be diagnosed with heart disease because of something that happened to me as a child that I had no control over. Seeing myself simplified into a depressing statistic makes me feel like all that's left for me to do is to wrap myself in industrial-strength bubble wrap for the rest of my days and hope for the best.

For a long time I felt that there were only two options being presented to me when it came to CSA and my health:

- ▶ Option A: My abuse was something that stayed in the past and might impact my present emotions but not my health or body.
- ▶ Option B: My trauma was destroying me from the inside out, and I was fated to a lifetime of health problems and being spoken about like some fascinating medical statistic.

It has taken me many years to learn that my truth is actually secret Option C:

My history of CSA impacts every aspect of my health, and even if people make me feel otherwise, it isn't anything for me to feel shame or self-blame over. I know that CSA has been associated with an increased risk of a variety of health conditions, like fibroids, digestive conditions, and chronic pain, and that knowledge can help empower us instead of making us feel a sense of doom. We can be our own health care advocates and remember that even if health care providers fail us, we deserve shame-free, holistic care that makes us feel supported and understood.

As always, I'll walk through just how I got to that secret Option C, and hopefully none of us will have to groan too much along the way.

I'm in this with you—I, too, have had a lot of questions about how health and my CSA relate to each other

When we talk about the mind-body connection, it can sometimes bring up (very justified!) fears that people, including me, are implying that our pain is "all in our heads" or somehow isn't real. Your pain is very real. You did not will it to be. You did not cause it. Your pain is real, and it is not your fault that you feel pain.

Ten years ago, I was navigating being a young professional and living in geographic proximity to my father for the first time in many years. To give you a cultural touchstone, it was a time when it was very important for me to know all the dance moves to Robyn's iconic "Call Your Girlfriend" music video. If you don't know it, stop reading, go watch it, and then come back. You're welcome.

As I was busy trying to learn important things like how to be an employee (lessons I now try to impart to my only employee, Franklin, my dog) and that I could no longer drink like I did in college (ugh, thank God), I was also trying to learn how to have boundaries with my abusive father. It wasn't going well. He wanted us to spend more time together, when I was traumatized by his presence.

About six months into my return to DC, I fucked up my Achilles' tendon when simply walking up a flight of stairs trying to get to a train. The podiatrist told me I had put a bunch of micro tears in it and surgery wasn't an option, but rather, I would need to just spend six weeks in a walking cast moving as little as possible.

I remember being frustrated and worried about how I would get around (yes, kids, this is before Uber/Lyft), not having a car and living in a pedestrian city. I also remember thinking that I could use this injury to keep some distance from my dad. There was no way he could expect me to get to him, and maybe he'd even be sympathetic toward me because I was hurt.

My father did not understand my emotions and boundaries, but he could understand an air cast and a torn ligament, and maybe that could buy me some cover. It worked for a while, and I got a few weeks of space. But then passed the six-week post-injury mark when I should've been better. The podiatrist noted that he saw no healing in my injury, so I'd need the cast for another month.

Within a few weeks of hearing the news, my dad emailed me an ultimatum. He said that either I needed to spend more time with him, specifically spending the night at his home, or he didn't want us to continue to have a relationship any longer. I decided that I wasn't going to give in to his ultimatum and I was done with him for good.

It would be years before I felt relieved that my relationship with my dad was over. What I felt those passing months was an onslaught of guilt and fear of what my father might do to me or to other people I loved.

The shiteous cocktail of guilt, self-blame, and betrayal

With each guilt-fueled month came my checkup with the podiatrist, where-upon he continued to tell me I was defying his medical knowledge by my body's refusal to heal in any way whatsoever. While I already felt so much self-blame for, in my mind, ruining and blowing up my entire family, I came to dread my doctor's appointments where my doctor continued to shift the blame to me. He accused me of not resting, even when I swore I wasn't walking at all. I felt my body had betrayed me in causing me to have triggers around my dad, and now my body was betraying me by refusing to heal an ordinary injury.

I know I'm not alone in struggling with feeling like my body was betraying me. I have heard many stories like this one from Disa: "Living without clear memories of my abuse yet experiencing extreme anxiety and physical reactions to triggers that I'm not aware of makes me feel like my body is literally suffocating for seemingly 'no reason.' It feels like my body is betraying me."

Have you ever struggled with feeling like your body is betraying you? What words might you put to those feelings?

As months passed, I grew accustomed to a life where I couldn't walk more than a block or believe in my own right to feel legitimate pain. I couldn't believe in my relationship with my own body.

Then, just shy of a year after my initial injury, my doctor gave me what he called a hail Mary of a recommendation for a new physical therapist. I couldn't get through briefing the new PT on my injury history without bursting into tears. She told me I was responding to the injury in a way that someone with PTSD would and had unaddressed trauma I needed to be working through in order to heal from the injury.

I felt defensive and angry: I immediately interpreted her message through the trauma lens that told me everything was my fault, my body was betraying me, and I was too sensitive to function in the world. But despite my defensiveness, I felt she had rung an undeniable bell. I went back to ther-apy to process what it felt like to lose control of my body and feel like my body had never been mine. I needed an expert to remind me each week that none of this was my fault and that I had done nothing wrong.

No, I don't think my trauma caused my injury

It took me many more years to understand what I needed to learn from that experience. Do I think my trauma caused my injury? Absolutely not. A recent history of being prescribed way too much of the antibiotic Cipro, which later became well known for causing spontaneous tendon ruptures, definitely caused my injury. My pain was real and my mind didn't cause it. But my trauma was actively impacting my healing process. Knowing that caused shame at first but later brought the relief of understanding my body better. Does thinking about your abuse impacting your body also fill you with a whole heap of emotions?

I invite you to consider what untrue stories you may have about your health and CSA

If you've felt at war with your body, betrayed by it when it reveals signs of trauma or doesn't allow you to move on when the world tells you that you must, know that you aren't alone. We have complicated relationships with our bodies. Our bodies were the home of so much of our mistreatment. When triggered, our bodies recognize our memory of trauma before our minds do. And while our bodies can be the site of harm and long-term health impacts, they can also be an entry point to our healing, a way to find home within ourselves.

"I have a facial tic that really flared up about four years ago. My face would physically be sore at the end of the day, and I felt so embarrassed, nauseous, and desperate," shared Elizabeth. "I chased all kinds of physical remedies, but there was nothing anyone could do. But then I saw a therapist who understood trauma, and they said they weren't surprised at all by my tic as a trauma response. The tic hasn't gone away, but just having that new framework has helped me to accept it."

What does it feel like for you to consider the possibility that your past abuse is impacting your present health? What kinds of emotions do you observe arriving with that? What are some of the fears that may arise when you think about the relationship between your health and trauma? Remember, none of these questions should lead us to ever blame ourselves or minimize the validity of our pain or health challenges.

It is totally normal to feel frustrated and angry at the thought of our trauma impacting our long-term health, while at the same time feeling validation from putting the pieces together. If you are hearing any unkind internal voices, don't worry. We are about to explore them and really understand where they come from and what we can do about them.

What are the origins of the bullshit?

There were people I trusted who reinforced my untrue story

While everyone's become a lot more trauma-informed than years ago, back in the day, the people who loved me wanted me to be all better, because they desperately didn't want me to suffer more. I remember some questions from family members like, "Do you think you'll ever be able to move on from this?" and "Look at you! You've healed yourself!" I get it. I too would wish my loved ones to not suffer long-term pain. But this contributed to my desire to hide the ways I was still being impacted by the CSA, because I didn't want to disappoint the people who loved me that I still wasn't *better*.

Their questions reinforced this idea that the abuse was like a wound that was really gnarly and bad, but with time it would scab over and fade away until all that was left was a faint scar and a memory of a more painful time. But the reality was that I had a wound that had taken over my entire body that I hadn't known about for years. While parts of it would scab over through the healing process, my body would forever be impacted by the wound.

It was me—I reinforced this untrue story too.
The call was coming from inside the house, if you will

But when I really dig in, I see how the most influential person reinforcing my untrue story was me. I had long felt that my body was betraying me by displaying so many undeniable signs of my trauma. My body was forcing me to face the difficult shit.

I didn't want to deal with the idea that the abuse could impact me, to some degree, for the rest of my life. I feared that it meant I was a broken object without any agency over my life. I intensely feared a binary that either

I had to be totally healed and absent of any ongoing trauma, or I was fated to a doomed lifetime of despair and a textbook of problems.

It's a very human response to wish for ourselves to not be in pain anymore and be free from long-term effects! We all deserve that, but unfortunately it's just simply not how this shit works. It's not fair of me to ask myself to not have any more symptoms after all I've been through.

And then there's all the people who told us our pain wasn't real when we spoke up throughout our lives

So many times in my formative years I tried to communicate that something was happening in my mind and body that wasn't okay. Those efforts were met with minimization, dismissal, and claims that I was overreacting and a drama queen. Whether it was adults in my family who I tried to confide in or a disastrous child psychologist who dismissed my cries for help, I learned from an early age that I shouldn't trust my own intuition about when I wasn't safe or okay.

That's led me as an adult to totally distrust my body's wisdom. Every time I am sick, from something as mild as a cold or as serious as an antibiotic-resistant bacterial infection, I find that it is only a matter of days until I begin feeling triggered and hearing invalidating voices in my mind that tell me my pain isn't real, I am being overly dramatic, and maybe I'm making all my symptoms up. This has led me to not get the medical care I need sometimes because I worry that I should just "suck it up" or that my symptoms may somehow be "fake."

While I am unable to fully prevent those thoughts from showing up when I am sick or in pain, I do now understand at least why I feel that way. I can accept that the invalidating voices will come and go. It's totally understandable why any of us would be worried that our pain wouldn't be taken seriously, distrusting our body's signals and fearing misplaced reactions from others. Do you feel this way when you are sick? If yes, you are in such good company, don't worry!

What are some forces or people who taught you to not trust your own body's wisdom? How has it affected your relationship to your body, pain, and illness?

Western medicine's insistence on seeing the mind and body as totally separate entities

Trauma encompasses our whole health, from mental and emotional well-being to nervous systems and hormones. Yet our medical institutions are designed to keep emotional and physical health as two totally separate things, which means they are set up to fail everyone.

Our health care system needs a comprehensive understanding of the relationship between trauma and health. One 2018 study in *Human Reproduction* on cisgender women showed that those who had suffered from childhood trauma were 79 percent more likely to develop endometriosis than their peers.[1] Yet, many of us have experiences of going to doctors who are completely ignorant of the way our trauma may be impacting our current-day health, believing abuse is only relevant to therapists and psychiatrists.

Elizabeth shared this example: "I have vaginismus, and one doctor said that I was lucky to have a boyfriend that would put up with intimacy without penetration. I knew that was a bullshit thing to say, but it still hit a chord. She encouraged me to take home a speculum to practice and referred me to a physical therapist to get dilators. The doctor's entire diagnosis and treatment was based around the physical without any curiosity of what could have been behind my physical symptoms."

Too often, we find ourselves in conversations with medical providers who respond to us in one of two ways:

- ► They make us feel like we are crazy, and they blame everything that's wrong with us on our trauma.
- ► They completely ignore the ways our trauma may be showing up in our health.

Both options totally suck and can leave us feeling denied of the reality of what we observe in our minds and bodies. They teach us to distrust our own instincts about what's happening within us, a sort of medicalized gaslighting where we are being told our bodies can't be acting in a way a doctor doesn't understand. We need and deserve clinicians who can understand the mind/body connection.

Health care providers who make us feel like statistics

When I speak with doctors, I often experience pathologization, which is when a medical professional treats a person or people as psychologically abnormal. It is the way medical professionals sometimes talk about survivors coldly and with a distant professional fascination. It makes us feel like some weird science experiment or just a statistic.

I had to stop reading medical articles about CSA survivors and our health because it made me feel like shit. It increased my own internal stigma and made me afraid to identify as a CSA survivor. It made me feel like I was medically fucked for the rest of my life. Even now, as a professional in this field, I brace myself when I am at conferences and have to hear doctors talk about survivors. They rattle off a laundry list of horrible medical conditions and leave me with a sense of doom. Not cool, doc, not cool.

It is even worse for survivors who have experienced medical abuse of one kind or another. The patient-doctor relationship necessarily has a power imbalance in our health care system. And unfortunately, that means we can be made vulnerable while trying to seek care. Ideally, medical workers would partner with us and actively work to recalibrate the power imbalance of health care. They would be trauma-informed enough to speak to us with compassion and understanding, instead of reinforcing stigma. They would consider mind and body holistically and acknowledge our authority as experts on ourselves.

Lucy shared with me how having a practitioner who knew how to ask the right questions radically changed her health trajectory: "I have had health issues for the past 15 years and now understand that my body was screaming at me to deal with past childhood trauma, and I just kept ignoring it and was getting sicker until I saw a new medical nutritionist who thinks and practices outside the box." When she went to fill out the intake form, there was a question about past traumas.

"This nutritionist was the first person in 15 years to ever ask me that question. Everything changed for me that day, as I had never previously connected my physical health with my trauma. I have been working with him, and my physical and mental health have improved greatly. I am forever grateful to him for asking that one question that no one else ever did," she said.

Are there experiences you've had within the medical world that contribute to your untrue story? In your ideal world, how would those experiences have been different? How should talking with a medical professional feel, versus how it may have made you feel in the past?

Strategies

STRATEGY: Learning more about the relationship between CSA and health conditions

My goal in sharing the following information is *not* to make us feel like our bodies are totally fucked. Nope. I just hope that if we learn more about this topic in a nonstigmatizing way, greater understanding of our bodies can lead to more self-compassion regarding health needs.

I FOUND IT HELPFUL TO LEARN ABOUT COMPLEX POST-TRAUMATIC STRESS DISORDER (C-PTSD)

C-PTSD is a diagnosis developed by Dr. Judith Herman in the early '90s: "In survivors of prolonged, repeated trauma, the symptom picture is often far more complex. Survivors of prolonged abuse develop characteristic personality changes."[2] When discussing the need for this C-PTSD diagnosis, as opposed to the already established PTSD diagnosis, Dr. Herman specifically uses the example of childhood abuse: "Survivors of childhood abuse, like other traumatized people, are frequently misdiagnosed and mistreated in the mental health system. Because of the number and complexity of their symptoms, their treatment is often fragmented and incomplete. . . . Survivors of childhood abuse often accumulate many different diagnoses before the underlying problem of a complex post-traumatic syndrome is recognized."[3] C-PTSD as a diagnosis attempts to encapsulate the layered and deeply interwoven physical, emotional, mental impacts of long-endured trauma.

In her memoir *What My Bones Know: A Memoir of Healing from Complex Trauma*, Stephanie Foo explains how the diagnosis of C-PTSD expresses the way trauma impacts all aspects of us: "Here's what makes *complex* PTSD uniquely miserable in the world of trauma diagnoses: It occurs when someone is exposed to a traumatic event over and over and over again—hundreds, even thousands of times—over the course of years. When you are traumatized that many times, the number of conscious and subconscious triggers bloats, becomes infinite and inexplicable. . . . The world itself becomes a threat."[4]

When I first heard about C-PTSD a few years ago from my survivor friend Amita Swadhin, I was excited to learn that there was a term that honors the difference between one traumatic event versus a long traumatic period. It isn't that one trauma is worse than the other. It just means that the trauma from surviving a car crash looks different in our minds and bodies than a trauma of years of danger throughout childhood.

If you've found trauma resources that are specifically for PTSD to be *limited* (cough cough), with websites that have American flags and stock photos of veterans and descriptions that don't feel totally like you, then join the club! While there isn't nearly as much out there for people about C-PTSD, what exists feels much more relevant to my life—yours too?

WE'VE COME TO THE TIME WHEN I GET TO TELL YOU ABOUT DISEASES AND CONDITIONS! HUZZAH!

A quick overview: experiencing sexual abuse as a child can be associated with certain health conditions for us as adults, including these:

- ► Chronic pain conditions like headaches, joint pain, or fibromyalgia.
- ► Gastrointestinal conditions such as irritable bowel syndrome (IBS).
- ► Mental health conditions like C-PTSD, eating disorders, addiction, depression, anxiety, dissociative identity disorder, and borderline personality disorder. All of which are, no doubt, fun and sexy times.
- ► Gynecological issues such as ovarian cysts and pelvic pain.[5,6]

Unfortunately for all of us, rarely do our health care providers make the connection between our CSA and our current health issues.

The connecting link between these differing health conditions is increased inflammatory activity in the body, which is associated with CSA and other forms of childhood trauma.[7] Thousands of studies have demonstrated a relationship between childhood trauma and inflammation, so the medical failure to connect the dots is all the more unacceptable.

This all may sound like medical mumbo jumbo to you, which is cool because you're in great company. The last science class I took was in my freshman year of college. Regrettably, while at the University of Michigan, I didn't follow in my roommate's footsteps and take the Dinosaurs and Other Failures course for my mandatory science credit. I took an infectious diseases class, where I learned just enough to make me a germaphobe and yet not enough to understand anything useful. So, just like with the last chapter, I'm going to explain sciencey things in the plainest layperson way possible. If you are into science and want to learn more, I encourage you to follow my citations for more detail.

IT'S ALL ABOUT THE CORTISOL, BABYYYY

Okay, so there's this thing in all of us called the hypothalamic-pituitary-adrenal (HPA) axis. It is a complex system made up of, perhaps you guessed it, our hypothalamus, our pituitary gland, and our adrenal glands. Together, they do very important things, including controlling our reactions to stress and regulating our immune system, metabolism, sleep patterns, and digestion.

The HPA axis regulates and produces the hormone cortisol, our body's stress hormone, sometimes called the body's alarm system. When we are in times of stress, our bodies produce more cortisol to help us stay safe and healthy. If we are sick, our bodies produce more cortisol to help our immune system work. If we are in danger, our bodies produce more cortisol to help us respond to the danger with our fight/flight/freeze/fawn responses.

Freeze means that during the traumatic events or triggers, we freeze up and do not move and/or speak. Fawn is when we engage in people-pleasing to survive, often being affectionate, kind, or agreeable to the person harming us. All fear responses are totally normal, not anything you have control over or get to choose, and nothing to feel ashamed of!

Many studies show that due to our trauma, our bodies had to produce a lot of cortisol during our childhoods. Studies suggest there are long-term impacts to childhood cortisol overproduction, including becoming resistant to cortisol or not producing enough of it in adulthood. This affects our level of inflammation and our body's immune system and has been linked to heart disease, diabetes, autoimmune diseases, and lots of other fun and sexy things!

Snarky aside: Wouldn't it be great if our health care professionals (a) understood this themselves and (b) could explain it to us to help us understand our own bodies better?

I hope this helps you connect the dots between your own observations. It helped me understand the mind-body connection. Being in a prolonged state of fear impacts our glands and hormones, which has a ripple effect on health.

Please remember that none of this is your fault, and you've done nothing to cause any of this! Our bodies did pretty extraordinary things to try to keep us as safe as possible while experiencing things we never should have had to, and that work has left traces behind. But that lasting impact is nothing for us to feel shame about (although frustration is welcome!).

STRATEGY: Learning more about the relationship
between CSA and chronic pain

Pain, both as a concept and as a medical condition, is deeply intertwined into the intersections of sexism, racism, and oppression. Whose pain and suffering counts and is validated and cared for by the institutions and people we depend on is determined by privilege.

We know Black women's pain, in particular, is misdiagnosed, dismissed, and invalidated constantly throughout the health care system and society.[8] There is a clear thread between CSA and pain: just as some survivors' victimhood (like mine as a white cishetero woman) is more likely to be believed and considered real and important, some survivors' pain is more likely to be validated than others'.

I cannot say this enough: If you are in physical pain, I know your pain is real and matters. I want to make it abundantly clear that your pain is very real and that it is absolutely, in no uncertain terms, not your fault. All pain, no matter how it originates, is worthy of treatment and care.

Now I get to introduce you to a friend of mine, Anna Holtzman, LMHC, who has helped me so much on my chronic pain journey. Anna is a licensed therapist and chronic pain expert whose expertise is at the intersection of chronic pain and trauma. She is also a childhood sexual trauma survivor, and you know we love survivor-to-survivor wisdom!

A year ago, I was dealing with chronic migraines. At my request, Anna sent me information about how chronic pain works in the body, along with resources like guided imagery and journaling prompts. One of the coolest things I learned was that research shows that simply learning about how chronic pain works can in and of itself be an effective treatment for pain. So many fellow CSA survivors struggle with physical pain, like shoulder/neck/back pain, migraines, and pelvic pain the way I have. It isn't a coincidence, and it certainly isn't our fault.

WITHOUT GETTING TOO PHILOSOPHICAL ON YOUR ASS, WE ARE GOING TO ASK OURSELVES, "WHAT IS PAIN?"

Anna explained to me, "Pain is nothing but a danger signal and triggered by fear. Sometimes the danger is physical, like a broken leg; sometimes the danger is emotional, like emotional abuse." She continued, "Pain is a danger alarm created in our brains when our nervous systems feel unsafe. This is a process that doesn't happen consciously, nor is it based on decisions we make."

There are loads of examples of how this mind-body connection works. If we are nervous about a job interview, having a difficult conversation, or awaiting results of an important test, we may get stomach pains, nausea, loss of appetite, tightness in our neck and back. Or, if you're me, you get the nervous bubble gut and you're just grateful to make it through without pooping your pants. We don't decide to get an upset stomach or back pains during these high-stress experiences; they are things that happen subconsciously.

There are these one-off stressful experiences, "but when you are dealing with chronic stress or chronic trauma, it can cause chronic pain. We can see examples around us, like having a super stressful job, which is an everyday experience, which may lead us to have headaches or back pain most days," said Anna.

It all sounds too simple, right? Well, that's kind of the point, she said. "This is all actually very simple. We all intuitively understand the connection between pain and trauma and our mind and body. But we've been conditioned to distrust our own knowledge of our own emotional and physical experience. We have been gaslit into believing our emotional feelings are not valid."

While the world outside of us tells us that physical and emotional pain are completely different things, one being considered "real" and provable and the other constantly invalidated and dismissed, they are interwoven inside of us.

Anna explained, "Physical pain and emotional pain are created in very similar parts of the brain, so the two are inextricably connected. They are coordinated aspects of stress response, so we cannot divorce one from the other, not ever. Even if you have pain from a bone, there's an emotional response to that from the physical sensation of the broken bone." I can personally attest to that as someone who, as a kid, all on separate occasions, broke her leg, three toes, one finger, and an arm (from literally, I shit you not, napping on the couch while watching *Baywatch* reruns and slowly rolling over onto the floor, landing on my arm. Yes, it was just a regular couch).

Anna continued, "Chronic pain is a result of the chronic tension between the part of us that wants to fight back and the part of us that has learned to be afraid to fight back, probably for good reasons, at least in childhood or before you had allies to support you."

To illustrate the point, she offered us this prompt:

- ► First, let's imagine lots of angry energy inside of you, the kind of fury of fighting back against all that is wrong. Tap into the anger and fury that is a part of each of us.
- ► Now that you've tapped into that feeling of righteous anger, try suppressing all that fighting energy with all of your might.
- ► What does your body feel like when you try to suppress your anger and fighting energy? It may feel pretty tense and tight in your body. If each of us sustained that for a while, we might start to feel some pain.
- ► Now that this little experiment is over, give your limbs a light shake or do some deep exhalations to release all that tension and discomfort, because that isn't a pleasant feeling!

Presumably, if we continued to suppress and silence the natural fight in us for long periods of time, say our whole childhood, we can see how some pain would start to develop. So this prompt is helping us understand a little better how chronic pain comes from this tension of suppressing our healthy natural emotional selves. Whether the prompt was illuminating to you or not, that's okay; we have more to learn together!

COMMON SURVIVAL BEHAVIORS THAT CAN PERPETUATE CHRONIC PAIN (NONE OF WHICH ARE ANYTHING FOR US TO FEEL ASHAMED OF!)

In further exploring the chronic pain and CSA survivor relationship, Anna explained to me that there are some common survival behaviors that we survivors engage in that can perpetuate chronic pain.

1. **Vigilance and preparing for the threat of danger.**
   Many survivors experience hypervigilance as a part of their trauma. I feel I am often on high alert, playing worst-case scenarios in my head as a way to anticipate danger and prepare for ways to deal with the fallout. Do you observe yourself being constantly on high alert? No shame if you do! This was developed for good reasons!

   "The habit of vigilance perpetuates chronic pain because it keeps our danger alarm on high alert all the time. Pain is a danger signal, so when we fear we are in danger, our body sends us pain as a message," Anna explained. If we spend a lot of time with our danger alarms going off, this can continue our cycles of pain.

2. **People pleasing and suppressing anger.**
   Many of us can relate to being conditioned to suppress anger, because if we tried expressing it when we were younger, we may have received explicit or implicit signals that it wasn't safe for us to be angry. Have you observed any people-pleasing/appeasing tendencies within yourself? Again, no shame if you have! This was developed for good reasons! (Yes, I will repeat this again because it is worthy of repetition!)

"The people-pleasing/appeasing/suppressing anger survival behaviors perpetuate chronic pain in a few ways, including that when we have the urge to fight back but have to suppress it, it is as though our internal gas pedal and brake pedal are being slammed on simultaneously, which causes physical tension," Anna explained.

3. **Perfectionism and self-criticism (I am the best at this one!).** My therapist says I am the best at criticizing myself for things that aren't my fault—which also fulfills my perfectionist tendencies, so take that. We can be so hard on ourselves in hopes that it prevents us from "inviting" (we never actually invite abuse from someone, hence the quotation marks) abuse from someone else. Do you join me in having a lot of perfectionism and self-criticism tendencies too?

When I asked Anna how this survival behavior contributes to chronic pain, she explained, "When we are perfectionists and intense self-critics, we are terrorizing ourselves all day long, and that turns on our danger alarms and sends signals of pain within us." I did a true, honest-to-God spit-take when she said this last one, because it was so real to me that my only option was to hysterically laugh.

It's no wonder so many of us deal with chronic pain! Look at all the coping strategies we had to develop just to try to stay safe and function in the world as survivors. Those same things can cause us pain. Thinking about all this together fills me up with a deep feeling of compassion for all of us.

HOW PAIN CAN SHOW UP DELAYED FOR US, LIKE A FUN SURPRISE FROM HELL!

A really important aspect of pain for us CSA survivors is that sometimes danger is a present-time threat, like touching a hot stove, but other times danger can be a conditioned response that reminds us of past danger or abuse. We can be going about our days and then get a headache or back pain and not know why, but it could be because we smelled or heard or saw something that subconsciously reminded us of our abuse. Anna explained that this can be a confusing part of pain, especially if we are trying to explain it to people who don't know what it's like to have trauma and experience triggers.

"An example I like to use is that when we get near a flame, our body automatically recoils from it because we know it's dangerous. How do we know it's dangerous? We aren't consciously thinking about how fire is dangerous, so we must move our hand. We aren't thinking about the first time we learned fire is dangerous. We may not consciously remember how and when we learned fire was dangerous, but our nervous system remembers fire is dangerous to touch, so our nervous system is recoiling our hand from the flame," Anna said.

For some of us, we experienced chronic pain throughout our childhood. For others, we didn't experience it until adulthood. Sometimes people ask, "Why now?!" to their pain who didn't experience pain in their childhood.

"Often with chronic pain, we experience the pain when our bodies are safe enough to relax our survival mechanisms a bit and we determine, in a subconscious place, that it's safe enough for us to fully feel the pain connected to the stress," Anna explained.

WE CALL BULLSHIT ON THE NOTION THAT
OUR EMOTIONS ARE "TOO BIG" TO FEEL

I've heard some people imply that we have chronic pain because our emotions are too big, or too hard, for our minds to process, so our bodies store them. When I asked Anna about this, she told me that every one of her trauma teachers has said that people suppress their feelings because they are too overwhelming, and that's what leads to chronic pain.

"In my opinion, that is bullshit," I was surprised to hear her say. "I don't think we are unable to handle big feelings. Or that there are feelings too big for our nervous systems to handle. But rather, it's that we can't handle big feelings in isolation. We need companionship in order to safely process our feelings."

We weren't born suppressing our emotions. We learned to suppress our emotions because we learned from the people around us that we were not going to receive empathy and companionship with our feelings. Expressions of our feelings were met with silence, criticism, denial, and even punishment. Bad fucking things. At the same time, we learned that our physical pain would be taken seriously and met with some sympathy and support. So our bodies brilliantly channeled all our pain and emotions into the parts of us that would receive care and support when hurt. Fancy, smart moves from our bodies.

"We feel physical pain because it has a greater chance of being socially validated than emotional pain, and we stuff emotional pain down because we know we aren't going to get empathy for it and the world around us has shown us it isn't safe to process it," Anna shared. Are there ways you've seen your physical pain garner more support and empathy than your emotional pain throughout your life?

The good news is that, as adults, we can seek out empathetic witnesses to our pain, like a trusted friend or a good therapist, who can offer us companionship that allows us to safely express our big feelings.

"Feeling our feelings *without* the presence of compassion makes our nervous system freak the fuck out because it feels exposed and vulnerable to potential threats. But feeling our feelings in the presence of compassion makes our nervous system feel safe," Anna told me.

What is most important is for each of us to know we aren't alone in our pain. "You are not crazy, and none of this is your fault. It is possible for you to find relief, and while you can never prevent all pain, it absolutely can get better," Anna offered.

I know that was a lot of information about chronic pain and trauma! What kinds of emotions, including potentially unpleasant ones, does all of this bring up for you? However you feel, it is totally normal.

STRATEGY: Let's keep finding ways to get into our bodies

Our next strategy is to explore ways to intentionally come back home into our bodies. During my time in therapy while healing my torn Achilles', I realized that I had never felt safe or at home within my own body. The disassociation from my body helped me to survive in order to get to this point. For a long time, being in my body wasn't a safe option.

As we transition from needing to be deep in survival mode to experimenting with other ways of being with ourselves, we can start to build a sense of neutral familiarity with our bodies. My hope is that this kind of neutral familiarity can lead us, over time, to strengthen our trust in our bodies and all the wisdom they store.

WE DON'T HAVE TO LOVE THEM—INSTEAD, CAN WE AIM FOR BEING NEUTRAL TOWARD OUR BODIES?

This idea of body neutrality is one that I have learned from fat liberation activists. The movement for fat liberation, created and led predominately by Black fat queer women, including Sonya Renee Taylor and Tigress Osborn, taught me how to interrogate the way anti-fatness, ableism, and racism work together to oppress people and create policies and systems that uphold the idea that there are good, worthy bodies and there are bad, unworthy bodies. This is illustrated in the way fat women often do not receive the medical care they need and deserve because doctors dismiss all their health problems as being because they are fat, whereas someone in a smaller body with the same symptoms will receive different treatment and have their symptoms validated and taken seriously.

My understanding of fat liberation is that in order for us to be in a world without fatphobia, we need to understand fatness as a natural, morally neutral way of being. Currently, as a society, we see thin people as morally superior—their thinness implies self-control, health, and discipline. We see fatness as a moral failure, as though a person is fat because of some sort of lack of self-control or unhealthiness, and not that fat people have always existed and will always exist, and fatness has nothing to do with health.

Fat liberation and ableism both tell us that the difference between our bodies can be categorized as "morally good and valuable" or "morally bad and not valuable." It is important for people and policies to treat all bodies as morally neutral and valuable. I find it much more manageable to consider working on seeing my own body as morally neutral and valuable versus having to fall in love with my body. Neutrality is much more feasible and I think a more useful goal for me to work toward.

What do you think about the idea of working toward seeing your body as both morally neutral and valuable, worthy of respect and care?

EXPERIMENTING WITH WAYS
TO CONNECT TO OUR BODIES

I experiment with finding ways to feel more connected and safe in my body without any pressure or expectations for myself. Those experiments will necessarily look different for each of us.

"I feel the most connected to my body when I'm listening to what it needs, whether that's bingeing an entire series in one sitting, spending the day with friends, or taking a relaxing bath," shared Carla. "When I take the time to be silent, ask my body what it needs, and then actually give that to myself, it feels like all the past parts of me that begged to be heard but were ignored finally feel acknowledged and can relax."

Sam offered another way of thinking about repairing her relationship with her body: "I try to appreciate my body, and wear clothing that is appealing to me, or just be naked, get comfortable with myself in my flat—on my own. All this has helped me develop a relationship with my body, independent of any negative experiences that it has experienced. These activities have resulted in a significantly kinder, welcoming, and accepting attitude towards my body."

I've experimented with loads of different things to get me to feel more at home in my body. I practiced yoga for years; I use drugs like weed that help me feel in my body. I obsessively buy, propagate, and repot my approximately 50 houseplants, whose leaves and soil remind me what is capable with care from my body to another living thing. I snuggle my dog, like a lot, and his puppy kisses (yes, I'm that white lady who lets her dog lick her face) remind me how joyful it is to be in my body and be able to connect with him. I've gone through periods of doing guided visualizations and meditations a bunch, then not, then picking it up again when it's helpful for me.

In addition to all of this, there are some therapeutic approaches that focus on the body as a way of healing trauma that may be of interest to some of you, which are generally called somatic (which means related to the body) therapy, including Somatic Experiencing, sensorimotor psychotherapy, and craniosacral therapy.

It is totally okay if the thought of connecting with your body feels overwhelming or uninviting. We have had to spend a lot of time disconnected from our bodies in order to keep ourselves safe. We need to honor the pace that feels right for us and not force anything that doesn't feel safe to us, even if conventional wisdom tells us it's "good" for us.

Elizabeth shared what she finds challenging: "I find anything that calls for me to be present in my body incredibly triggering, even breathing exercises. The best thing for me to connect with my body has been acknowledging to myself that I don't want to force my body to do anything. Whether it's canceling a dentist appointment or taking the elevator instead of the stairs, I make choices now based on what my body does and doesn't want." I love Elizabeth's wisdom because it serves as an important reminder that sometimes it's not about what we are actively doing with our bodies, but rather what we *aren't* asking our bodies to do.

There's no right way to connect with our bodies, and the way that's right for you will be so specific to you.

Perhaps you are already doing things that help you feel at home in your body, and you may have not noticed it! What are some things you are doing in your life that help you be more in your body? Are there new things you'd like to experiment with while practicing patience and self-compassion?

WE CAN EXPLORE HOW BODY-CENTERED GRATITUDE PRACTICES FEEL FOR US

In learning to be more neutral toward my body and no longer see it as betraying me, I've taken to trying to intentionally thank my body for allowing me to do things that are important or pleasurable for me. It's nothing fancy or formal, but whenever I notice that I am happy, I try to take a moment to say to myself, "Thank you, body, for allowing me to experience this."

Sometimes I do this when I'm delightfully drunk with my friends, having sex, going on a beautiful hike, or feeling the warmth of wrapping my arms around someone I love. I try to take a beat to thank my body for allowing me to be present to get to do the shit that means the most to me.

Is a gratitude practice something you'd like to experiment with for your body? What comes to your mind when you consider ways to befriend your body?

STRATEGY: Becoming our own health care advocates

While our health care systems shouldn't require so much self-advocacy labor, it doesn't look like they will radically improve anytime soon. In the meantime, we can practice identifying our needs, creating safety plans, and asking for what we need.

LOOKING FOR PATTERNS IN OUR TRIGGERS AND HEALTH.
IT'S A DATA-COLLECTION OPPORTUNITY FOR DATA-LOVING FRIENDS!

One way is to observe patterns in our health and use that information to better advocate for ourselves during appointments with health care practitioners. Examples of my patterns:

- ▶ I tend to get cold and flulike symptoms a few days after processing a big trauma trigger.
- ▶ Whenever I have a lot of fears around trauma stuff, my chronic migraines return.
- ▶ When I go through periods of hypervigilance and anticipating triggers, my digestive system goes to hell and I get insane poop attacks that make me feel like one of my kidneys just fell out of my butt.

By noticing these patterns, I am not diminishing the validity of my physical pain, nor am I implying that I somehow caused it by having high stress levels or anything of the sort. But the knowledge of my own patterns helps me have conversations with my doctors that are more useful to me—for example, asking how to fortify my immune system during triggering periods, or options for medications to interrupt trauma trigger cycles.

Knowing my patterns also helps me to proactively offer myself care and support, as opposed to always feeling like I'm responding to myself in crisis. By being observant, with as little self-judgment as possible, I noticed that every time I did a professional speaking engagement where I spoke about CSA, no matter how great the event went, I felt physically ill for two days after. I've tried so many things to prevent those two days of feeling sick.

But then I spoke with my friend Ignacio Rivera, the founder of The HEAL Project, which works to end CSA through holistic sexuality education, and I realized that it was completely normal that this work would have this kind of impact on our bodies and health. Ignacio modeled for me being proactive and planning on taking the day or two after an event fully off so I can rest and recover.

Knowing that someone I look up to plans for their health this way really helped reduce my feelings of shame or being hard on myself for having my needs. I still feel sick for 48 hours after an event, but I now anticipate it and build it into my schedule, which helps me recover with greater ease and self-compassion.

Our patterns will be specific to each of us, but my hope is that we can observe ourselves, while tapping into deep wells of self-compassion, and understand that this information can be useful to each of us.

I invite you to reflect on these questions:

> ► What are some patterns or trends you've noticed about how your triggers and health may be linked together?
> ► What opportunities may there be to build support or advocate for yourself with that knowledge of yourself?

You don't need to know right now! For now, I invite you to welcome a judgment-free curiosity with yourself.

STRATEGY: Pushing through the discomfort to advocate for our boundaries when dealing with health care providers

We deserve so much more than the medical system currently offers survivors. It is unacceptable that so many people cannot afford to go to the doctor or don't have options for safe, trauma-informed doctors.

While we may not be able right now to overhaul the entire health care system to be in alignment with survivors' healing, we can use our words to communicate for boundaries! Here are examples of language we can use when dealing with providers:

- ► "I am not going to be weighed today. I would like for us to focus on a wellness/treatment plan that is not focused on changing my weight."

- ► "It is not clear how this question is relevant to my health care."

- ► "I came with a prepared record of my history/symptoms/analysis, and all the questions I feel comfortable answering are already addressed in the document."

- ► "I am uncomfortable with xyz procedure (exam, x-ray, test, etc.). Is it medically necessary at this time?"

- ► "I need a break. We can continue after I have a few minutes to myself."

- ► "Can you explain each step of this exam before we begin and check in with me at each step of the exam?"

- ► "I am getting the sense that you may need additional information about providing health care to trauma survivors. Is that something you can do some learning about before our next appointment?"

What phrases or boundaries would you add to this list? Are there any new ones you can think of that could meet your needs or increase your comfort?

Being our own health care advocates can sometimes feel like we are being too "pushy" or "demanding." I think it feels that way because we are challenging the power dynamics between provider and patient that traditionally tell us that doctors have all the power and we have no agency. By being our own advocates, we are saying that we want our providers to be partners in our health. By being your own advocate, even if it's uncomfortable, you are taking wonderful care of yourself, which is truly what all health care providers should want for their patients.

Great, now let's put this knowledge to work and do whatever our bodies tell us they need

I hope we can all get more curious about the relationship between our minds and our bodies. I will say it one more time because I never tire of it and I think it's too important: There is no shame or self-blame that our trauma and our health are invariably linked. We all deserve compassionate, fully trauma-informed care that honors the complexity of our health experiences.

Our bodies have been through so much and have done a wonderful job getting us here and keeping us alive. Now we get to put all the pieces of our own internal jigsaw puzzle together, pieces that were pulled apart without our permission, and explore what happens when we allow for our minds, bodies, and spirits to be reconnected together again.

So, let's listen to our bodies as they tell us what we need right now. A bathroom break? A bite to eat? A walk around the block? To put on some cozy PJ pants and watch TV? Whenever you're ready, the rest of this book will be here for you.

4

We Are Delightful Friends

UNTRUE STORY
We have too many needs to be a good friend

BUT TRUTHFULLY
We can have needs and still have meaningful friendships

As the legendary Barbra Streisand said in *Funny Girl* via serenading a mediocre fuck boy, "People, people who need people, are the luckiest people in the world."

We all need people, and also, people are a tricky business, which is why the next couple of chapters are devoted to different kinds of relationships in our lives. We are starting with friendship, as I find friendships the most interesting, yet underexplored, form of relationships. They are a source of intimacy, romance, and love that are built on two people's continued consent. They are not founded on a familial obligation or a legally binding contract; instead, they are love and support given freely. That shit is beautiful to me.

But friendships are fucking hard. Often they mean more to us than our romantic relationships, and in following in the leadership of trans women of color, including survivors Sylvia Rivera and Marsha P. Johnson, who for decades have shown the world what it means to create a chosen family, often our friends do become the family that we build for ourselves. It is also likely that if we are going to disclose our abuse to someone, it is going to be to a friend.

Yet there isn't a whole lot out there that helps us to navigate these relationships, especially when living in a society that tells survivors that our trauma is a liability we need to protect others from. The complicated truth is that we need people, that interdependence is real and necessary for healing, yet our experiences with trauma direct us to either hide our pain or isolate ourselves from human connection. Let's walk step-by-step together to unpack those feelings of shame. Each of us is capable and worthy of healthy meaningful friendships.

I'm in this with you, and I still worry sometimes that I am "too much" to be a good friend

Let's travel back in time to 2008, when Lady Gaga had just hit the scene and no one yet had the sense to be exhausted by the Black Eyed Peas. I was a junior in college and a director of the biggest student organization on the University of Michigan's campus.

The summer before junior year, Jack, my stepfather, died, triggering not only grief but repressed memories of child sexual abuse from my biological father. Back then, I was diagnosed with PTSD for the first of many times.

My overachieving tendencies, at once a comfort, also led me to isolate

I returned to campus in the fall fully traumatized, dependent on Klonopin (What doctor prescribes this to a college student and doesn't explain to them that it's habit-forming and not to be taken with alcohol?! Hello, 2008), and crushingly determined to keep moving forward. Overachieving had always been a part of my coping mechanisms, as it offered me a distraction from my pain and a way to find a false sense of control. So many survivors develop these perfectionistic tendencies as a coping mechanism. Shout-out to fellow perfectionists—are we having fun yet?!

As these old type A–style coping mechanisms kicked into high gear, a value system arose in me to try to make sense of what I was enduring: "Look how strong I am. I am in such unimaginable pain, and the people around me have no idea. If they ever found out, they'd be so impressed by how strong I am." I remember thinking this with such intensity, as it never dawned on me that hiding my trauma was not in my best interest, nor a good foundation for building friendships. I told myself that if friends ever found out, they'd admire me and look up to me in amazement as some sort of hero.

The trauma math I had been doing wasn't adding up anymore

I made it to the end of the school year and decided to confide in one of my organization teammates, Eva, about what the last year had actually been like for me. Here was my big moment—she was going to be so floored by me and my strength!

But I was confused. Instead of looking at me with awe, Eva's eyes were filled with sadness. I wanted to shout at her, "Are you not amazed?!" Reader, she was not amazed.

Eva told me how sorry she was that I had to endure all that I had and, in a way that did not make it at all about her, lovingly expressed a sadness that I hadn't shared this with her and our friends the entire year.

My mind was swirling, recalculating the math I had been relying on for a year that said: hiding trauma – burdening/depressing anyone with your needs + being present for them in a way that I wouldn't let them be for me = good friend. That calculation left a person I really cared about feeling like maybe we weren't actually close friends.

I'm not saying anyone is deserving or entitled to know about our trauma and pain. No one is. But I would've loved for Eva and our team to have known what I was going through. Not necessarily any details: just to know I was really struggling with mental health. If I had known I could show up without a sparkling smile on my face, then I wouldn't have spent so many nights isolating myself from a healing community.

I began to see the binary I had set up for myself:

- ► Option A: I was strong and admired.
- ► Option B: I was honest and a depressing burden.

Not only was this binary unhelpful and isolating to me, but it didn't benefit my friends either. Over the years, I've learned to recognize when my brain is thinking that there are only these two polar options and to challenge myself to find secret Option C, where I get the support I want and need while honoring my boundaries and the boundaries of the people I love.

It isn't always easy or cute, but we need people, and they need us. Learning to deconstruct the walls of isolation that trauma causes is one of the most radical and powerful things I've learned to do for myself.

Other versions of untrue stories about friendship and trauma

Since our untrue stories aren't a one-size-fits-all thing, here are some other survivors' versions:

Dani shared with me that her untrue stories around friendships told her that it was best to keep distant, for fear that people would see her as a human disaster. "They'll see me as a big mess, and there is so much shame attached to that fear." The world has taught us, as survivors, to feel shame about how we simply exist in the world.

Teagan, another survivor, expressed that their untrue story is that "I'm 'too much' and people won't like me if they see my true self" and shared a fear that their relationships will be one-sided, with them taking more than they give. But support isn't a zero-sum game, where if one of us is being supported, then it means others aren't.

What does your version of the untrue story around friendship sound like? Maybe the words don't come quickly to the surface. That's okay! Below is a list of questions to gently explore the fears:

- ► What are some times when I've been afraid of appearing too needy?
- ► What fears come up for me when I consider confiding in a friend?

▶ What pressures may I feel to be "healed enough" to be able to build reciprocal friendships?

What are the origins of the bullshit?

There are people I trusted who reinforced my untrue story

One important question comes to mind when I think about who reinforced my untrue story that I should hide my pain: Who are the people who taught me to prioritize other people's comfort over my own emotional needs?

I specifically recall going to see a child psychologist when I was in fifth grade to help me manage all the hurt and confusion I felt around my father. I remember telling the psychologist calmly that I didn't want to harm my father, but I just wished he was peacefully dead, without him suffering and without anyone being upset. A pretty eloquent solution for a fifth grader, don't you think?

Unfortunately, her response to me was to make me name one thing my father was good at, to which I replied, "Cooking, I guess," and then she instructed me to focus exclusively on that one good thing about my dad when around him. (Frequently, I play a fantasy out in my mind of finding that child psychologist; handing her this here book, with this page highlighted because I am petty and also operate with the subtlety of a hurricane; furiously stuff my pockets with all her good fidget toys; and dramatically slam the door on my way out.)

I remember being grateful to that now-loathed child psychologist. As a kid, I felt she had "saved" me, because in learning how to repress and deny my true painful emotions, I was able to continue to have a relationship with my father, which, to child-me, was the most important thing I could do. I learned in that experience to prioritize making sure that everyone was comfortable over my very real and urgent needs. My father also reinforced this lesson in the next paragraph, which you may wish to skip if you're triggered by emotional gaslighting.

That lesson continued to be reinforced in all my interactions with my father. When I would reveal to him little droplets of my deep resentment and hurt, he reacted with such severity, which often involved crying his tears of victimhood, that I learned it was safer for me to fake my emotions and plaster on a smile while dying inside.

Are there people who taught you to prioritize other people's comfort over your own needs? How has that affected how you approach relationships?

Other survivors also untangle survival messages from their childhood in their adult friendships. Teagan shared, "It comes from living with abuse and secrets and learning at a very early age to pretend. As a young child, I tried to act 'normal' and perfect so no one would suspect the abuse and learned to act like things were okay when they weren't. It was a part of my survival mechanism. Even after years of therapy, it can still feel like 'too much' to be my full self with friends."

Repression is not the answer. And still, I have a great deal of empathy for the younger version of me, and the younger version of all of us, who had to navigate staying safe and who learned from adults to repress our trauma and go with the flow rather than be the "difficult, dramatic" child. I want to hug the child-me who had to find a way to make sense of carrying around a hidden world of pain, and so she made it her own valuable superpower, her nifty trick that she convinced herself others would admire if only they knew.

It can be so difficult to recover from a friend's failure to support us during a disclosure or from their saying something hurtful to us that reinforces our fears around our trauma. If past experiences like that are weighing heavy on your heart, please know you are not alone. That pain matters.

Are there people you can identify in your life who upheld or influenced parts of your untrue story around friendship? What messages did you receive? What do you think may have been those people's motivations for telling you those messages? How can you feel compassion for your past and present self?

The social stigma around mental health

While I spend all my spare time on TikTok watching Gen-Z teens speak powerfully and openly about their own mental health experiences, in 2008 those messages were not a part of my lived experience. This isn't to say that there haven't been disability and mental health activists who have been fighting for decades, just that in my little bubble, we were not talking openly about this shit.

If everyone around me had felt safe being open about their own mental health struggles, I wouldn't have felt I had to hide. Nowadays, if I have plans with a friend and feel an instinct to cancel because my trauma is really present, I'll give that friend a heads-up: "I'm having a rough mental health day, but I still want to chill and eat delicious food together—is that cool?" It helps relieve the pressure I feel to either fake a smile or stay home alone. But I didn't know, until others modeled it for me, that it was even an option to be so honest and unashamed about my mental health.

When I did eventually share my trauma with friends, I navigated a lot of their misunderstandings about why things don't just get better. Although everyone's trauma awareness has grown, those misunderstandings made me share less for a time. All of us were being negatively impacted by the lack of cultural understanding around the long-term impacts of trauma.

Ableism and individualism at work make us feel shame for living with trauma

Ableism, as Jaden Fields of Mirror Memoirs defined it to me, is "a system that creates the idea of what is a good right kind of body and mind and 'other' minds and bodies. The 'others' get pathologized or made to be seen as bad, unhealthy, difficult, something to fix or something to dismiss."

Ableism and capitalism work together to tell us that people who do not have disabilities are more valuable in our society, and people living with disabilities are a burden. You may or may not identify as someone living with a disability. Personally, I often identify as someone with a disability (PTSD is defined as such under the Americans with Disabilities Act), and I have found the leadership of people with disabilities fighting against ableism to be of tremendous benefit.

Before I understood my own disability and began my disability justice work, my internalized ableism told me I was more valuable if I could deny my disability and fake "normality." Most of all, my internalized ableism told me that not needing others was an admirable and valuable trait.

This is rooted in the lie of American individualism, which tells us that the goal of being a good and valuable American is to lift yourself up by your bootstraps and be self-reliant and not need community, accommodations, or social safety nets. And it's a total scam.

Powerful movements in the United States challenge this scam. "Disability justice, a queer and trans people of color–led liberation strategy, understands that ableism is a form of oppression," Jaden explained to me. Per Jaden, part of the disability justice strategy is to give people full access to their autonomy to create networks of care that center people's needs—"for people to not treat disability as a burden, but rather to understand that there's so much wisdom that comes from understanding your body and mind's different needs." For more on disability justice, I invite you to explore the works of Mia Mingus and Patricia Berne.

In what ways have stigma, shame, or ableism fueled your untrue story? In what ways could stigma and ableism impact millions of other people living with trauma? I ask this not so that you feel overwhelmed by the magnitude of hurt, but rather so that you see you aren't alone in this and see that it isn't your fault that you feel these ways!

Strategies

STRATEGY: Let's do a cute little imagined role-reversal scenario

One strategy for fighting the untrue story that we burden our friends is to do a hypothetical role reversal with the friend in question. When I put myself in my friend's shoes, I am able to see that I am giving my friend an opportunity to meaningfully show up for me in a way that honors everyone's needs.

This is a strategy I developed after talking a few years ago with a survivor friend, Lauren, who had told me that she was struggling to make friends. "I was in such a trap; I was stuck in a cycle of making a little progress with making friends, and then being triggered and having a couple of hard days and losing all that progress," Lauren told me recently as she looked back on our conversation. "It was so demoralizing, to the point where I started to wonder if I should even bother trying anymore."

To help her navigate this, I asked her some questions, which I'll share with you here, so that if you want, you can ask yourself them too:

Question 1: What, in your ideal world, would you want from this friend?

Is there a particular friendship that's coming to mind for you, and if yes, what would you like from it? As for Lauren, she wanted the friend to not take it personally if she had to ghost for a while to take care of herself, and for that friend to keep inviting her to things even if she couldn't join for a while.

Question 2: What are you comfortable sharing with this friend?

When you ask yourself this question, remember that no one is entitled to our truth, and we should only ever share what we want to share. Sometimes we want to clue a friend in about what we are going through, while still honoring our boundaries and privacy. I find that all-or-nothing thinking can show up when considering disclosing to a friend. We may think we have to either pretend we are totally fine or list all our traumas in alphabetical order with citations included. But there is so much space between those polar options.

As for Lauren, she found it challenging to think about what she wanted to share, so I offered her some examples, which I've listed here in case you may find them useful:

- ► "I have some mental health challenges that impact my day-to-day life."
- ► "I am navigating healing from past trauma, and it still impacts me today."
- ► "Sometimes things are shit for me because of long-term impacts of what happened in my childhood. It isn't anything I want to get into at this time; I just wanted to give you a heads-up."

What might a message that honors the amount of information you feel safe sharing, put in your own words, sound like?

Once we have the answers to the two questions, we can put it all together to practice an imagined role-reversal conversation with a friend.

I asked Lauren how she'd feel if a friend told her, "I'm going through mental health challenges from past trauma, and while I don't want to get too into it, I want to give you the heads-up that I tag out for weeks at a time to focus on my healing. When that happens, please don't take it as a sign that I don't want to be friends. If you don't hear from me, could you still keep inviting me to things so that when I am better, we can hang out? Does that work for you?

Lauren smiled and replied, "I'd feel important, like she trusted me and was invested in our friendship." A very sweet, lovely light bulb had gone off over Lauren's head (she's a very lovely person, so of course the light bulb would match), and in doing the role reversal, she realized what I had learned with my friend Eva: that it doesn't have to be all-or-nothing.

She continued, "Recognizing my black-and-white thinking was so key for me; because of my experience with trauma, I am so used to living life on a scale of extremes that I forget that there is a middle ground, and allowing myself to access it can be so profound and stabilizing." We can create our own boundaries for friendships—sharing what feels right to us, communicating our needs, trusting that our friends can do the same for us too. All of that often makes people feel valued and connected to us.

What is it like for you to imagine your friend telling you exactly what you'd like to say to them? I encourage you to be as specific and direct about what you'd like from your friend as possible. It may be uncomfortable to be honest and direct with yourself about exactly what you want, and it can bring up big hard feelings about feeling shame about our needs.

But we are modeling for our friends ways of being open and transparent while honoring our boundaries. The more explicit my friends are with me, the more I realize it's okay for me to be that way too. So by engaging in these kinds of strategies with our friends, we may be doing them a favor by expanding their own ways of thinking about their needs and their friendships!

STRATEGY: Using the spoon theory to
help us communicate with less shame

"What is the spoon theory?" you may ask. Well, it is a theory developed by Christine Miserandino in an effort to describe to a friend what it was like for her to live with a chronic autoimmune disease. As she describes on her website, ButYouDontLookSick.com, the spoon theory says that people have a limited amount of energy, and that energy is represented by spoons.[1]

People start the day with a set number of these metaphorical spoons. Christine starts with fewer spoons because of living with her chronic illness. Every activity in the day costs spoons (aka energy), like showering, working, and preparing a meal. The fewer spoons available, the fewer activities a person can engage in.

Christine's spoon theory spread like bananas on the internet as a way for people dealing with chronic conditions, from lupus to clinical depression, to communicate to people what it is like living in an ableist world that doesn't make space for people living with chronic illness and disability. It gave people a new way to talk about the realities of limited energy or capacity in a way that doesn't bring guilt or shame upon the person who is dealing with differences.

I learned about the spoon theory when my bestie Kate texted me, "Do you have spoons today to give me advice on something?" I responded that I had all the cutlery in the world for her, and when we got on the phone, she explained the theory to me. It felt like such a relief to have language that helped me understand my own capacity and share with others without shame.

If someone without a chronic condition or disability starts the day with 20 spoons, I'll say that with my C-PTSD I start the day with, let's say, 15 spoons. If I had nightmares the night before, that automatically takes half of my spoons. If I experienced an intense full trigger, then that's like 8 of my spoons already gone at the start of the day. Working takes 6 spoons, exercise another 2, and feeding myself another 2. It means that some days I have no spoons left to socialize with someone, to take a shower, or to clean up my home.

Instead of feeling hard on myself that I need to reschedule plans or that I cannot bring myself to go to the grocery store, I can understand that I simply have the spoons I have, through no fault of my own. The spoons are limited and there's no shame in that.

"Spoon theory is so helpful because it allows us to build a friendship based on mutual consideration. When we request support from a friend, we ask them to consider if they're able to give it," shares Dani. "When practicing spoon theory, I never feel like I am a burden. If I'm asking someone about their available spoons, I trust that they'll be honest with me."

Applying the theory like this has also been an awesome way to practice consent with my friends, especially with my bestie Kate, who I met on my very first day of college. Not only did Kate teach me about vintage clothing, model for me what it's like to not exist for the male gaze, and show me that even when you think there's nothing in the house, there's always enough ingredients for a soup, but also she taught me that it's okay if we don't have the same amount of needs.

For many years, I worried that my needs eclipsed hers and that I was "too much." I think it took a good eight or so years of friendship for me to confess my fear of having more needs than her. Kate replied, matter-of-factly, "Yeah, so?"

Here I thought she was going to comfort me by denying that I had more needs than her, but instead Kate did something way more powerful and critical for me in my healing: she told the truth. She told me that I do have more needs than her, and that is okay. We aren't the same person; we haven't gone through the same shit, and our brains are wired differently. And that's okay.

In telling this truth, Kate dramatically reduced the shame I had felt for needing the way I did, whether it was needing to cry on the phone more or needing to leave a coffee shop because they were playing a triggering song. By being honest about our differences, I no longer worried as often that I was steamrolling over her feelings.

I will text her, "I'm dealing with some triggers/struggling today, do you have spoons to chat?" This gives Kate enough info to be clued in but allows for her to consent before I dump heavy shit on her. Her reply might look like, "I have spoons but not availability time-wise, but I can text with you, it'll just take me a few hours to respond. Is that cool? I love you."

It isn't our fault that our brains are wired the way they are, and it isn't shameful that we have these long-term impacts of trauma. We don't need to all be the same. What matters is the story we tell ourselves about those needs and whether we can accept people's love and support without keeping score.

What would your version of the spoon theory look like? What are the activities you do in your everyday life, and how many spoons does each of those things require? This is an opportunity to whip out the fancy markers, the glitter pens, and the washi tape, my office-supply-loving friends. Go bananas.

What are ways you can imagine communicating with people in a way that allows for everyone's needs to be honored?

STRATEGY: Putting our eggs in multiple baskets

My relationship with Kate had me proverbially putting all my eggs in her basket for many years. For at least three years, Kate was the one friend I shared my CSA trauma with in detail (except for my therapist Connie, who wasn't a friend but was a very important part of my support system. Remember, friends are not therapists and should never function as our therapists! Boundaries!).

I got all too lucky with Kate. Since she was 16 years old, she volunteered at rape crisis centers, and she now devotes her life to the anti-violence movement. All this goes to say, she isn't just a good friend, she is a professional bestie to this lucky survivor. In the early stages when I was processing my CSA, Kate was able to give me critical information, like the fact that it was normal to not remember CSA clearly. She was trauma-informed before I even knew what that term meant, and our already extremely close friendship was even lifesaving at one point.

One month into writing this book, I visited Kate. While hiking with her dog somewhere outside of Oakland, we talked about that terrifying time of my life. She shared that while she knew all the "right" things to say to a survivor in a professional context, it felt totally different to her when it was her closest friend going through it. Kate told me it was hard when I looked to her for all the answers. She had to learn for herself that it was okay to not know. While she glided with ease up the mountain and I tried to pretend I wasn't sucking wind, Kate shared that she had to make peace with the reality that she was one person who couldn't fix my trauma for me. In many ways, I was looking for her to replicate the role of my therapist, which isn't an appropriate or fair thing for friends to do to one another.

Being young 20-somethings and learning how to have boundaries with friends is hard enough, but then doing it while navigating trauma is next-level tricky. In time, I learned that I needed to widen my bench and not just rely on one person to fulfill all my friendship emotional needs, especially since as an extroverted person, I needed to talk with people about my shit. I don't mean to say that I don't need Kate—I do—but in order to honor the needs of both of us, I cannot put all my eggs in her basket. It isn't what is good for either of us.

While Kate offered a specific kind of emotional support, when I expanded my thinking, I realized that I actually had a lot of friends who loved me and I could trust, even if there were things I wouldn't talk about to them in the same way I'd share with Kate.

Have you found yourself in a scenario where you're putting all your eggs in one basket in terms of looking toward one person to fulfill your emotional needs? What are some ways that you can practice honoring that person's boundaries and making space for them to express their needs?

APPRECIATING THAT PEOPLE
SHOW LOVE IN DIFFERENT WAYS

About five years ago, Sarah, one of my best friends from childhood and college, moved back to DC. While Sarah didn't have any experience navigating trauma and didn't love talking about feelings, she loved me in her own very meaningful way.

In high school, Sarah wore a sandwich board for an entire day to campaign for me to be elected as student-body vice president. It was a winning strategy. In college, when I found that my stepfather's cancer had returned, I lay on the floor of our apartment unable to move, and Sarah, having no words to offer me, panic-baked me a chocolate cake and served it next to my face-planted head on the ground. In her own special and specific way, she had loved me for a really long time.

I knew that it wouldn't be honoring Sarah, her needs, and who she was for me to talk to her in the same way I spoke to Kate. But we grew to meet each other where the other was at. She learned to sit and be present with me and just listen when I needed to talk, and I learned to appreciate being heard by this person who cared about me, even if she didn't have the "right" words. She had her own language, which, as she was a classically trained chef and a fellow Jewess, often involved a lot of awesome food.

I accepted Sarah for who she was, and she also accepted me as I was, while still learning from one another. I taught Sarah to stop telling me that things were going to be okay, and she taught me to get out of my head and into my body, both through nourishing myself with a good friend and by snuggling her angel puppydog Clive. We learned how to understand and appreciate each other for who we were.

EXPANDING NETWORKS OF CARE

This idea of expanding our networks of care so that we aren't putting all our needs onto one person is one that Jaden Fields has been thinking a lot about too. "Through the leadership of other folks in the Disability Justice lineage, I've been learning that building a network of care means you aren't depending on one person to meet all your needs, but that your needs are interconnected." He reminded me that networks of care aren't a new concept; people have been learning to lean on their communities since forever. "I learned about the tenets of this growing up in the Black church, because while the church was the site of a lot of trauma and fuckery for me, I did see that it did everything for the community, since we knew we couldn't depend on the state."

We can invite people in to be a part of our support team in a way that honors everyone's boundaries. People have to have the option to say no, and we have to be okay with that. And as Jaden has taught me, not everyone in our network of care has to be a super bestie. Our coworkers don't have to be emotionally close to offer us professional support when we need it. Or maybe acquaintances have pets we can visit when we need animal time. Think creatively about who can support you.

Are there ways you can see yourself widening your bench of people you can turn to for support and community? Are there people in your life who may have their own unique ways of expressing love and care? What does it look like for us to consider all the different gifts and capacities of people, so that all our emotional needs do not fall squarely on one single person?

STRATEGY: Practicing addressing
harm that occurs in our friendships

This strategy is a hard one. And that's okay, we can handle hard shit—look at us! As I've learned from leaders, namely Black queer and trans women of the transformative justice movement, including Mariame Kaba and Aishah Shahidah Simmons: all people are capable of and do cause harm. Being in relationships with people means we fuck up, hurt people's feelings, make mistakes, and sometimes make bad decisions. The question is, when that happens, how do we hold ourselves accountable for that hurt?

I remember a few years in my life when I felt deeply connected to my victimhood in a way that made it difficult for me to hold myself accountable when I inevitably crossed a boundary or hurt a friend (We all do! It's part of being human!). For so many years, my victimhood had been so intensely denied by the world around me, and as a result, I began to crave the specific kind of validation that comes when people see you as a victim.

But when I fucked up and didn't honor a friend's request for some space from me as they processed their own personal struggles, I took their feedback as an invalidation of my victimhood. Instead of simply saying to that friend, "I am sorry, and I will honor your boundaries," I felt a strong internal resistance where something within me wanted to scream, "I am a victim too!" I struggled to not center my own feelings in this simple exchange between friends.

For a lot of us who had childhoods where boundaries either didn't exist or were not honored, it may be challenging for us to experience other people asserting their boundaries with us. Even today, I sense those initial impulses to feel fragile and make their boundaries about my feelings. With practice, I have learned how to take a breath, create space from the moment, prioritize the feelings of the person I hurt, and meaningfully apologize when I do inevitably fuck up.

More on this to come, but I encourage each of us, very much myself included, to understand the ways we unintentionally hurt people we care about, explore how we can prevent future hurt, and meaningfully apologize while centering the feelings of the harmed.

I'm not asking that we hold ourselves to a higher standard than others; I certainly think the whole world would be a hell of a lot safer and healthier if everyone did this! I do think we have a unique opportunity to model for people in our lives what holding ourselves accountable for hurt in relationships looks like.

What has it felt like when a friend asserted a boundary with you? What might it look like to safely explore any feelings of discomfort so that, over time, you can respond with even greater ease and respect when friends communicate boundaries?

STRATEGY: Accepting that sometimes
we may have to release a friendship

I KNOW IT IS PAINFUL, BUT SOMETIMES WE HAVE TO RELEASE A FRIENDSHIP

Sometimes when we focus on our healing, including creating boundaries and showing up in the world without shame, it can bring us clarity that some of our friendships aren't working for us anymore. You make the rules. You get to decide what friendships you continue and what friendships are no longer the right fit.

If you're dealing with a friend who is failing to support you in a meaningful way, especially after you've tried communicating with them clearly about needs, please remember that their reaction likely has nothing to do with you. I know this is easier said than done! But I've seen just so many times that someone's bad reaction to our trauma is really about them: their own triggers, unresolved trauma, or emotional challenges.

Releasing friendships can be so painful. I still obsess over friendships that ended years ago. I feel guilty when I think about all the good times. We survivors have an incredible ability to blame ourselves for any and everything. I blame myself for what I see as a failure of those friendships. Which is a super harsh and unfair way to see things!

I don't need to wish that my obsessive thoughts over these old friendships will suddenly disappear. Instead, I just interrupt those thoughts by asking myself questions like these:

- ► Was that person able to give me what I needed?
- ► Am I entitled to need what I need from my friends?
- ► Am I the only one responsible for maintaining a healthy friendship, or should both people be equally responsible?
- ► How do I feel when I think of my current healthy friendships versus how it feels to think about these old friendships?

I remind myself to tap into compassion and understanding for myself, trusting that I have made the decisions I've needed to make. It's okay if it doesn't feel neat and tidy, because relationships are complicated.

When thinking about friendships you've released or may need to release, what kinds of emotions arise for you? What do those emotions remind you of? I invite us all to get curious about a path toward accepting that not all friendships get to come with us, and it may be no one's "fault" but just a natural progression of life.

NEW EXCELLENT FRIENDSHIPS CAN EMERGE FROM OUR HEALING WORK

When we focus on our healing, some new and very cool friendships often begin to emerge in our lives. When we are clear about who we are and the importance of healthy boundaries, we develop new fulfilling and transformative friendships.

Sometimes all we can see is everything we've lost to our trauma. I totally understand if that's where your heart is today. Even if it's hard to see it right now, I firmly believe there is some deeply cool shit for you coming your way friendship-wise because of all your amazing healing work.

STRATEGY: Remembering all the great and totally delightful things we bring to a friendship!

Be clear with yourself about all the gifts you bring to a friendship. I know that when I am deep in the shit and dealing with triggers, I feel so far away from the light that lives inside me. My all-or-nothing thinking kicks in and tells me I am a garbage person living on garbage island and have nothing to offer. It is in these moments that I have to rely on a practice of literally listing out all the ways I've been a good friend.

By now, you've probably picked up on my personal dislike of trauma silver linings. I am not interested in glorifying the shit we've had to go through. But I cannot deny that there are some really important gifts we specifically can bring to our friendships as a result of our experience with healing work. Gifts like these:

- The way we show our friends how to have open conversations about needs, boundaries, and consent
- The ways we can help our friends advocate for themselves by seeing how we advocate for ourselves
- The way we model self-compassion and emotional honesty, which gives our friends permission to do the same

Tools from our healing help us show up for our people in a way that is meaningful and so important. Clare shares, "I think the act of doing therapy makes it easier for me to be a friend. It's easier to listen without judgment. It's easier for me to spot dysregulation in others and learn how to navigate it."

What does it feel like for you to consider what specific gifts you bring to your friendships? How do compassion, empathy, and emotional intelligence, for example, show up for you in your friendships? Is there some resistance to placing value on these skills? If yes, that's okay! It can be new and uncomfortable to think of ourselves in these ways, and hopefully in time it gets a lot easier for us!

Phew, look at us! Diving into the good and fucking tricky realities of needing and loving our friends. Great job, everyone!

It's hard fucking work to be honest with each other about the ways our trauma impacts our friendships. I'm sure there are so many ways I didn't even mention that your trauma has impacted your friendships, all of which are valid and important.

As for me, I've learned over the years to release my untrue binary that I either have to fake that I'm totally fine in order to be liked, or be honest and a bummer of a burden on my friends. A decade later, and I am grateful to Eva for waking me up to my own untrue story, and grateful that I now have a more honest relationship with myself and with my friends.

My hope is that in time, we are able to offer ourselves the compassion and understanding that we'd like to give to our friends and remember that there is no shame in needing people. Barbra is right: we need people, and that's a good thing.

5

Our Bodies Are Wise about Sexual Healing

UNTRUE STORY
*We are having too much sex because of our trauma and
are also having too little sex because of our trauma*

BUT TRUTHFULLY
*Our sex lives ebb and flow with us as a part of our healing,
and we have nothing to be ashamed of!*

My friend, do you feel like you're desiring the right amount of sex? What about the right kind of sex? Blink once if you feel like you're "broken" from the CSA and it's causing you to not want *enough* sex. Blink twice if you feel like you're "broken" from the CSA and it's causing you to want *too much* sex. Blink until your eyes are just closed from exhaustion if you struggle to make sense of all the voices in your head telling you conflicting stories about how your trauma is impacting your sex life. Then open your eyes again so I can tell you that you are not alone in the way you feel, and we are going to navigate it together.

In conversations with thousands of survivors, I've found that all of us feel some form of pressure around sex and our trauma. Sex is a part of the very nature of how we were harmed, so it is inevitably a part of our hurt and healing. But its significance extends beyond that; sex often becomes a yardstick with which we and others measure our progress on the mythical road from broken to healed. We can end up lost in our minds trying to parse out what is our own sexual autonomy and what is trauma.

Each of us has different untrue stories that dance inside our heads about who we are and the sex we do and don't want. While the voices in my head may sound like they're shaming me for banging someone, those voices in your head may sound like they're shaming you for abstaining. Even though the words in our heads may be different, they stem from the same forces at play: blaming survivors for the ways we endure and heal. No matter what our untrue stories tell us, we each have to navigate turning down the volume on them so we can hear our own body's wisdom more clearly.

In the first half of this chapter we'll talk about being slut-shamed for the sex we want, and in the second half we'll talk about being prude-shamed and the pressure we may feel for not desiring sex. I've felt all of these things and everything in between, so stick with me and we will cover it all!

PART 1: Shaming survivors for the sex we want

Untrue stories say things like, "My sexual desire isn't *real*, it's just a symptom of my trauma," "Am I even attracted to [insert any kind of person], or is it all a response to my CSA?" and "Something's wrong with me that I want this much sex or I want to engage in these types of sexual fantasies."

I encourage you to identify which ones are popping up right now (with as little self-judgment as possible!). Remember, we are just gently looking inward to see what comes up for us, and it's totally cool if nothing is coming to mind right now.

I, too, have worried that I was having "too much" and not the "right kind" of sex

The untrue story that used to dominate my thinking in my early 20s was that I was sleeping around because I had "daddy issues." While I craved casual fun relations, I worried that others might see me as being too broken to have deeper connections. The stigma from the CSA told me that my sexual desires were only products of my trauma. I was feeling all the intense impacts of some really shitty slut-shaming, which made me distrust my own desires and the wisdom held in my body.

What are the origins of the bullshit?

There is one specific person, Joey, who told me I had daddy issues and made me feel super fucked up for having a lot of sex while healing. Joey and I were friends with an unspoken agreement that we would not acknowledge that I was in love with him.

I was 23 years old and living in Washington, DC, trying to figure out what it meant to return to my hometown as a young professional, which included getting discount drunk at happy hours and ghosting and being ghosted by guys on dating apps. After one weekend when I had dalliances with two different guys, I debriefed with Joey, who was living on the other side of the country, over the phone about it Sunday night.

That was when, in a self-serious tone, Joey warned me, "Be careful. You are starting to behave like you have daddy issues, and you're better than that."

He was someone I trusted deeply who meant more to me than, in retrospect, I wish he had. If he had been some internet troll or some asshole, I think I could've told him to fuck off. But it was so much more confusing to hear words like this from someone who mattered so much to me. Not only was I not-so-secretly in love with Joey, but also he was one of four people, including my therapist, who knew that my father had abused me. This meant that at least 25 percent of all people who knew my truth thought I was an embarrassing mess of a girl with daddy issues.

When we disclose to people we love, we often have to deal with their own internalized rape culture. Please remember that their reactions are not about you. I didn't know then, like I do now, that, as my friend Amita Swadhin says, "when people stigmatize CSA survivors, it says much more about them than about survivors." Joey's words marinated in my mind until the voice saying I had daddy issues over and over again sounded like my own.

Who are the people who may have influenced your untrue story about how much or the kind of sex you may be desiring? What may have been the motivation behind their words? In what ways do their motivations reflect something about them, and not you?

Paternalistic sexism that spits in our face and tells us it's for our own good

There was a specific kind of paternalistic sexism at work with Joey that took me several more years to identify. He fashioned himself after Aaron Sorkin characters (should've been a huge red flag) and saw himself as the kind of cishetero good guy who is the only person in the room who sees the woman in question clearly and knows what is best for her. Think Drake: *'Cause you're a good girl and you know it. I know exactly who you could be.* These same men love to write songs about how the most beautiful woman is one who doesn't know she is beautiful (confidence is so unflattering) until a man identifies and informs her of said beauty.

His behavior also reminded me of the TV show *How I Met Your Mother*, which was extremely popular with white people at the time of my conversation with Joey. Neil Patrick Harris's character, Barney Stinson, a caricature misogynist finance bro we were supposed to find lovable, systematically sought girls with daddy issues because they were crazy, easier to sleep with, wilder in bed, and desperately eager to please men. Instead of looking at girls and femmes who were mistreated by their fathers with respect or, dare I even wish, compassion, the show turned them into a punchline for surviving. I see now that it made Joey's words dig even deeper into my brain.

In what ways have sexism and paternalistic behavior of people who think they know "best" reinforced your untrue story about the sex you desire?

Can doctors please stop talking about "hypersexuality"? It's weird, creepy, and unhelpful

An institutional force upholding my daddy-issues story was the medical establishment, whose warnings about hypersexuality in survivors were everywhere. Article after article written by academics described girl survivors as hypersexual, saying our desire to have sex was a symptom of our trauma. Many researchers even said adults should look at "hypersexuality" in girls as an indication that we may have been abused.

It always seemed like hot garbage to me that academic researchers and medical experts were discussing girl CSA survivors' sexuality in terms like "hypersexual" while knowing they weren't asking the same questions about boys. It is particularly harmful for Black and brown girls because, as a result of the compounded oppressions of racism and sexism, these girls are not afforded the youthful innocence that white girls are, and even as children, they are often discussed and sexualized as though they are adults. As a result, girls of color are disproportionately at a higher risk of experiencing sexual violence and are less likely to be believed when they speak out about it.[1]

Even though it seemed highly questionable to me that mainly white male researchers were worrying about and measuring girls' sexual activity, it still seeped into my brain. There're only so many times you can read about doctors pathologizing all the things that were "wrong" with how we survived and had sex, without feeling stigma.

We have to talk about purity culture . . . oof

Another enormous place that perpetuates our untrue stories around wanting too much sex as survivors is the purity culture found in various religions around the world. Some religious traditions impose strict gender and sexual roles onto young people. While it varies by religion and community, the broad strokes of purity culture are that children assigned male at birth learn that their sexual thoughts are evil, and girls learn that their bodies are evil, as by just existing they are "tempting" men. Sex is reserved for married heterosexual couples with the potential for creating a baby and expanding the patriarchal heteronormative clan.

I spoke to two survivors who grew up in different religious traditions with purity culture on how it impacted their experiences with sexual abuse and healing.

Sarah grew up in an Orthodox Jewish community in New York and was taught from a young age that they had to change their behavior and dress in order to prevent men from having "impure" thoughts: "I was told that once I turned twelve, I would no longer be permitted to sing in public because it could cause men to get aroused. Even when my cousins would come over, my mom would tell me I couldn't be in my pajamas because it might make my cousins 'uncomfortable.'" Betty grew up in an Evangelical

Christian church and family and was taught at a young age by the adults in her life that her body was dangerous and that everything remotely related to sex was extremely sinful.

Purity culture is deeply connected to CSA because children are taught that their sexual selves and bodies are not their own. In particular, purity culture tells us that girls' bodies are to be saved for certain men or to be controlled by men. Their bodies are objectified as family property and a constant potential threat to the sanctity of boys and men. The part that most breaks my heart is that purity culture fuels and justifies blaming children for the sexual violence they experience, as though they did something wrong to invite the abuse.

Both Sarah and Betty shared with me how purity culture fueled so much harmful victim-blaming they received from the adults in their lives. Sarah explained that they were taught that it was their job to not tempt men: "I thought that the abuse must've been my fault and that I did something wrong to provoke it." Similarly, Betty told me she was sexually abused by a family member when she was six years old: "It didn't stop until my mom eventually 'caught us.' And that's how it felt to me, that I was caught in the act too and like I had done something wrong. I feel like if my parents hadn't been so entrenched in purity culture, they would've taken what happened to me more seriously."

For these survivors, it is a continuous journey to unlearn the harmful messages they received throughout their childhoods. Sarah shared, "I still often struggle with compulsory heterosexuality and questioning whether I'm really gay, because for so long I was taught that my sexuality could not exist independently of the male gaze." As for Betty, she told me that she still feels shame sometimes before, during, and after sex and self-pleasure: "I don't think I'll ever fully unlearn everything, but I know that liberation is possible, and I am relearning new things about myself and my sexuality every day."

If you are a survivor who is working through the impacts of purity culture, know that you are not alone in that journey! Sarah offered, "My advice to other survivors working through this is to remember that the shame is not yours to carry. It belongs to your perpetrator and to the culture that kept you silent." They also shared this critical reminder: "We are not bad or wrong or broken; we have nothing to atone for. We are worthy of compassion and healing."

What is it like for us to continue to take the shame we feel and place it where it correctly belongs: on the people and culture that perpetuate abuse?

Strategies

STRATEGY: Examining the shame
we feel around our sexual desire

My friend and fellow survivor Ignacio Rivera, founder of The HEAL Project, has helped me to challenge and release sexual shame. Ignacio told me, "As a society, we believe that relationships, love, and intimacy are an absolute formula, and if you don't fit within that formula, then something is wrong with you." They explained to me that anyone who deviates from the status quo is shamed. It isn't a coincidence; shame is used as a tool to keep people "in line" and prevent them from changing the status quo.

In what ways do you not fit the narrow societal constraints of what relationships, family, sex, and intimacy "should" look like? How are those parts of you connected to the shame you may be experiencing?

For me, I was feeling shame over my relationship with my father in large part because I was challenging the societal norm that we must protect our biological family no matter what. When I deviated from how Joey believed a survivor, and a woman, should act, Joey's words reminded me that I should still feel humiliated and silenced by my trauma. Not only was he saying that my desire to have sex was a symptom of my abuse (cool sex-positive perspective, bro!), but also, by his logic, I was supposed to be "better than" my fellow survivors who were unable to hide the signs of their trauma. The stigma of being a survivor was overwhelming.

By considering my sources of shame, I was able to see that it all was a trap. There was no way to correctly express or conceal my abuse. There was no way to cope better or worse than my fellow survivors. There was no way to perform my trauma so that I would always be granted compassion over shame. Some would pathologize me, no matter what choices I made.

WHILE WE ALL EXPERIENCE SHAMING AROUND
SEX, WE DO NOT EXPERIENCE IT EQUALLY

While all of us experience shame around sex, survivors who most deviate from the heteronormative, monogamous, vanilla sex status quo have to navigate through more shame. Even though I've been shamed for the sex I desire, I am often seen by others as a "good" survivor because I'm a white cis woman who is interested in having what I would describe as some pretty basic-ass heteronormative boring sex.

Others may be deemed "bad" survivors because they engage in sex work or are into kink, are polyamorous, or are queer. Ignacio explained that queer and trans survivors experience a specific kind of shaming and pathologizing, "Our identity is locked into our survivorship because people think the reason why we are queer or trans is because we were sexually abused. People try to find reasoning behind why we are who we are, rather than understanding gender and sexuality as fluid, growing things."

While it can impact us differently, dealing with shame is an inevitable part of being a survivor. "Even as a poly, kink sex educator who teaches people not to have shame, shame still visits me sometimes. The work to get out of shame is our work, it is our self-realization," Ignacio shared.

FANTASY AND ROLE-PLAYING CAN BE
CRITICAL TOOLS IN OUR SEXUAL HEALING

I know so many survivors who've found healing in exploring rape fantasies in safe, supportive ways, but when they talk to me about it, they struggle with stigma and may feel ashamed. We have no time and no space for shame over here, only healing! Talking about fantasies that replicate our abuse is a wonderful time for us to practice our principle that if it feels like it's healing to us, then it's healing to us.

Jaden Fields, the codirector of Mirror Memoirs, has advice for survivors who explore rape fantasies. He says it is critically important for people to recognize that exploring rape fantasies as an adult in a consensual situation with another adult is a completely different scenario than our abuse. "The most important part is that the survivor is making the choice and therefore is in control. Even in a situation where we may be in a submissive role, we are in power because we've chosen that role. In many ways, we are using a reengagement tool, and even beyond kink, we may be experiencing reexposure therapy, as we are going back to a moment with more control and more awareness to heal some aspects of ourselves. That can be a therapeutic tool," Jaden shared.

When I asked him where he might advise someone who is curious to start, Jaden said it is important for survivors to spend time sitting with what we hope these experiences will bring us so we can communicate clearly with our partners about it. "I also advise people to do their own research before they dive in so they have all the information they need in order to tell their partners what their yes/no/maybes are and also create an aftercare plan so each partner gets what they need to feel supported."

The world loves to shame survivors for everything. But engaging in fantasies while practicing boundaries, open communication, and consent is the complete opposite of what we went through with our abuse. "It is important to remember that we are setting the scene with a partner in a way that is in our control, and we can stop it whenever we want. Between the conversations of boundaries before and intentional aftercare following, we are creating environments where we are receiving the kind of care we actually need and be held in a way that is so radically different from the abuse we've experienced," said Jaden.

"It is always important to check in with yourself to see if the fantasy or kink still works for you because it might shift for you, and it's okay to let go of something that may not be in service of your healing any longer," he added. We get to make our own rules, and we get to change those rules when it's right for us too.

WE AREN'T DAMAGED GOODS.
SHOCKINGLY, WE ARE HUMAN BEINGS

If you have ever been called "damaged goods," I have some important words for you. You are not a busted-up old VCR or a hideous vomit-colored moldy vintage chair, or some other object that once upon a time was useful to society and now can sit in a corner falling the fuck apart and not being cherished or valued by the world. I understand why you may feel that way sometimes, because the world tries to objectify us constantly, and maybe someone even told you that before.

But you are a human fucking being. A human being, who, by the way, has survived some shit that no one should have ever had to endure. And does that shit, through no fault of your own, still impact you in various ways today? Yes. And, also, that is okay. What you had to go through was totally fucked up, but you aren't totally fucked up. You are trying to do your best to heal and live a full life navigating conditions you never should have had to navigate.

I encourage you to remind yourself as often as you need to that you are not damaged goods, you are a person healing, and you deserve to be surrounded by the loving embrace of people who honor that. If they don't, it's their shame and loss, not yours.

STRATEGY: Looking to the wisdom of our bodies
to understand what's best for our sex lives

Our bodies hold so much invaluable information when it comes to figuring out what we need for our sex lives. Our bodies talk to us about what feels safe and good, but it can be challenging (through no fault of our own) to hear what they're telling us.

As CSA survivors, many of us learned at a young age to disconnect from the ways our bodies felt as a means to protect ourselves. It is a deep survival mechanism and nothing to judge ourselves for; it is how our brains learned to endure. As a result of this coping mechanism, which was necessary for our survival, we often have decades of practice blocking out the information our bodies are communicating to us. But that's what's so dope about healing: We get to practice new ways of prioritizing the messages from our bodies.

Joey's "daddy issues" comment rocked me. As I worked to get my feet on solid ground again, I knew I could count on my body to tell me the truth, as it had always tried to do, even when it wasn't safe for me, as a child, to listen to it.

When I reflected on what my body was telling me, I saw undeniable signs that the sex I was having actually was healing for me. I was enjoying sex for the first time in my life specifically because I was feeling more in control and empowered in my own skin.

When Joey made his comment, I was enjoying distance from my abusive father for the first time. As I got farther away from my father, something truly thrilling had started happening within me. I began to want sex more. It wasn't like the opening of the floodgates (the metaphor works on multiple levels) with an exploding sexual appetite, but rather, I quietly felt my previously paralyzing fear of sex began to lessen.

I started having sex with more guys and found it really helpful to not care very much about them. I was always so afraid of the high possibility of being triggered mid-hookup, but I realized that my fear became more manageable when I banged dudes for whom I had no feelings. I knew that if I'd have to stop mid-sex and the boys took it badly, I wouldn't have to see them again and it was no sweat off my back. The stakes had never been lower, and for the first time in my life, sex felt liberating, thrilling, and messy, instead of terrifying and shame-inducing.

But when I took the time to step away from all of the slut-shaming and judgment from this supposed friend and focus on what my body was telling me, I discovered that I was finding healing through sex, and it didn't matter if anyone else understood that. Through sex, my body was showing me that I could be resilient, and maybe it wasn't just about surviving, but things could actually get *better* for me.

What are some of the signs your body shows you that it feels good and safe? What are things you do that make it feel like that? Remember that we do not need to feel shame for prioritizing what makes us feel so good deep in our bones.

It has taken years, but I can now confidently wrap my arms around my truth: sex has been a part of my healing, not just a part of my hurt. Casual, delightful, carefree, mediocre, plentiful sex gave me my first glimmers of hope that healing was possible for me, and I now see there is no space for me to hold shame about it.

I know that you too can explore the truth about your relationship with your own sexual self, and I am here cheering you on, each step of the way. The wisdom we can glean from honoring what feels good in our bodies can lead us to more safety than we've ever known before.

PART 2: Shaming survivors for the sex we don't want

Just as many of us are struggling with the untrue story that we are having "too much" sex, there are many feeling shame for not having "enough" sex. Plenty of survivors deal with versions of both these stories at different times. While it's common, even dare I say normal, for the relationship between our healing and our sexuality to ebb and flow throughout our lives, that fluctuation can leave us feeling disoriented and discouraged. Healing is very nonlinear. Things that weren't triggering can become triggering and vice versa.

I, too, have worried that I was broken for not wanting to have sex

A couple of years after I found joy in casual sex, my sexual desires shifted. I was 25 years old and very often experiencing triggers during sex. Since I didn't know why things had changed, I worried they would stay that way forever. That was when my brain came up with a new untrue story:

When I'm triggered during sex, it's a sign that I haven't found the right person. When I find the right partner, the triggers will stop and sex will be safe, pleasurable, and desirable again.

I desperately wanted to believe that with the right partner, all my trauma symptoms would disappear. It was a lot more appealing to me than facing the complicated truth that the impact of CSA would, in some form, always be a part of me. That untrue story kept me optimistic in the face of dating so many shitty dudes and comforted me from my fears that the CSA had permanently "broken" me.

But then I met the love of my life, and all my trauma sex shit did not magically disappear. And I was fucking furious.

Falling in love didn't fix my triggering sex stuff. What a scam!

I met Charlie on OkCupid, right before Tinder became a thing. I showed up to our first date jaded from going out with so many seemingly nice guys who had ended up being just as shitty as the overt assholes, as well as physically exhausted from an acute bladder infection I had developed that required me to pee, in agony, every 20 minutes. I said something funny and found the sound of his full-hearted laughter instantly addictive.

We became serious quickly, in large part because Charlie had no game and it never occurred to him to try to play it cool with me. His kindness and sincerity were equally refreshing and unsettling to me, as it had never dawned on me to value those traits in a partner.

For the first three months of our relationship, my untrue story was holding up. Charlie was the right person for me because we were having loads of sex and I wasn't being triggered. Then, on one day that seemed no different from the 90 days that had gone before, I saw my abuser's face instead of Charlie's gorgeous green eyes while we were in bed.

I was devastated from the instant I felt the trigger in my bones and, despite Charlie's overwhelming compassion for me, couldn't muster any compassion for myself. In the following days, my story evolved from believing that if I found the right person, my trauma would disappear, to believing that even with a dreamy partner, I was too broken to ever have a "healthy" sex life.

My untrue story had put way too much pressure on me

My untrue story left me feeling like a failure each time I was triggered while hooking up. Putting this outsized significance on feeling safe during sex made me feel discouraged about all my healing efforts, as though each trigger meant my healing efforts weren't working.

It was also hurtful because it made me feel like I was disappointing my partner. Wasn't I holding him back from all the sex he must've been desiring? There was no way he imagined being in a committed relationship with someone who didn't want to have sex for months and months on end. I ascribed frustrations and emotions to Charlie that he not only never expressed, but vehemently and exhaustively denied.

As survivors, so many of us have been conditioned to prioritize the desires and comforts of others over our safety and health. I was conditioned by my abuse and also by misogynistic messages that a man's pleasure and happiness was more important than my basic well-being. It ran deep. That old way of thinking was still really close to the surface for me, and it was all too easy for me to revert back to where Charlie's assumed desires were more important than my needs and falsely believe I was a bad partner.

Finding my true story: that it's okay and natural for my sexual desire to ebb and flow along with other parts of my healing

As I developed deeper friendships with other survivors, I was able to see that it's okay for my trauma to still impact my sex drive. These friends would speak openly about how some years sex felt liberatory and other years it was the complete opposite. Reflecting on it now, what strikes me the most is how matter-of-fact they all were about it all, saying things like, "Well, of course the trauma still impacts our sex lives—trauma literally changes the makeup of our brains, that shit doesn't just magically go away, and it's nothing to be ashamed of; it's just always a part of us."

This is the kind of survivor-to-survivor wisdom that we could never read in a textbook or see in some clinical study; it is the wisdom that casually, yet permanently, changes the way we've viewed ourselves and our entire lives for the better. They helped me see that I don't have to feel shame or self-blame simply because sex can still be tricky and triggering for me sometimes.

What are times when you've felt conflicted between what you think you *should* want around sex versus what your body is telling you that you need? How can you learn to accept your real needs?

What are the origins of the bullshit?

Fuck boys really messed with my head for a long time

When I think about the people I trusted who reinforced this untrue story, Isaac comes to my mind. I dated Isaac for a few months when I was 24 years old, before I was old enough to know that cishetero men who brag about being feminists are actually the worst. I was nervous about sleeping together, since I had been experiencing a lot of sexual triggers at the time. I remember feeling so confused and discouraged that something that had been so healing only a year earlier was now filled with fear and pain again.

I felt pressure from Isaac and decided to give it a try, and I was triggered mid-act. The next day, when I saw him, as I tried to explain why I had that reaction mid-hookup, he accused me of making up my history of abuse to hide the fact that I clearly wasn't into him. He told me that if I were really attracted to him, this wouldn't have been an issue. My God, toxic masculinity is exhausting.

That experience fueled the binary thinking that either I am a sexy young person triumphing over my trauma or I am broken with nothing to offer a partner. It led me to feel like a failure each time I had to abstain from sex because of a trigger. I was back to thinking I was that shitty broken VCR, a damaged, useless object who couldn't function or engage in the modern world.

Who are some of the people, whether past partners, friends, or loved ones, who come to mind when you think about your untrue story?

There is so much social pressure that says we are fucked up if we don't desire sex

We live in a world where we have a lot of overwhelming expectations for young people to want sex. Heterosexual people hear warnings of the decay of our sex lives as we get older, especially if we choose to marry or have children. Nearly every '90s sitcom has some story line about entering a monogamous relationship and the sex dying. We also see this with queer women who have to contend with the trope of "lesbian bed death." It felt particularly scary to not be having sex in my 20s because, according to pop culture, once you hit 30, it all just stops! What a cool way for us to collectively understand sexuality, age, and the passage of time!

And this is coming from a woman. I cannot begin to imagine how much pressure there is on men of all sexual orientations to want sex. Every pop culture depiction of young men is that they are obsessed with having sex. We definitely live in a society that doesn't have any real understanding of young people's varying sexual desires, and asexuality is marginalized in particular.

What are some of the ways you see social expectations for young people to desire sex show up, including in pop culture? How does it affect how you feel about your sex drive?

When doctors make us feel like a
healthy sex life is off the table for us

I've had conversations with clinicians who have repeatedly made me feel like
a healthy sex life shouldn't be a priority for CSA survivors. In conversations
with doctors about the medications that help me manage my C-PTSD and
their effects on my libido, my sexual desire is always seen as this acceptable
sacrifice for the sake of my mental health. Many clinicians resist helping me
address libido symptoms, acting like I should just be grateful that I'm mentally stable. It's not too much to want a healthy sex life while living with
trauma.

The health care system also fails survivors in addressing how physically
painful sex may be for us. I went to multiple gynecologists when I was trying to have sex with my first boyfriend who could not help me successfully
navigate the excruciating pelvic pain I was experiencing.

One doctor prescribed numbing cream, which in retrospect is hilarious. Here was a doctor prescribing a 17-year-old girl numbing cream that
blocked her pleasure so that her boyfriend could have more. Like, is that
okay that my boyfriend gets to enjoy sex but I don't? Not helpful.

Many survivors are getting amazing
support from pelvic floor therapists

While I know I just knocked on the health care system, I have to shout out
pelvic floor therapists.

In recent years, I've heard from so many survivors that they've had really
positive experiences with pelvic floor experts, including trauma-trained pelvic floor therapists, who can help survivors experience reduced pelvic pain.
I wish access to pelvic floor specialists were available to all it would benefit.

We should hope for much, much more than numbing our bodies to be
vessels for someone else's pleasure! There are so many reasons why sex may
be physically painful for us, and none of it is anything we should feel any
shame about! We deserve healing, not shame.

Strategies

STRATEGY: Finding power and healing
in the times we've chosen to not have sex

There are times I've felt really good about not having sex! I think it's important to celebrate those times and remember that there can be so much beauty and power in honoring that sometimes we don't want to bang.

I once spent six months intentionally abstaining from sex while living alone, and it was awesome. I learned so much about how to be in my own company. Previously, I had been so afraid that in the silence of solitude I would become overwhelmed by the noise of my trauma screaming at me. But it wasn't so scary anymore, once I approached it in an intentional way.

With the extra energy saved by not trolling for peen, I learned there were so many other things that made me feel really good, like strengthening existing friendships and making new ones, learning to cook and host my first dinner parties, and developing a yoga practice like the good white millennial woman I am.

The solo time during the first six months in my apartment was the first time I experienced positive effects of abstaining in a longer-term way. I didn't set out to have six sexless months, but as each week passed, something inside me said it felt nourished. It felt so healing to learn how to not just tolerate but actually derive pleasure from being alone.

Abstaining can be an expression of agency. When I was 23 and in the middle of my casual-sex era, I went home with a guy, and in the middle, like truly the middle, of intercourse, I started feeling exhausted and a little hungover. It dawned on me that I didn't have to prioritize whatever this guy wanted over my own comfort. I withdrew my consent and he withdrew what he needed to, and I was out the door on the way home to sleep in my own bed and relish in delight over how powerful it had all felt.

In what ways are we tapping into our power when we choose to not have sex? If you're feeling curious about intentional abstinence, then I encourage you to experiment! Do it for as long as it feels good and healing. You make the rules.

STRATEGY: We have to call bullshit on our
all-or-nothing thinking around our sex lives

If you find yourself thinking about your sex life in unhelpfully all-or-nothing terms, then you are in the best company. Even Ignacio, in all their sex-positive glory, has struggled with all-or-nothing thinking when a trigger hits during sex: "I go through my 15 minutes of pouting where I want to shout, 'What the fuck! I've been doing this work for so long—why does this keep happening?' Then it passes, and I remember that this is all a part of the process."

It is easy for me to identify this kind of thinking within myself because if I'm trying to have sex and feel as dry as the desert, I shout at Charlie, "Oh my God, we are never going to have sex ever again!" I go from either having intercourse at this moment or never boning ever again. That is definitely some binary thinking. What does your version of all-or-nothing thinking sound like?

Charlie has helped me talk back to those voices, replying each time, "You always say that. And it's never true." Often he follows it up with an assurance that when the time is right and I feel safe, sex will happen again. He models compassion for me in a way that gently reminds me that I should have some compassion for myself.

INSTEAD OF ALL-OR-NOTHING,
WE ARE RIDING WAVES IN THE OCEAN

Ignacio recommends resisting viewing our sex lives in terms of "successes" versus "failures" and explained that they see sexuality and triggers as waves in the ocean. "Sometimes the water is beautiful and I can float without worrying about the waves taking me out. Some days those waves are so powerful that I can't stay in because it's too much. When I have those moments, it is a chance to pay attention and learn how to better navigate those experiences, so, over time, I don't have to stay out of the water for so long. But no matter what, I always know that, in time, I'll put my feet in again."

When we find ourselves on the sandy shoreline taken out by the waves, this is an important time to talk with trusted people in our lives in order to continue to normalize the highs and lows of our libidos and trauma,

Ignacio said. They also suggested trying little experiences to help stay connected to our bodies, unless being disconnected for a little while is what we need. Those activities to stay connected to ourselves can look like spiritual work, writing, baths, yoga, meditation, looking at ourselves naked in the mirror, touching ourselves, and paying very close attention to how different things make us feel.

It's okay if our trauma impacts our libido and sexual preferences, as well as what kind of sexual partners we desire. It previously was really difficult for me to openly acknowledge that there were some specific features in men that I couldn't tolerate and that, despite my best efforts, I would still be triggered with another person, including a specific body type, a particular kind of facial hair, and even some words that a partner may use. None of these features, qualities, or actions are bad or an indication that someone isn't a good person; it just means they aren't the right partner for me, and that's okay! We can make space for our fears and also be mindful that we don't participate in the oppression and stereotyping of marginalized bodies because of triggers.

It can be liberating to resist all-or-nothing thinking when it comes to preferences in partners. My trauma neither fully defines who I want to bone (for example, my sexual orientation is how I was born) nor exists completely independent of who I want to bone (I can't be with people who remind me of my abuser). So many people will try to pathologize us and question *why* we are the way we are; queer folks especially are gaslit this way. We are allowed to have preferences shaped by trauma—which is, of course, completely different from harming others with stereotyping comments.

Are there ways you can invite some space and ease for finding your truth between your all-or-nothing thinking?

STRATEGY: Let's broaden our understanding of intimacy, pleasure, and boundaries

WHAT DOES INTIMACY MEAN TO YOU?

For the vast majority of my life, I've had a pretty narrow understanding of what constitutes sexytime activities. I was socialized to define sex as when a penis goes into a vagina and a dude reaches orgasm, which is bullshit for a whole host of reasons. By having such a limited understanding of the scope of sexuality and intimacy, I've diminished the opportunity to identify and value a whole world of pleasure possibilities.

What makes us feel closely connected? Are there ways for you to express desire that are more accessible than sex?

I had a conversation with a fellow CSA survivor I'll call Berta, who finds physical contact of any form extremely triggering. She shared with me that she and her partner like to grab onto either end of a scarf as a way to hold hands, which gives them both a sense of closeness while honoring her boundaries. Berta's idea elegantly fit her specific desires and oozed intimacy to me.

"Intimacy can happen with sex and without sex. It can happen with touching and without touching. With someone you just met or have known for 15 years. What is intimate to one person may not be for another. Like sex and gender, intimacy is subjective," Ignacio explained.

I discounted many intimate things Charlie and I were doing because of my bullshit narrow ideas. Things like spooning, the way I like to hold his pinky finger when we walk, all the times we grab each other's asses in delight, how each night he kisses me while placing a cup of tea on my night-stand. What things are you doing in your life, with someone or with your-self, that you could newly consider intimate?

As adrienne maree brown quotes Audre Lorde in her anthology *Plea-sure Activism: The Politics of Feeling Good*, "For the erotic is not a question of only what we do; it is a question of how acutely and fully we can feel in the doing. Once we know the extent to which we are capable of feeling that sense of satisfaction and completion, we can then observe which of our var-ious life endeavors bring us closest to that fullness."[2]

Like so many of us, I had been viewing sex as an accomplishment. Think-ing sex was a goal led me to "power through" triggers and caused me to disas-sociate during intercourse. Leaving my body during sex was the opposite of intimacy, because I was totally disconnected and numbing out. If we were to consider how acutely and fully we could feel in the doing, as Audre Lorde's words suggest, then that would mean we would stop trying to have sex when it didn't feel good. It would place much greater value on the everyday actions that make us feel fully alive. For example, when I come out of the shower and affectionately rub my hands along the tattoo that lies across my ribs, when I wake up in the morning and feel my muscles and feel the joy of knowing I'm getting stronger, or when I delight in Charlie spooning me.

How might you experiment with expanding your definition of intimacy? What are some things you already do that are intimate? How might we continue to experiment with and grow that list?

USING BOUNDARIES TO HELP US EXPLORE NEW THINGS

"Sometimes experiments are failures and you make note of what didn't feel good, and sometimes they're amazing and you learn you want to replicate it or add something to it," Ignacio shared. Maybe you're thinking that trying something new is scary. I totally understand. I've noticed that when I establish boundaries, I feel a lot more enthusiastic, and less fearful, about experimenting. Until pretty recently, I had thought of boundaries as inherently negative and associated boundaries as synonymous with saying no. Then I read adrienne maree brown's words, "Your no makes the way for your yes. Boundaries create the container within which your yes is authentic. Being able to say no makes yes a choice."[3]

And a light bulb went off in my head.

I realized I could experiment with a boundary by saying, "I want to try this new thing in bed, and if I start to feel anxious and overwhelmed, then I'm going to press pause," and that made me more enthusiastic to try new things.

Every person, regardless of whether or not they're a survivor, has boundaries that deserve to be honored. I remember one time when Ignacio plainly asked me, "Have you ever talked to Charlie about his sexual boundaries?" And I realized that I had been assuming I was the only one who had any parameters. It inspired me to open more dialogue with Charlie about what new things we may want to try, what it would take for us to feel safe doing them, and what steps we'd want to take to build up to something different. Those conversations have helped me to not feel like I'm the one bringing all this baggage into our bed; instead, we are in it together.

Now is a great time to ask yourself what are some new boundaries you'd like to try out. What would you need in order to feel enthusiastic about trying something new?

Okay, we just finished a mega chapter— we definitely should take a beat

If you've read this chapter and are thinking, "But wait! I'm still confused about the truth of my sexual self and my survivorship." know that this all takes time! While aha! moments can happen in our healing, lots of the time things swirl around in our heads and hearts for a while and slowly start to make more sense for us.

As for me, after these years of soul-searching, I have come to understand my sexuality as something alive within me. My desires ebb and flow and live and breathe and are not stagnant, even when I fear they are. Just like all other aspects of my healing, my sex life is going to be nonlinear. When it gets hard, I remind myself that I am not damaged goods, but rather, I am a human being and I deserve to feel good and safe in my body.

You don't need to have all the answers for yourself right now—I certainly don't for myself. How about we take a break, get some food and hydrate, and let all this marinate for as long as we need.

6

It's Unbelievable How Fucking Lovable We Are

UNTRUE STORY
We cannot love someone until we love ourselves

BUT TRUTHFULLY
We are capable and worthy of all the love we desire

Welcome back, friends! Hope you've drunk some water, maybe did a little gentle stretch, got a yummy snack—whatever feels good to settle back in for some more fun and sexy times together.

Let's talk romantic partnerships. Broadly speaking, there is an enormous amount of societal pressure (rooted in patriarchal structures) for all of us to find a single partner and get married. There are some specific ways that pressure gets applied to survivors.

Let's get a head start calling bullshit on these three big ways we are pressured to live untrue stories about romantic love and trauma:

- ▶ Let's call bullshit on the idea that a healthy relationship is some sort of litmus test for how "healed" we are. Like, if we are in a loving and supportive relationship, then it's proof that we are healed.

► Let's call bullshit on the idea that if we find the right romantic relationship, then all our trauma shit melts away and we are magically healed.

► Let's call bullshit that a healthy romantic relationship is some sort of reward for all our hard healing work.

Do any of these pressures feel familiar to you? What would you add to this list?

I'm in this with you, and I have felt many pressures around romantic love and healing

My God, I have had to call bullshit on so many untrue stories I've had about romantic relationships and my trauma.

I thought there was a magical point in my healing where suddenly I would be able to receive love, and the question of when and how that would happen was all in my hands. I pressured myself toward this magical healing point and blamed myself when it didn't happen. By now you must be tired of me saying it, but no more impressive group of people exists than CSA survivors for our ability to blame ourselves for *any* and *every* single thing. It's our worst party trick.

I also believed that when I reached the magical place of healing, trans-formative love would make all my residual trauma bullshit melt away.

I simultaneously believed that I needed to be "healed" to find this life-changing love, but also that love would instantly do all the rest of the healing for me. I never said any of this was totally logical, but ooof was it powerful for me.

I spent time searching for a mythical point in my healing where I'd suddenly be worthy of a healthy relationship

I thought a mythical soulmate would make the trauma finally go away. With that magical love, I would stop getting triggered during sex, I would be unafraid to explain what I had been through, and my truth would be received with validation and support. The scary things would be less scary.

The parts of me that were overwhelmed by the stigma of being a survivor and afraid of how much the CSA had royally fucked me up would go away too. I could finally see myself as the high-functioning thriving survivor and distance myself from the pop culture cautionary tale of the young woman who was sexually abused and then had fucked-up relationships for the rest of her life.

I wanted all of that for myself. And I was inundated with Instagram wellness influencers who were insisting on everything I had to change in order to be "open" to love. Apparently I needed to love myself before someone else would love me, even though the chemical balances in my brain and my neurotransmitters were not permitting me to love me.

I viewed each failed situationship with a lens of self-blame. Instead, I could have recognized that I was trying to date 20-something hetero dudes (God help any of you in that boat), many of them with the emotional maturity of a Teletubby, none of whom had done any work and meaningful reflection on themselves. As a result, there were going to be a lot of shitty experiences.

To be fair, I was shitty sometimes too. It took me time to learn how to end something with the right words. As much as I hated being ghosted, I was a hypocrite and did it to plenty of people too. For many years, I had no idea what I wanted and didn't value what I now know was important. For example, I didn't value kindness. I thought that if a guy was confident and funny, it wasn't important if he was kind. Yikes.

Experience showed me that balance, compassion, patience, and softness were all important to me. But instead of valuing the experience, I viewed the end of each dalliance as an opportunity to increase self-blame for a failed almost-relationship. I told myself it was my fault and maybe I just didn't love myself or work hard enough on my healing. Each time, I felt increased shame that I was just a fucked-up girl who fucked-up things happened to, and that was how it was going to be. Does the dedication to self-blame sound familiar to you?

We are all capable and worthy of love. Dating is fucking tricky, and it isn't a reflection of our worthiness of romantic love. I could do everything possible for my healing, read all the books, collect all the gold stars from all the therapists, go on all the fancy retreats, shout my story to the world, journal, meditate, and shit out words of affirmation with my coffee each morning. And none of those things could ever make the impact of my CSA disappear, nor could they make the right partner appear in my life.

When it comes to dating, in what ways might we be blaming ourselves for things that are beyond our control? How does it feel to consider that you've always been worthy of the love you desire?

I was drinking my own bullshit Kool-Aid

When I met Charlie, my now-husband, I felt really cynical and distrusting. He was kind, open, and genuine, so naturally I thought he must be full of shit. Or have a secret family. I waited for the other shoe to drop for many weeks. It took me time to allow myself to fully fall in love with all of him.

As we fell in love, it became clear to me that our relationship was unlike anything I had experienced previously. The parts of me that felt scary and dangerous just didn't seem that scary or dangerous when I was with him. I was with someone who accepted me for everything I was, and that kind of understanding and patience made all my rough edges soften so that I no longer feared that my trauma would puncture our little love balloon.

It became too tempting to believe my own untrue stories. I was buying my own bullshit: I believed I had achieved the "right" level of healing to be capable of romantic love and that love erased the leftovers of my trauma. There were moments when my trauma momentarily burst my love bubble, like when I'd have occasional triggers during sex. But the bubble's walls would be repaired after each trigger. I came to believe that Charlie was my reward for all that I was able to do to put my trauma in the past.

My love bubble burst, and I learned the hard way that the story I told myself was untrue

Shit hit the goddamn fan about two years into our relationship. My father was trying to reenter my life in a harmful way, and simultaneously I was in a toxic workplace dynamic with my boss.

I was overwhelmed by the way trauma quickly took over every aspect of my life and was so terrified that I hadn't seen all of it coming. By my logic, all my healing work brought me my healthy relationship and meant I was done cooking. I was a phoenix who had risen from the ashes of bullshit to fly high with the man of my dreams.

So to see myself spiraling into previously unknown depths of pain, shame, and fear meant, among many other things, that I had to let go of my idea that my trauma was in my past and I was done healing. While I was in love, no partner could prevent me from going through new levels of life-upending trauma healing.

I spent a year in enormous pain as I quit my job, had conversations about accountability with family members that made things worse before they got better, navigated moments of suicidal ideation, and began to try to imagine another way for myself to be in the world.

Charlie's support, patience, and kindness never wavered during those terrible times. But it was so hard and so heavy for both of us. For the first time, I had someone I was in a committed partnership with who saw the ugliest and scariest moments, and it led me to feel so much guilt that my trauma was impacting him too. I feared that my trauma made me a bad partner.

I had to face the truth: neither was I healed before meeting Charlie, nor could Charlie's love heal me. I had to recognize that those untrue stories, at their core, reflected my belief that my history of CSA and the way it still impacted me was something I should feel ashamed of, as though I were unfit to love someone, as though loving me would be a burden on another person instead of a gift.

I learned then that the best thing I could do for our relationship was to continue to take care of myself. I couldn't look to my partner to "save" me from anything. But I could allow Charlie to be present in my life, to believe and trust him when he told me how he felt, instead of pretending I knew what was best for him. I was committed to my healing work, which at the time looked like allowing myself to lean on my friendships, going to therapy as often as I needed, taking my meds, boxing, feeding myself, and giving myself space to feel all my difficult emotions.

I now believe I am worthy and capable of giving and receiving love. While Charlie and I are different people, with different histories and needs, we both bring a whole lot of wonderful shit to our relationship. Yes, he is a mensch, but I'm a goddamn delight and no one's charity case. My healing isn't done, and I'm not sure it ever will be. My trauma is a part of me, and I'm done wishing and hoping it will all disappear. But I no longer fear my trauma torpedoing my relationship and permanently bursting my love bubble.

When you think about romantic relationships, what are some of the untrue stories that come up for you? Some questions to consider:

- What are some pressures I feel around romantic relationships and my healing?
- What are some fears that come up for me when I think about my romantic relationships?
- Have I ever observed feeling guilty and ashamed in the context of my romantic relationships? What experiences brought up those emotions?

What are the origins of the bullshit?

There are so many people I dated who contributed to these harmful pressures

As much as I may not want to admit it, my exes' words have influenced my thinking. I spent time with some pretty not-great guys in my early 20s. They had not done their own healing work, and I was often treated in a way that further stigmatized me and my survivorship.

Besides accusations of daddy issues and making up abuse covered in previous chapters, I also had a couple of different experiences of disclosing to guys I was seeing and never hearing from them again. Even trusted guy friends would describe women they were dating as "crazy" for expressing their emotions. All these experiences signaled to me that my trauma made me an undesirable partner, and getting rid of it fully was the only way to find love.

I am not alone in hearing these harmful messages while dating. CJR shared, "One night I was crying a lot about a recovered memory. After listening to me for 30 minutes, my ex called me a basket case and told me nobody would want me if I couldn't figure out my issues." Fortunately, CJR is no longer in that relationship. "My current partner reminds me how strong and worthy I am every single day," they told me.

Elizabeth also had a hellish experience with an ex-partner, who weaponized her trauma as a manipulation tool to keep her from leaving. "An old boyfriend tried to talk me out of breaking up with him and told me that he was the only one who could help me through my issues. He said I couldn't do it alone, and not everyone would be as 'caring.'" In my opinion, this kind of patronizing, condescending concern-trolling shit is just as harmful as the partner who rejects us because of trauma.

It is so natural for us to wish that we could easily dismiss our exes' harmful words. But when we are honest about how our exes' behavior may be contributing to our untrue stories, it can help us understand that the ways they've hurt us are their fault, not ours.

In what ways have the people you've dated contributed to your own untrue stories around romance?

When it comes to matters of love, our families may have done a real number on us

I experienced so much gaslighting by being told from the moment I was born that the person harming me loved me more than anyone else in the world, and *that* was what love was supposed to feel like. It is immensely confusing to be experiencing feelings of ickiness, violation, and unsafety and being told by everyone around you that what you are experiencing is unconditional love.

I spent the first 20-plus years of my life being told that my dad loved me more than anyone in the world and that it was my fault that he doubted my love for him. I had to repress my true "difficult" emotions or be swiftly reminded that I was a bad person for having such dangerous emotions. Of course that shit was going to continue to impact me for years and leave me with a lot to unlearn about love.

Real love means that someone allows us to be our full selves: including feeling our hardest feelings. We don't need to love every part of ourselves—that sounds exhausting and, for me, unrealistic—but we can give ourselves permission to stop hiding away our real emotional selves from the people we love.

Emotional honesty is not a burden on the people we love. In fact, it can be a real gift. When we are able to be emotionally vulnerable in a way that honors everyone's boundaries, we are giving other people a gift of trust and space for them to also be open with us.

My friend, the brilliant Aishah Shahidah Simmons, who is the author of the groundbreaking 2019 anthology *Love WITH Accountability: Digging Up the Roots of Child Sexual Abuse* and the filmmaker of the 2006 *NO! The Rape Documentary*, has some wisdom on these issues I'd like to share.[1]

Aishah can trace her past romantic experience of settling for exponentially less than she deserved as rooted in her childhood experiences with her family: "I was raised to care more for my parents than for myself and was taught that love meant caring for others more than for myself. I do not say that as a badge of honor. It led me to allow some people to take advantage of me, and I became some of my past partners' caregivers without receiving what I deserved in return and believing that was what love was supposed to feel like."

What are the ways your family has influenced your ideas about what love is, how it should feel and look, and perhaps what you may desire from another person? It is impossible for a child to not be impacted by the ways adults we trusted framed what we were experiencing as love. If you have dysfunctional beliefs, it's not your fault.

Pseudo–wellness influencer nonsense messing with our heads

When I think about cultural forces reinforcing my untrue stories, I immediately see images of pseudo–wellness influencer girlies preaching, among photos of green smoothies and boho rattan furniture, that we cannot find real love until we love ourselves. I know this notion has reached a lot of us. In my 2019 Google survey for CSA survivors that I mentioned in the first chapter, 80.6 percent of the 949 respondents said they had heard the untrue story in their lives that "we can't love someone until we love ourselves."

This particular kind of internet-influencer "wisdom" is my favorite because it is simultaneously seemingly inoffensive and apolitical, and it just sort of sounds good. But when we examine it with a critical eye, it is actually kind of a fucked-up message. (When you think hard enough, you can ruin anything!)

This kind of message ends up placing a sort of litmus test on people of how healed they have to be in life in order for someone to love them. Self-love as a prerequisite for romantic love is a tall fucking order. Some of us simply do not have the required chemical balances in our brains or particular neurotransmitters firing in such a way that permits us to love ourselves.

I also worry that if we embody the message that we have to love ourselves before someone else will love us, then it can lead us to self-blame when we are victimized by others in relationships. I would never want someone to have had a terrible, and perhaps abusive, experience in a relationship and believe that the responsibility of that harm lived within themselves because they did not love themselves enough. That's not on us, ever.

As CSA survivors, we carry with us so many strange curves and dark edges because of what someone did to us and the failure of everyone around us to adequately care for us in the aftermath. I used to worry that someone would only love me if I could love the traumatized bits of myself, and since I knew that wasn't possible for me, I then believed that someone would only love me once I erased the remnants of abuse within me.

I'm never going to love the traumatized aspects of my personality—to me that feels too close to finding a silver lining in my abuse—but that is different from hating or dismissing them. I can respect myself and respect how I've survived, and I can have compassion for the parts of me still carrying that trauma within me. I have found it personally more effective to work on cultivating self-compassion than self-love.

How does it feel to consider focusing on self-compassion compared with focusing on self-love? Your answer may be different from mine, and I encourage you to focus on whatever feels most useful to you.

*There was an endless parade of movies and TV shows
that reinforced my untrue stories about romance*

I fucking love rom-coms. If I could live in a Nora Ephron film or inside a Nancy Myers set, I would be so happy.

But lord, I have consumed so many narratives about a "broken" woman who dates terrible people, who is beautiful but somehow doesn't know it, and then finds a mensch of a man who heals what hurts. For the first time, the woman sees that she is beautiful and capable of love—but only after she goes through a montage of acts of supposed self-care, which are legally required to include scenes of her in a spinning class. The love interest remains heroic in his selflessness to love such a complicated woman with emotional baggage.

On the gender flipside, I have also watched so many movies featuring a brooding, damaged young man who wasn't loved enough in his childhood and therefore treats women as disposable, having to hurt them before he can be vulnerable enough to be hurt. He is gorgeous, which is undeniable with his bone structure, but we pretend he isn't by making it look like he hasn't showered in a long time. Then, he finally finds the one person who "gets" him, calls him on his bullshit, takes him seriously, but doesn't take herself seriously (where would the fun be in that?). Her real talk and undeniable sex appeal are enough to awaken his soul, heal what hurts, and transform him into a fully healed and happy man.

Popular culture tells us that romantic relationships fix us and that we are broken and require fixing in the first place. I still am devoted to rom-coms, but even the most committed fan must ask themselves what the impact of this kind of media has on beliefs about trauma and relationships. As Robby asked, "Wouldn't it be great if we could see portrayals that show that most of us are just normal people, with a shitload of baggage and not enough time, money, resources to slow down and deal with it? We're tired, moody, needy, burnt out, but can still be fun, engaged, creative, and successful." I'd like to see more of that, for sure.

What are some movies or shows that come to mind when you think about your untrue stories about romance and trauma?

Our old friend ableism is back for more

The last, and very important, factor that contributed to my untrue story is our good old friend ableism. My internalized ableism tells me that someone would love me only if I could hide or erase my C-PTSD. This is total garbage, but the impact of living in a world that tells us that having mental illness or a disability makes us a burden on other people adds up within us.

Jaden Fields explains, "The idea that needs are burdens can be a real hindrance to even considering relationships. Many people may not feel safe enough to be honest about their needs and disabilities."

Even Aishah Shahidah Simmons has said she has to contend with her own internalized ableism: "I can feel guilty about having depression and dealing with trauma triggers. My default is 'It can't be done,' and I am constantly preparing for the worst, because the worst has happened to me."

Our society lacks proper safety nets for people with disabilities and fails to support people's financial and accessibility needs. This leads us to having to rely on a partner for financial and logistical support, which in a better and just society would be provided for by our social systems and communities. While we may not be able to shift these enormous systems beyond our control, Jaden says we can push back against ableism by being honest with each other about our needs. "In queer and trans relationships, I see the ways we create visions around creativity and intimacy, and these are already a starting place to be transparent about our needs, which disrupts ableism."

It takes a lot of work for us to push back on ableism and remind ourselves that our worthiness as a romantic partner is not determined by any disability or mental health condition we may have. We are not a burden, and loving us is a motherfucking gift for anyone lucky enough to be in that position.

Strategies

STRATEGY: We get to make all the rules about what we disclose

We get to decide with whom we share, how much we share, and when we share. I don't care if you've been married 40 years or are in the talking stages with someone, there is no person in our lives who is entitled to know our history of sexual abuse. We may determine that it is in our best interest to share, or we may decide that it is in our best interest to not share, that part of ourselves. Or, we may find someplace between those two choices that feels right and true for us.

The key point I want to get across to you is that you are in charge. You are the decider. You are the captain. The captain of what? That's another decision you get to make! A ship? A rum distillery? A team of Power Rangers? You tell me. The point is, you are the boss. My wish for you is that the decisions you make about what you share with a partner come from a place of centering your own safety, needs, and desires.

DISCLOSURE ALWAYS INVOLVES SOME LEVEL OF RISK BECAUSE WE CAN'T CONTROL HOW OTHER PEOPLE RESPOND TO US

Whenever we are sharing about our trauma, we take a risk because all vulnerability is a risky business. When we consider any meaningful relationship in our lives, it has, at some point, required taking a risk to count on that person, without a guarantee that they would rise to the occasion.

To use a non-trauma-related example, in college I had a boyfriend who broke up with me a mere 72 hours after I told him I loved him. It only took about five years to find it hilarious. For a long time after that experience, I told myself that I shouldn't have been so vulnerable. But years later, I don't think that was the right lesson to take from the experience. His response was very disappointing, but I think it is good to be honest about my feelings and take risks to try to potentially deepen relationships that are important to me.

Only you can decide what the right risks are for you to take, at the right time, and with the right people. It's okay that sometimes we will be wrong about people—that's inherent in trying to build meaningful relationships! Please be gentle and resist blaming yourself (I know, I know, we all do it) if people disappoint you.

LET'S ENVISION OUR IDEAL SCENARIOS TO HELP
US FIGURE OUT WHAT BOUNDARIES WE NEED

These disclosure conversations are an opportunity to practice creating and enforcing boundaries that prioritize safety and well-being. I've found it helpful to ask myself, "What would the ideal scenario, best possible outcome look like for me going into this?"

If that question feels unnatural to you, then know you aren't alone! It feels intensely uncomfortable to ask myself that question because it touches on all the hypervigilant parts of me that say I have to be prepared for all the worst-case scenarios. Don't worry, we all have plenty of time to plan for those too.

When I spend time drawing out my best-case scenario, it helps me to see what I really want and build boundaries around those desires. It can help me see what details I want to share and what I don't want to share at this time. It helps me identify that I want my partner to respond with questions like "What can I do to support you?" and not questions like "But how do you know it really happened?"

In seeing all of that, I can start to build some boundaries for myself that don't guarantee any sort of outcome but do help me practice prioritizing my own wishes and well-being. Examples of boundary language:

- ► "I experienced sexual trauma as a child and it impacts me today." But I may not want to say who harmed me, the details of how it went down, or anything more.
- ► "I'm going to share some things with you, but I don't want to answer questions right now. I just want you to tell me you believe me and support me."
- ► "I want to share some things with you, but before we talk, would you be willing to read this article/book/letter that helps explain about CSA?"
- ► "I am worried you'll reply to what I have to say with xyz (e.g., questions, doubt, asking for proof), but what I really need is for you to reply to me with abc (e.g., support, validation, understanding); is that something you will be able to do for me?"

▶ Sharing desires for aftercare, like "I'm going to feel vulnerable after this, so I'd like you tomorrow/a week from now to ask me how I'm doing after all this and ask me if there's anything that I need."

What boundaries are aligned with your own ideal scenario? Even if it feels challenging, can we communicate what we need from that person? Robby put it this way: "Don't be afraid to spell out exactly what you need from the other person while you're being vulnerable. This is important shit, so it can be good to lay some ground rules out."

Boundaries do not guarantee that things will go a certain way, nor is there a guarantee that the people we speak to will honor them. As Prentis Hemphill says, "Boundaries are the distance at which I can love you and me simultaneously,"[2] so having these boundaries is a loving act for both you and the other person.

IT ISN'T YOUR FAULT IF THINGS ARE MESSY; IT'S JUST THAT PEOPLE ARE A VERY TRICKY BUSINESS

If things don't go well, please know that other people's shitty responses are not about you. I know! I know! You told them something and then they were shitty, so how could it not feel like it's about you?

There are loads of reasons why people are terrible at responding to disclosures of sexual violence, especially child sexual abuse. They may be survivors or have survivors in their families, and so talking about abuse may be triggering or overwhelming for them. They may have consumed popular culture that stigmatizes CSA and have internalized that stigma. They may be emotionally immature people. So many possibilities! And literally none of them have anything to do with you! Even though it feels intensely personal!

Elizabeth advised, "It's possible you will be discussing something that means everything to you with someone who hasn't thought about that topic in their whole life, which may lead them to say stupid things that can range from well-meaning but useless advice to more damaging things. You need to remember that you're the expert and have a plan in place to prioritize yourself no matter how the other person responds."

You get to decide what comes next. You get to determine whether you want to continue conversations with the person or not. It may be possible that the dialogue between you and your partner may need to extend beyond a single conversation. Robby offered that it may be helpful to move slowly and recognize that it may take time for us to establish for our partner the framework of our trauma and have them understand.

Your instincts may be telling you that the person's reaction shows they won't be able to provide you the support and respect you deserve. Elizabeth shared from her experience, "If someone doesn't love you the right way, it doesn't reflect badly on you. It's really tough to face that this person you care about has let you down, but you've got to face that. Otherwise you'll endure something you don't deserve."

If things do not go as you hoped, remember that you've made the best decisions for yourself with the limited information available (i.e., not knowing how someone else will react), and you haven't done anything wrong, even if it hurts really bad.

As Robby said, "How someone else reacts to our trauma is entirely on them, and we cannot allow ourselves to take any responsibility for that." If we find ourselves feeling self-blame for a disclosure that has gone poorly, Robby encourages each of us to redirect our energies to immediately putting ourselves in a supportive situation: "Go to the people who love you, schedule that emergency therapy appointment, get yourself to a safe space and protect yourself."

I agree that the best management for dealing with a poor experience with disclosure is to take whatever steps we can to combat the feelings of self-blame and shame. The truth is, we did something that required a lot of courage and put us in a vulnerable way, and that is something we should feel proud of ourselves for, even if the people receiving our disclosure miserably fumbled the ball.

What might your care plan to support yourself after disclosing to another person look like?

STRATEGY: Everyone has needs, and it's the responsibility of each of us to communicate about those needs.
It isn't glamorous, but it is necessary

I often hear from people (and the voices inside my own brain) that we have too many needs to be a good partner. But the truth is, every person has needs, and it's okay if ours differ from our partner's. The key is to be honest with ourselves and each other and communicate as best we can about what we need and want out of our relationships.

I know that can be easier said than done. During the hardest moments, I've feared that my needs take up all the oxygen in the room, and my partner's needs are left to suffocate without proper air supply. It leads me to want to keep some sort of relationship scoreboard of our needs so that we can be equal. I find that this thinking is founded in a scarcity mentality, like love and support being a zero-sum game.

Aishah shared with me that she's had to navigate similar fears in her relationship: "Even after all these years, I have to be vigilant around making sure I speak up around my needs because I have a real fear that I will be abandoned or our relationship will rupture from me simply being myself." Aishah's relationship with her partner, Sheila, is one that I've admired from the outside, so it was really comforting to know that even they have to work through balancing and honoring everyone's needs.

I found couples counseling to be a valuable tool for making sure that both Charlie's and my needs could be honored in our relationship. Talking about scary things in couples counseling was like going bowling and putting on the bumpers to ensure that the ball didn't end up in the gutter. In our first session together, I lobbed 10-pound balls one after the other down the lane, saying things like "I am afraid my needs are so big, there's no space for yours" and "I'm afraid you're going to resent me and the way my trauma shows up in our relationship," but with the bumpers up, none of my words fell into the gutter. It felt so freeing to be honest with Charlie about my fears.

Charlie acknowledged that our needs looked different, which surprised me, just like how Kate had surprised me years earlier when she acknowledged the same thing in our friendship.

I expected Charlie to say, "No, it's all in your head, that's not what it's like at all." But he didn't. Instead, he was honest. Charlie said, "Something happened to you that wasn't your fault, and you are doing your best living with the impacts of that. That same thing didn't happen to me. So yeah, we have different needs." It is so refreshing when we can be honest with each other about these things! He wasn't downplaying the needs I had, but he also wasn't blaming me or stigmatizing me for having those needs. He's a good egg.

Is there a way you can be honest with yourself about your needs without allowing that to cause misplaced feelings of shame or feelings of guilt? If shame and guilt do come up, can we practice talking back to those emotions and reminding ourselves that it isn't our fault? It is the long-term impact of shit we've been through that we never should have had to experience.

IT CAN BE CHALLENGING TO BE HONEST
WITH OURSELVES ABOUT WHAT WE NEED

The hardest part of these conversations is where I have to be transparent with myself about my own needs. It brings up old shit about feeling like I'm too much or super fucked-up.

Is the thought of being honest with yourself about your needs too challenging? If yes, what might it be like to create a little distance from yourself and imagine that instead it's a friend who is talking to you about what they've been through and what they need? I find that, on the whole, we survivors are super great at showing up for other people's needs but find it super hard to do it for ourselves, so let's tap into that a bit to make it useful for us!

WE CAN TRY OBSERVING OUR OWN PATTERNS
TO BETTER COMMUNICATE ABOUT OUR NEEDS

From our conversations, Charlie knows to offer me lots of tea and water when I'm triggered, since I get dehydrated then. When Charlie's had a bad day, I know he needs his own space to process internally, listening to music or reading comic books on our balcony. It's really helpful to make care plans like these not during crisis and pain, but during calm times when we can talk proactively.

This includes a plan for when I go to the extremely dark places of my trauma. A few years ago, I was having a night that brought me back to the absolute worst feelings of my life (I know you know those ones). Charlie was beside me in bed, but I didn't want to clue him in to what was happening to me because I felt ashamed and worried that I'd scare him. As a result of that experience, in the calm light of day, Charlie and I planned what to do if I returned to that kind of dark place again.

The plan is hyper-practical, detailed, and very specific to me. The process of identifying what I needed in my safety plan made me feel super vulnerable, but after we had it agreed upon, I immediately felt relief. I'll share some of it with you, in hopes that it may inspire you to create a safety plan with your partner if you haven't yet:

1. The first step is that I clue Charlie in by saying something like "I'm in a bad way; I need you to enact our safety plan."

2. Charlie gets me my emergency meds and then puts me into a cold shower, which helps shock me back into my body. Charlie sits in the bathroom while I shower.

3. After the shower, Charlie sits with me while I call my therapist.

4. He sends a message or calls my mom to let her know what's happening so that he isn't alone in worrying about me or having to figure out what comes next.

5. He puts me into bed and gets the dog to snuggle up with me and him.

We've enacted the plan at least once since creating it, and it works very well for both of us. I know Charlie really likes knowing exactly what to do, and it brings both of us comfort to know we have a clear-headed plan for the catastrophic times. People who love us generally appreciate being told exactly how to support us.

What are the ways you can proactively plan for your needs that are inclusive of your partner? In what ways can your plan honor the needs of both of you, include consent from both people, and help reduce the barrier to giving and receiving support during your worst moments?

LET'S MAKE SURE WE PAY ATTENTION TO ALL THE
GOOD THINGS WE BRING TO OUR RELATIONSHIPS

Those couples therapy sessions also helped me see that I had been downplaying my contributions to our relationship and Charlie's well-being. During those sessions, Charlie shared about all the ways I had supported him during difficult times in his life. Yes, Charlie is an aforementioned good egg, but I'm a pretty fucking great partner too and no one's charity case, and sometimes my trauma distorts my ability to see that clearly.

Until those conversations, I hadn't realized that for years I had been modeling for Charlie how to have healthy boundaries with people and how to be honest about dark and difficult feelings. I had no idea that by unapologetically being myself, I was influencing how Charlie wanted to live in the world.

How can we place a higher value on all the wonderful things we bring to our relationships? What are some practices, like caring for yourself, having healthy boundaries, and being compassionate, that you may be modeling for your partner?

STRATEGY: This isn't always fun, but we have a chance to practice real accountability in our relationships

Relationships are messy—have I said that enough? Every person is capable of hurting someone else's feelings. While it can be incredibly difficult to deal with either guilt over hurting feelings or expressing hurt feelings, it can also be an opportunity to build something different from bad past experiences.

Many of us will never receive a meaningful apology for the abuse we experienced as children. We may have grown up around people who were unwilling to acknowledge the hurt they caused without layers of defensiveness and denial. We may be just now learning what it feels like to both offer and receive a meaningful apology.

Aishah Shahidah Simmons is someone who has done extraordinary work around accountability and healing, as in, she literally wrote the book (if you haven't read *Love WITH Accountability* yet, get on it!), and she shared this with me: "I constantly am reflecting on the idea that, even in the midst of the hardest moments of my trauma, that pain does not give me a license to cause harm."

WE MAY HAVE DIFFERENT WAYS OF DEALING
WITH CONFLICT THAN OUR PARTNER

Understanding conflict styles helps with accountability. My style is to get very reactive—I am quick to yell, be totally exasperated, fire off a million questions, and berate Charlie for not answering me quickly and clearly. I become obsessed with being "right" even if it hurts the people around me. Whereas Charlie is an internal processor. He needs time to think through a conflict, figure out what he is feeling, and then calmly articulate his feelings. When I would raise my voice, I thought Charlie was silent because he didn't want to engage with me. But when we were able to have open conversations about it, I learned that my yelling was triggering Charlie to fully shut down.

Jaden Fields and his partner also process differently from one another: "My partner needs space before they feel safe enough to communicate. Without that space, their language will be sharper and more hurtful because that's how they navigated communication with their abuser as a kid. But my style of communication is completely different, and I want to squash any issue immediately and get anxious when I don't understand exactly what's going on, which also stems from my experiences of abuse in childhood," he shared.

Recognizing that Charlie and I were experiencing different needs in communication was huge: I've learned to not raise my voice even when I'm super mad, and he's learned to validate my feelings while also asking for the time and space that he needs for his own.

How would you describe your conflict style? How might you and a partner talk about your conflict styles and identify some ways to honor your differences?

WHEN IT COMES TO HURTING PEOPLE, WE HAVE TO
PRACTICE FOCUSING ON OUR IMPACT OVER OUR INTENTIONS

While I never meant to hurt Charlie when we were arguing, I had to accept the impact of the way I responded in those heated moments. "Recognizing the difference between intention and impact in the midst of a trigger is so important," Aishah told me. Offering me examples from her own relationship, she shared, "I have to honor the impact of what I've done to cause harm to Sheila, even if it wasn't my intention to hurt her. I've learned to say, 'It wasn't my intention, and I am sorry how that hurt you.'"

But this can bring up really challenging feelings! I felt defensive when Charlie first told me that my yelling triggered him. In my guilt, I felt a desire to rely on my own victimhood as justification as to why what I did couldn't have been *that bad*. But I tried to resist all of that and instead focus on how my actions made Charlie feel, regardless of intent.

Aishah assured me that the internal resistance I felt is common, even for her! "There are times I don't want to practice accountability. I am a Buddhist practitioner, and while meditating I'll notice resistance within myself to recognize that the way I may have treated Sheila was wrong. The silence of my meditation practice is very illuminating for me and helps me to see what steps I need to take to hold myself accountable with Sheila and apologize to her," Aishah shared. Practicing accountability is uncomfortable sometimes for everyone.

I apologized to Charlie—but that wasn't all I needed to do. Words are important, but not the whole ball game. "The big thing is practice," Aishah told me. "It is important to be verbally accountable, but the practice is the truth. It's not just about the words we say, but also accountability requires us to explore how we can prevent ourselves from causing harm again. We have to ask ourselves, 'How do we unlearn the habits that cause harm?'"

It isn't perfect, but I am working hard at catching my harmful behaviors and doing the work I need to do to avoid hurting Charlie again. While uncomfortable, it is getting loads easier with more practice.

If you're having a hard time starting to think about these ideas of accountability and hurt in relationships, Jaden recommends taking wisdom from the long-term friendships in your life. "If you can be friends with someone for 15 years, then it means you've been through it. It means you do know how to apologize, how to navigate conflict, and how to cultivate connection," he shared. "Look at what happens in those relationships, because those are people who probably have called you out on your shit, who, over the years, you have probably had to meaningfully apologize to and vice versa."

What are some lessons you can take from your friendships that can help model for you ways to address hurt within romantic relationships?

STRATEGY: We all have to be responsible for our own healing

No one person can "save" or "fix" us, and no one should ask that of us either! There is no magical love that solves the problem of trauma all by itself. I've been on both sides. As tempting as it is to be "saved" by someone, it's even more tempting for me to think of myself as a savior for another.

But the fun, sexy, and flirty truth is this: everyone is responsible for their own healing *and also* all people need people, and that isn't a bad thing!

In our conversation, Aishah put it this way: "I believe everyone is responsible for their own healing. But, at the same time, in the words of Audre Lorde, 'Without community, there is no liberation,' so both of these things must be true at the same time."

Our desire to heal, our desire to take responsibility for our lives and do the work to grow, has to come from inside of us. "People have to take the first steps to heal themselves, but we can be cheering them on and walking beside them," Aishah said.

We need a boundary that we should never try to save or fix someone, and also a boundary that we won't ask that from another person either. We can stand beside one another, we can soften the loneliness of the pain and celebrate in the good moments, we can share our lives with one another, and I think that's all pretty great.

Have you ever had experiences of looking to someone to fix something within you? Have you ever experienced someone looking to you to fix them? How did it make you feel? Were there conflicting emotions, maybe of being important and valued, but also feeling overwhelmed or other feelings?

STRATEGY: Let's widen our bench so that more people can sit with us

Too often, the world gives us this heteronormative bullshit about "the one" being a single person who is supposed to be our everything. Jaden said he gets a particular kick out of watching straight dating shows like Netflix's *Love Is Blind*: "Heteronormative culture really loves to push this idea that you have this one person, your soulmate, and they are supposed to be the only person you need and you just got to stick it out until you find them."

He pointed out to me that shows focusing on finding your "better half" perpetuate the idea that all our needs should be met by one single person, which leads to codependence, not interdependence.

This has led Jaden to ask the question, "What about our friendships? What about those ride-or-dies?" So much of the way love is discussed in our society diminishes the significance of meaningful friendship in our lives.

I have lots of best friends! To paraphrase Mindy Kaling: a best friend isn't a person, it's a tier.[3] Has Charlie made it into that tier? Sure, but he's in excellent company up there. It's unrealistic to think that there's one human on planet Earth who could fulfill all my emotional needs. Also, I wouldn't want it to be true! That's too much pressure on a person, and it may be setting us both up for failure.

Luckily, Charlie values the importance of deep, meaningful friendships as much as I do. I remember one night when Charlie brought me a snack while I was lying in bed. In gratitude I said, "Oh thank you! You are my favorite person!" Without missing a beat, he said, "I know that isn't true. I know your favorite person is Kate. But I love you too."

He was 100 percent correct about my bestie, Kate. Charlie didn't say it bitterly or with any resentment in his voice. Charlie was being very loving, and one of the ways he was loving me was by honoring the significance of one of my most precious friendships. It made me love him even more.

When it's been a particularly difficult time for me and Charlie's played the caregiver role in a really intense way, sometimes the best thing I can do for myself and for Charlie is to invite myself over to a friend's for dinner or go spend time with my mom. I allow my friends and family to help take care of me. In turn, Charlie is able to recharge his batteries and care for himself in the ways he needs to: playing video games, reading comics, FaceTiming with his besties. I allow for other people who love and care about me to be present for me. In doing so, I allow for both Charlie's and my needs to matter.

STRATEGY: Not everyone can come with us in our healing

It's important to understand that not every person will be the right person to have beside us in our healing. Listen, I know it's easy for me to say this, as though having to make that discernment isn't a big fucking deal. But I think maybe that saying it plainly is helpful, because it might be simple in our minds but complicated in our hearts.

Sometimes ending a romantic relationship can be an act of love. Jaden shared that in his relationship, his and his partner's commitment to love doesn't mean they have to stay together: "If the most loving thing for us is to shift from a romantic relationship to another kind of relationship or friendship, that's okay too."

Aishah shared, "Life necessarily involves impermanence. Things are constantly changing, and what may have worked at one time may not work now. It's only a bad thing because of our attachments of wanting things to be the way they were, but this change can be a really good thing."

For all the time we may spend worrying that we are not "enough" for a partner, it's important to remember that we do not settle for crumbs. We are not lucky to find someone who will love us *despite* our trauma. Yes, we have trauma. And yes, it impacts our romantic relationships. But it isn't something that taints us or makes us damaged goods. We are not a defunct home appliance. We are people who have to navigate some shit that wasn't our fault with some bomb-ass gifts to offer the world.

And so, like in friendships, not everyone may be worthy to get to come along for the ride. Only you can be the judge of who is worthy of getting to be beside you.

What I can offer you is a list of some qualities that survivors may find healthy and important in a romantic partner:

- ► A general sense of willingness to learn about what living with trauma and CSA is like and how they can be a good partner for you
- ► A lack of ego and healthy humility when discussing trauma and your needs from the relationships—aka, they don't make everything about themselves
- ► Someone who demonstrates that they respect boundaries (their own and yours!)
- ► Someone who, through their words and actions, generally does not increase your feelings of shame, self-blame, and stigma

▶ Someone who is willing and interested in taking accountability for their behavior and impact

These are just trends I've observed from supporting survivors through various partnerships and dating experiences. How would you remove from, add to, or edit this list?

When we find ourselves in relationships that aren't right for us, it can trigger the shame and blame we feel from our child sexual abuse. Any shame you may be feeling is not yours to hold. You are worthy of a love that offers you a sense of safety, support, and deep recognition.

What have the relationships you've had to let go of taught you about what needs are important for you to honor?

Time to find some off-season candy hearts, get a sugar rush, crash, and then take a nap

If there's anything you remember from this chapter, please let it be this: you are the fucking tits. You are not someone's charity case. You are a human fucking being who has been through shit that no one should have ever had to go through and still impacts you today, and that's okay and totally normal. If you crave more connection with others, then that is only a good thing because people need people! It is messy not because there is something fundamentally wrong with you but because dealing with people is a messy business!

Dating is a nightmare, even without trauma. We are just bags of flesh throwing our bags of flesh at each other and hoping for the best. It is necessarily messy. My hope is that, with the right person, your trauma does not feel like a liability to the relationship but just another layer of life to navigate with someone caring.

Now time for rest, k?

7

Our Healing Journey Invites Our Families to Heal

UNTRUE STORY
We are ruining our families

BUT TRUTHFULLY
*When we focus on healing ourselves, we are also healing
our families because we are a part of our families*

Well, friends, we have arrived at the family chapter. Cue the ABBA, start the disco ball, and put on your best dancing shoes, because here is where the party really gets going.

Regardless of whether our abuser was inside or outside our family, CSA is a family issue. Our families were in charge of protecting us and did not prevent the abuse from happening. Our families responded or failed to respond to our trauma and its aftermath. Many survivors abused by someone outside the family found the lasting impact of their family's failure to support them in some ways more harmful than the initial sexual abuse. So I will first discuss abuse within families, then move on to the topic of familial response to abuse.

Harm within families has unique impacts because when we are harmed by a trusted adult who is charged with protecting us, on whom we are financially, emotionally, and socially dependent, the ramifications of that hurt reverberate throughout our entire lives. While it is still incredibly taboo to talk about sexual abuse within families, statistically, kids are much more likely to have been harmed by someone close to them. Stranger danger does exist, but 93 percent of the time when a child is sexually abused, the harm-doer is someone known to the child, according to RAINN.[1]

This isn't the "Alisa persuades you to confront and/or cut off your family" chapter. That chapter doesn't exist! I am sharing my experiences, and you could be in the exact same situation with your family and find that what is best for your health and safety is completely different from the decisions I've made. I am not going to be encouraging you to take any actions: I truly do not know what is best for you and your family. My intention is to help ease feelings of isolation, gaslighting, and shame so that everyone can see their own path more clearly.

It is so natural to feel a swell of anxiety knowing we will be spending time talking about our families and our trauma. I want you to know I totally understand that, and I have taken every step I can to make this as easeful and the least triggering as possible.

There will be no descriptions of sexual abuse, but a lot about the really heavy emotional impacts of it, including mention of suicidal ideation (but no actions of self-harm). Take your time, read what feels right to you, leave what doesn't, and prioritize your well-being. If your body is sending you signals that you are triggered but you keep reading anyway because you want to "power through," I *will* know. These words will still be here for you after you take a break, I promise. Also, my jokes are funnier when you're not triggered, and my fragile ego wants you to laugh.

I'm in this with you, and I used to feel responsible for "ruining my family," but I now know that isn't the truth

I want to share with you what I've learned is my true story: I am not ruining my family by being honest about my abuse. When I take steps to protect myself, I am actually protecting my family because *I am part* of my family. By prioritizing my healing, I am offering space for healing within my lineage of past, present, and future members of my family. But for a long time, I held on to a false narrative that by being honest about my abuse, I was responsible for "ruining" my family.

So let's go back about 10 years, to an era when everyone did the "Gangnam Style" dance and guys hit on women by using the line, "Call me, maybe." What a time to be alive.

I was 23 years old, living in my first apartment in Washington, DC, and overwhelmed by how to navigate an ultimatum my father had just issued me. He sent me an email saying that he had observed me pulling away from him and resisting him ever since Jack, my stepfather, had died three years earlier. In the email my father said that either I spend more time with him, including weekends at his place, or we wouldn't have a relationship anymore, but the status quo was no longer an option.

I had spent two decades repressing my trauma in order to fake a relationship with my father. When I was growing up, he conditioned me to see him as the victim of every story and to believe that I should protect his feelings over my needs. When I was a child, he required me to care for him as an adult cares for a helpless child. Many of us were "parentified": as children, we were the adults in our relationships with our parents.

The first thing we need to call bullshit on is the lie that children are responsible for the happiness and emotional well-being of their parents. It is bullshit that so many of us are put in positions where, as children, we are the adults in our relationships with our parents.

This sort of parentification of children can look many different ways for us. I've found the psychological term *emotional incest* (also called *covert incest*) particularly helpful for understanding what I was going through. Emotional incest is when a parent treats their child as though that child is their romantic partner. While it doesn't necessarily include sexual abuse, emotional/covert incest describes the abuse of parents expecting their children to meet their needs like an adult or put their parent's needs first.[2]

Emotional/covert incest can cause long-term trauma for kids. While it is considered separate from sexual abuse, it is an incredibly important and relevant form of harm that many of us navigated. Folks who experience emotional incest without sexual abuse often face similar trauma and challenges as CSA survivors do. When I've seen those folks learn about emotional/

covert incest and recognize that they experienced abuse, they understand why their childhood felt bad, confusing, and traumatizing.

I can't repeat enough: children are children and parents are adults. Parents are responsible for their own emotional needs, for the harm they cause, and for protecting and caring for the needs of their children. Kids are responsible for being kids. And while we may recognize the humanity in the adults who harmed us and see ways they were unsupported, it doesn't mean their burdens should have been ours. As with all things, you are allowed to feel any way you feel about it.

If the existence of emotional incest is news to you, what new insights is it unlocking?

I was ready to prioritize my safety over my family's comfort

By the time I received my father's ultimatum, I had been in therapy long enough to understand that I was not responsible for his happiness. It took me countless hours to learn that no parent should put their child in that position.

I know that internalizing this understanding is easier said than done. It's one thing to intellectually know; it's another thing to try to override decades of learning how to blame ourselves.

It was really hard and scary, but I was ready to start protecting myself. There was no glory leading me to that point. It wasn't like I was hit with some sort of dramatic moment of heroism where I put on a cape, Katy Perry's "Roar" started playing, and I shouted, "Alisa bows to no man!"

Instead, what led me to that moment was that all my old coping mechanisms had stopped working. My old coping mechanisms that had allowed me to repress my trauma were broken, no matter how much I wanted them to still work. Have you ever found yourself nostalgic for past coping mechanisms, even knowing we shouldn't numb to our feelings? Sometimes feelings are . . . overrated. Many survivors wish they could've maintained "normality" instead of facing trauma. It's a completely natural desire, even if we know it's important for us to feel our feelings!

Since numbness wasn't an option anymore, I processed my feelings with my therapist, Connie. She helped me see that I was feeling trapped because I was operating under an untrue story that told me I had two distinct options:

- ▶ Option A: I live with unbearable trauma symptoms that are taking over my life.
- ▶ Option B: I take steps to protect myself and have boundaries with my father but am responsible for ruining my family. (Reminder, this isn't true! It was my conditioned self-blame and self-shame talking.)

No wonder I felt such an unbearable amount of pressure! I was operating under the false belief that the fate of my entire family was sitting squarely on my shoulders. My therapist wasn't pressuring me to cut off my father, just encouraging me to think critically about the idea that protecting myself meant I was ruining my family.

When I received my father's ultimatum email, I knew my life was worth fighting for. Even if I was vilified for my choice, I knew I owed it to myself to try to cultivate safety. I replied to his email with my decision and never spoke with my father again. I felt isolation and fear of judgment, but when I did confide in my close friends, I found that all they wanted for me was to be healthy and safe. Their support illuminated for me what I wanted my family to feel like: not feelings of guilt and shame, but a kind of love where we just want whatever is best for each other.

It's not like all my self-blame and guilt disappeared with my decision about the ultimatum. For years I doubted whether my safety was more important than protecting a narrow idea of the family institution. Over time, the guilt softened as I expanded my understanding of what family means to me.

By healing myself, I am not only contributing to healing my chosen and future families, but also contributing to the healing of the generations known and unknown that came before me. By caring for myself in a way that centers compassion for all, including me, and resisting calls for silence and shame, I am being a really good family member.

Questions to consider:

- ▶ Have there been times I've had a sense of obligation to my family when it comes to my abuse?
- ▶ How does my family's response (or lack of response) to my abuse impact my relationship to my trauma?

I know this shit is heavy. Is now a good time for some water, a snack, a snuggle with a pet, perhaps? Please take your time moving on to the next part of this chapter. It'll all still be here when you're ready to keep the party going.

What are the origins of the bullshit?

Our abusers and the trick they do to Deny, Attack, and Reverse Victim and Offender (DARVO)

It helped me understand my father's behaviors when I learned about DARVO. The term was developed by Dr. Jennifer Freyd, fellow survivor and badass researcher and professor, to describe the way perpetrators often respond to being held responsible for their harms.[3] The DARVO tactic is not reserved for abusers: sometimes we see it with adults who fail to protect us or are complicit.

The DARVO acronym stands for Deny, Attack, Reverse Victim and Offender. In my life, DARVO looked like this: every time I advocated for my needs, my father would first deny that he had ever done anything wrong; then he would attack me by saying I was a bad, ungrateful, unloving daughter. Lastly, he would reverse victim and offender by crying and telling me he was the victim and I was the one harming him.

DARVO denies our reality, making our abusers seem like the victims and not us. It makes us feel guilty both for our own pain and also for "causing" our abuser pain too. The long-term impact of DARVO for me has been that even after all this time, instead of feeling righteously angry at my father, I usually just feel sorry for him. It is so difficult for me to place the responsibility of my abuse rightfully on him. Due to my conditioning, I see him as a helpless, pathetic man who did his best but was a victim of the world. This view of him is different from recognizing my harm-doer's humanity: I wish I could just simply recognize my father's humanity, but instead, I only see the ways he is a victim and I am to blame.

What are some examples of people using the DARVO tactic from your life or from popular culture? How does it feel to learn that this is a well-researched and common tactic of abuse? How might DARVO be influencing our relationships to our families and fueling our untrue stories?

We have to talk about the parents who were unable to protect us from the abuse

With the exception of Aishah Shahidah Simmons's groundbreaking anthology *Love WITH Accountability*, where she writes and speaks about CSA within Black families, I rarely see public conversations about parents of survivors who were doing their best but were unable to protect us. It can be so difficult to talk about well-meaning parents who were unable to recognize the abuse and support us. But we must talk about it, because I know from my work that it's an overwhelmingly common experience in survivors' lives to have a parent in our life who loves us but really missed the mark on CSA.

It's so difficult for me to write about my mother, Diane, because I love her so much and she has become my greatest champion. I desperately want to protect her, but I know in writing all of this that sharing more about my struggles with my mom may be even more helpful to other survivors than talking about my relationship with my abuser.

My mom has chosen to do her own healing work, a decision that we cannot make for our loved ones, as much as we may like to, and her efforts have made it possible for her to be present with me through this process (you'll hear from her in her own words in a bit!). It's more important to my mom that she help other survivors who may be struggling with their parents than keep the most painful moments of our relationship private. She's a real one and a total badass and I love her forever.

Diane knew my dad wasn't a great guy and divorced him when I was a baby. She watched me struggle throughout my childhood, crying and anxious every time I had to visit him. I never told her that I thought my dad had sexually abused me; I didn't understand that for myself until I was in my 20s. But I was a child who was in a great deal of emotional distress. There were years that were better and years where it was truly awful, and I think the better years may have given my mom a false sense of hope.

I remember as a kid having frequent conversations with her where she would tell me that in my relationship with my father, I, emotionally, was the adult, and he was the child. She recognized that I was being parentified by him but didn't understand the damage of it. My mom encouraged me to grow a thicker skin and recognize that my dad was doing his best even though he was so "limited."

My mom was the person I trusted most—she was my superhero who could do no wrong—so her words impacted me profoundly. Unintentionally, she communicated to me that the pain my father was causing me was my responsibility, and it was my weakness that he upset me as much as he did.

My emotional distress was dealt with as though it were an interpersonal problem between two adults, when in reality, it was a structural family problem involving an abusive parent, a wounded child, and everyone else who ignored or dismissed her pain. I wasn't allowed to actually be a child— or a victim. Diane upheld the narrative that my father was a sad man doing his best, which reinforced my dad's DARVO.

We can recognize the complicated situations that adults may have been in, while still acknowledging how they reinforced our untrue stories

My mom, like so many of our parental figures, was in a complicated position. Her divorce had been really ugly, and visitations with my dad were part of the settlement agreement, which didn't give her much leeway. She wanted me to have a relationship with him, since parenting books on divorce advised consistent relationships with both parents. She was so afraid of being partial and poisoning me against my dad, she went too far the other way.

Diane gave me the option, when I was around 11, to stop seeing my dad and said we could go to court to try to change his visitation rights. But whenever I thought about it, it always felt like this was my problem, not our problem. I felt that if I stayed away, it meant I was too sensitive, not that it would be the right or brave thing to do.

My relationship with my mom struggled in the aftermath of the ultimatum and my decision to not speak with my father again. She had a difficult time accepting that he had sexually abused me. Her doubts fueled my feelings that I was responsible for my own abuse and the family repercussions.

I want to hold space for the complicated relationships you may have with parental figures in your life whom you love deeply, who have done so many wonderful or important things for you, but who have also contributed to your untrue story.

Do you have a parental figure like that in your life? How does it feel to allow for the good and hurtful stuff to all be true at the same time?

In addition to parental figures, are there other people close to you who have contributed to your untrue story around family and abuse? Identifying these people in our lives doesn't mean we don't care about them or love them (or it may—that's cool too!). We can allow for our understanding of them to be as nuanced and layered as feels true to us.

It may feel frustrating that the words of the people close to us in childhood still impact us so intensely as adults. If you're feeling that frustration, I encourage you to tap into patience and self-compassion. We have had decades of gaslighting and being conditioned to blame ourselves.

For some of us, healing may involve creating a new way for us to be a good family member—a way where caring for ourselves is seen as a sign of strength, where our pain is validated, and where people themselves are accountable for the harm they cause. And that's really hard work! That takes time! And sometimes it makes us feel terrible! But that doesn't mean you're doing it wrong. It's just what it looks like when you have to build the roads yourself.

The myth that CSA doesn't happen here in [insert literally any community]

A common force I see replicated for survivors across the world is the cultural narrative that CSA doesn't happen in *our* community; it is a problem in *other people's* communities. To be as clear as possible: CSA is a problem that knows no religious, geographic, ethnic, class, or gender bounds. CSA is a problem in every community across the world, without exception. As prevalent as CSA is throughout every corner of the world, equally prevalent are the lies that communities tell themselves about how they're the exception.

This cultural othering of CSA is a way for communities to do two things:

1. They can avoid having to address CSA in their community—or acknowledge that people they look up to abuse children.

2. They can invalidate survivors who choose to speak their truth, saying that the survivor must be lying since CSA does not happen here.

I come from a wealthy, highly educated, white, Jewish American family. I've never heard CSA addressed within Jewish spaces, and in my community child abuse was generally assumed to be a problem of gentiles. When I did come forward about my abuse, there was (and in some parts still is!) a lot of disbelief that this actually happens to us by members of our own community.

Those same beliefs exist in every other community. I work with survivors from all across the globe, from India to Australia, South Africa, Portugal, and Argentina, as well as literally every US state. CSA happens everywhere to every kind of family, and every community thinks they're the exceptional one where it doesn't happen.

Have you ever received the message that CSA isn't a problem that happens in your family or community? What might be the motives of people who uphold that myth?

Is blood actually thicker than water? Chemists, weigh in

Another cultural force that upheld my untrue story was what my friend and fellow survivor Amita Swadhin coined "blood supremacy." They explained, "Blood supremacy is the notion that blood ties are paramount, even at the expense of one's own well-being. It is used to underwrite patriarchy and every possible form of oppression."

Our entire social structures are built around family units of blood relatives. Who among us hasn't heard some sort of slogans upholding this, like "Blood is thicker than water," "Family first," or "Family over everything"? Think of every platitude you've ever seen painted in cursive on a piece of driftwood and sold at HomeGoods, for example.

We are taught from the jump that when we have nothing else, we still have our family. Loyalty to family is a highly admirable trait; people being close to their families is often viewed as a desirable quality in a potential suitor (amiright, Bachelor Nation?).

I'd like to never again see the story line of a parent who does a shit job but then redeems themselves

The messages of family over all else reverberate through a countless number of movies and TV shows. TV is my favorite self-soothing activity, but nothing makes me hate the love of my life, television, more than the following story line: There is a parent who does a terrible job caring for their child. Years later, said parent has a redemption moment with their adult child, who forgives them for being a flawed person doing their best, thus washing over the parent's abusive behavior for the sake of family.

I'm not saying that that story doesn't exist in real life or that people shouldn't forgive their family members—forgiveness is a very personal thing to each survivor. But because I saw this forgiveness arc so often on my screen, I thought it meant that someday I would be forced to forgive my father, because he is my biological family. I dreaded having my own TV moment of my father coming to me terminally ill, or fleeing a natural disaster, or looking death in the eye from the pending zombie apocalypse. I would have to forgive him to complete his regularly scheduled redemption.

It wasn't just me who was influenced by the story of family over everything. When I talked to friends about my painful relationship without disclosing the CSA, they often responded with "Well, he is your father" or "Yeah, family is tricky, but what are you gonna do?" "You don't get to choose your parents," and "At least he wants to be in your life!" These cultural messages left me feeling like I was bad and shameful for challenging blood supremacy.

What cultural forces do you see impacting your own untrue story about family? Maybe they are specific to a culture, an ethnicity, or a religion you may be a part of or perhaps a place where you live. What stories do they tell about what it means to be a good family member and person?

Strategies

STRATEGY: Reminding ourselves that we get to make our own rules

Now is a good time for us to remember that we get to be the deciders. We make all the rules for ourselves. You are the captain of your ship, the pilot of the plane, the driver of the Oscar Mayer Wienermobile, or whatever other transportation metaphor feels right.

If you're like my coaching clients, you might be worried that I will pressure you to take some big action concerning your family. That fear may be even stronger because I shared with you my personal story of refusing my father's ultimatum. But remember, I made that choice because it was what I personally needed, due to my specific safety concerns, at a particular moment in time. No one could've made that decision for me, just as no one can make any decisions for you. We are each the expert of our own safety needs.

OTHER PEOPLE MAY BE PRESSURING US TO HAVE SOME
BIG SHOWDOWN HIGH-DRAMA MOMENT WITH OUR FAMILIES.
BUT OUR LIVES ARE NOT A LOW-BUDGET NETFLIX MOVIE

We may also be dealing with other people's expectations for us. They may be thinking that, since we are open about our abuse, it means we should be confronting our families or making big moves. But these things are not necessarily connected. For some people, that confrontation will be healing; for others, it could be in conflict with their healing.

One of the most common questions I get from survivors is, "What was it like when you confronted your father?" To which I say, "Lolololololol. When did I say I did that?" I get why people are asking that! I'm a public survivor, so they assume that's all part of the process.

But I've never had a cinematic showdown with my father. I sent him an email telling him I was out and asking him to leave me alone, as a response to his ultimatum. I never sat across from him yelling, "I know what you did to me!" as music swelled in the background, and my mother, played by Meryl Streep, stormed out of the restaurant with me after pouring hot clam chowder in my father's face. I am confident that doing something like that would have been detrimental to me and not aligned with my safety or healing needs. But that conversation may be exactly what another survivor needs!

Remember, all you have to do is take things one day at a time. I know this shit feels very high-stakes. When I was in the depths of navigating all this, I kept thinking about what it would mean 20 years from now, or when someone I cared about would inevitably get sick, or what stories they would tell the younger generation about me. There was so much beyond my control, and it all felt scary. If you're in the midst of all that, I am here—I know how daunting all the unknowns are.

All each of us can do is make the right decision for ourselves today. We don't know what the future holds, and the good news is, none of us have to make permanent choices. All we can do is consider what we need for our healing today, knowing that the answer is allowed to change each day, month, and year. I know that might not make anything easier, but I hope it takes a fraction of the pressure off you.

It is totally normal to feel like all the options suck and are awful. It's not your fault: that's trauma, babe. The options suck because navigating our families after CSA is something no one should ever have to be doing. We never should've been harmed in the first place! It feels terrible because the situation is terrible, not because you've done anything wrong. You're doing great, I promise.

STRATEGY: When we push back on the abuser/victim binary, we create space for all our complicated emotions about the people who abused us

I've learned from the work of Aishah Shahidah Simmons that it is important to create space for complicated and sometimes conflicting emotions we may have about the people who abused us.

Society thinks about harm in a very narrow and limited way, seeing people as either good victims or monstrous subhuman abusers. This framing of harm is super unhelpful, in many ways helps perpetuate violence, and is particularly tricky when dealing with abuse within the family.

This binary was a barrier to my healing because I never saw my father as a monster, and the untrue story taught me that if I didn't want my father to rot in jail, my trauma wasn't real. Believing the false binary makes us feel like we aren't real victims unless abusers match the pure-evil stereotype.

Aishah taught me that having complicated feelings about abusive families is very common in a world that doesn't really allow for nuance. It is only now, 10 years after cutting my father out of my life, that I have begun to feel semi-okay admitting to myself that not all the memories of him are bad, and some of them may even be good. For the past 10 years, these neutral/ good memories have felt like a threat to me, like their very existence meant I should feel guilty for asserting my needs and protecting myself.

Aishah's work has shown me that everyone, especially nonsurvivors, needs to start understanding that ordinary people behave abusively and that people who harm us look like, act like, and actually are human beings. Sometimes people we love and respect abuse children. If we, as a society, could understand that, then maybe people would be more supportive of the survivors in their lives. We could have fewer people denying our abuse just because the person who hurt us looks like a normal person and not an eight-headed green thorny monster with knives for teeth.

What does it feel like to allow for it to all be messy and all be true?

THE TRUTH IS THAT PEOPLE WHO ABUSED US MAY ALSO BE VICTIMS, BUT THEY ARE STILL RESPONSIBLE FOR THE WAYS THEY'VE HARMED US

The other way I am trying to push back on the victim/abuser binary is when it comes to recognizing the victimhood of the person who hurt me. As a child, I recognized that the ways my father had been emotionally victimized as a child probably did a real number on him. Seeing my father as a victim ran really deep for me, because, as I described earlier, he worked very hard with immense intention to get me to see him as the victim. Although I have no reason to believe he was sexually abused, I thought that because I could see the ways he had been hurt, it meant he wasn't responsible for the way he was hurting me.

When it comes to CSA, it isn't uncommon for abusers to be victims too. They may not be victims of the exact same kind of abuse, but they can often be survivors of some form of abuse. We can't address ending CSA until we can talk about these cycles of abuse that can happen.

Lourdez Velasco has modeled for me how we can have a level of understanding for victims who may have victimized us, without erasing their responsibility for the harm they've caused. Lourdez learned that their family member who sexually abused them also had been sexually abused as a child.

Lourdez shared that they had compassion for the person who harmed them and recognized the impact of the intergenerational trauma passed down through their lineage since the colonization of their native island of Guåhan (often known by its colonized name, Guam): "I believe our land is our body and our body is our land. My people's autonomy has been completely violated through colonization and systematic oppression, and that creates more violence in our familial and interpersonal connections, furthering how colonization continues to permeate our lives."

Lourdez and I shared with each other how we feel careful in these conversations to not imply that any of us are fated to grow up and sexually abuse other people. Let's be super clear: loads of children, the vast majority of children who are sexually abused, do not grow up to abuse other people. We are not fated to any of this terrible shit.

While the history of abuse, intergenerational trauma, or mental illness may help us understand the context of the person who harmed us, it doesn't mean they are absolved of responsibility. Lourdez shared, "I can have compassion around all that my parents had to go through without any tools available for healing, while also choosing to have firm boundaries with them to protect myself from further harm."

Are there larger social and cultural factors that have contributed to patterns of abuse in your family? How does it feel to allow space for that, while still holding the person who abused you responsible for their actions?

STRATEGY: Understanding that our family's denial has nothing to do with us. This one is easier said than done, I know

By now, you've heard me say over and over again that people's denial of our abuse is a reflection of them, not us. But it may hit differently now that we are talking about our families. It is the most natural thing in the world to wish that our families would honor our truth. I will never tell you to stop wanting that kind of support and affirmation from the people who we've been told are the most important people in our lives.

But wanting and needing their affirmation are two different things. And as painful and difficult as it may be, we need to separate in our minds the validity of our abuse from whether or not our families are accepting of the truth.

If your family doesn't believe or support you, then please know you are not ever alone! Overwhelmingly, of the survivors I know who've talked to their families about their abuse, their families responded by denying it ever happened. There are a few exceptions here and there, but more often than not, the families are not supportive, at least initially. If this is your experience, then please know you are, like, in the best company with some of the dopest, most loving, badass survivors in the world, and it doesn't mean your trauma isn't real.

It's hard not to take our family's denial personally. It feels immensely personal and like a betrayal, because, you know, it is a betrayal. If I've learned one thing, it's that we can never ever underestimate the capacity of a survivor's family members to deny their trauma and how much that denial has truly nothing to do with the survivor.

Maybe you're considering these words and saying, "Hey, Alisa! Easy for you to say!" Okay, I get that. So maybe it would be helpful to hear about it not from me, but rather from my mom, Diane, who struggled with her own denial of my abuse for several years.

NOW COMES THE BEST PART OF THE BOOK, WHERE YOU GET TO HEAR FROM MY INCREDIBLE MOM, DIANE, ABOUT HER EXPERIENCES WITH ACCEPTING MY TRUTH

My mom said all the right supportive things to me when I was figuring out what to do about my father's ultimatum. She was navigating some challenging family dynamics, but Diane's words told me she had my back. It wasn't until four years later that I understood that my mom actually didn't get it. For four years, she denied to herself that I had been sexually abused.

The turning point was an upcoming complicated family function where my father was sure to be in attendance. It would be the first time I was going to see him since the ultimatum. While my mom was busy trying to make accommodations to limit my potential interactions with my father, I couldn't understand why she thought seeing him was an okay thing to expect me to do.

Diane recently explained to me that when I first told her about the nightmares of my father sexually abusing me, she told herself that my father had only emotionally, not sexually, abused me.

"I knew your father was a horrible person, and there was no doubt in my mind he had emotionally abused you. I felt as if I was supporting you, and I didn't feel like it was necessary for us to have the same idea of what the abuse had entailed. I couldn't allow myself yet to go to a place where I would accept that he sexually abused you," Diane shared.

I spent months trying to prepare to see my father, but the closer I got to it being a reality, my suicidal ideations became stronger than I'd ever experienced before. While I was able to prevent myself from self-harming one particularly terrifying night, in the aftermath of that night I realized that I needed my mom to finally get what all this meant to me.

At my wonderful therapist Susan's suggestion, I had my mom come to a session with me. Halfway through our session, Susan interrupted my mom and insisted that she hear my pain. I remember seeing a switch immediately flip inside my mom. I watched the horror flash across Diane's eyes as the truth of my abuse hit her. It affirmed all my suspicions that until that moment, she hadn't believed my father had sexually abused me.

"I remember coming home after that first session together, sitting at the kitchen table, and saying, 'Oh fuck me. He did it,'" my mom recalled.

That therapy session served as a wake-up call. It was not a magical moment where we suddenly had the beautiful relationship we do today; we both had so much healing we needed to do individually and together. While she never doubted my truth again, it took me a long time to make peace with my mom's denial. It's helped me to learn more about the origins of her denial to realize that it wasn't my fault.

LET'S HEAR FROM A PARENT ABOUT WHY THEIR DENIAL OF OUR ABUSE HAS TO DO WITH THEM AND NOT US

During a recent conversation, I asked Diane how she made sense of her previous state of denial. "I was overwhelmed by the stigma of CSA," she replied. "In my mind, I thought, 'This doesn't happen in our family. How could I have let this happen? I would've seen it. I would've known. How could I have married someone, and loved someone, who would sexually abuse their own child?' In that sense, it was all about me more than it was ever about you."

I recognized that my mom had to navigate her own shame: "As a parent, I have a deep-seated need to protect my child. If I was driving and we got in a car accident and you got hurt, I would be devastated, but the world around me would understand that accidents like that happen. But allowing for my child to be sexually abused by her father? No, it's just too horrifying for words. I am a perfectionist; I always have been [Alisa's note: I inherited this trait]. It was hard for me to accept that I was in a failed marriage, so to accept that I had failed my daughter?" my mom shared.

She and I both feel strongly about contextualizing our relationship journey, especially because we would never want someone to read about our story and feel like they should be able to get their parents to come to terms with the trauma like us. We both recognize that our story would look really different if my parents were still in a relationship, if my mom were reliant on my dad for anything, or if she held him in high esteem. She explained, "I had the privilege of getting out of my marriage, of being independent, of not needing a goddamn thing from your father." For many parental figures, they have other challenging considerations that impact their ability to accept our truths. It is never your fault if your parents don't ever have their own wake-up-call moment of accepting the truth of your abuse.

ADVICE FROM DIANE FOR FAMILY MEMBERS WHO WANT TO WORK THROUGH THEIR GUILT AND DENIAL IN ORDER TO SUPPORT US

If you have family members who are demonstrating a willingness to support you but don't know how to, my mom advises them to get their own therapists who have a good understanding of CSA and trauma. "The feelings of guilt are valid, and family members need space and resources to process them, as processing the guilt with the survivor is not appropriate. I received a lot of support from my therapist, who was able to help me understand how common CSA is—who could help me both with my own healing as well as help me understand my child's healing too. A parent's healing process must be a separate process from supporting their child in their healing."

If you're reading this and thinking, well, that's good for you, Alisa, but that's never going to be me and my family, I hear you. I am extremely lucky to have the relationship I do with my mom and that she was willing to do her own healing work to be able to show up fully for mine. I recognize that our relationship is the exception and unfortunately very far from being the rule. My hope, though, is that by hearing from Diane yourself, you are able to, in time, recognize that the shame your family may be experiencing is not yours to hold. Their denial reflects absolutely nothing about your truth. But I know that doesn't stop it from hurting.

SOMETIMES THE FAMILY MEMBERS DENYING
OUR PAIN ARE SURVIVORS THEMSELVES

In my coaching work, I've seen a common form of denial where the family member who is denying our abuse is themselves a CSA survivor.

In the Hulu original drama version of life, the survivor parent or sibling would hear that someone they loved was also sexually abused, and that would bind the two survivors together in resilience and support.

Which is cute.

But in reality, it is sometimes the people who themselves are survivors who have the hardest time accepting that a child or younger sibling they love also went through the same kind of abuse. That older survivor perhaps hasn't done their own healing work and is still repressing the impacts of their own trauma. Their coping mechanisms are in direct conflict with a survivor living in their truth.

Whatever the reason why a family member is denying our abuse, please remember that you deserve all the support in the world. I am so sorry that the people you love aren't able to give you what you deserve. That is their failure, not yours.

I asked Diane what message she'd like to offer all of us survivors. "What I really want to say to all the survivors reading this who are struggling with their families is that I'm really sorry your families cannot be there for you," she said. "It's not your fault—it is society's fault, and the stigma that we have put on CSA, that prevents people from not just talking about it, but accepting that it happens, and it happens all the time. It's not about you and your pain, it is about them and their inability to go there to address that pain. But your family's lack of validation does not change what has happened to you and the validity of your pain."

I totally agree, Mom.

STRATEGY: Finding power and healing
through building our own families

Okay, friends, I know this shit has been *heavvvvvy*. But I think it's safe for
me to say that the heaviest is behind us, and now we get to talk about beautiful, proactive endeavors of building our own families. So let's take in a deep
breath and exhale out all that feels heavy, and repeat as needed.

WE GET THE OPPORTUNITY TO REPARENT OURSELVES! HUZZAH!

As I've learned from Amita Swadhin, Ignacio Rivera, Aishah Shahidah Simmons, and others, healing can also include parenting ourselves. We can provide ourselves what we needed and didn't receive when we were younger.

For me, reparenting has looked like this:

- Constantly validating my feelings and my pain
- Encouraging myself to be as openly sensitive as I truly am
- Being emotionally honest without worrying that I am being
  too dramatic

What were some things you needed from the adults in your life that you
didn't get when you were younger? They may include material things, like
a safe home, or emotional things, like validation and being heard. We don't
need to have the answers to these big questions right now, but rather, I
invite you to simply get curious about ways to give yourself what you lacked
as a child.

WE CAN BUILD A FAMILY WITH
WHOMEVER WE'D LIKE!

I've learned so much from the leadership of queer and trans people of color
who have been modeling for decades what it means to create and build families that aren't based on biological relation. Blood does not need to be the
primary bond in families.

Over time, I've been building my own family full of people whom I love and respect and who love and respect me. It includes some people from my family of origin, people I've been friends with for decades, my husband, and several dogs. It doesn't mean my family is without conflict, but when there is disagreement, we can work it out in a way that invites accountability and growth. For me, my family doesn't involve unconditional love. No one is obligated to love another person, and it's okay for other needs, like safety and basic respect, to be more important than love.

I'm not alone in finding healing in building my own family. Katrina shared, "I've found healing in my new chosen family with my partner and our pets." She continued, "Also my partner's father has become such a safe father figure for me, which was difficult for me since I didn't feel worthy of his unwavering support and love. It's been healing to know there really are some good people who love and accept me, scars and all."

Katrina's words really capture for me how radical it can be when we experience what family love should feel like for us. It may feel disorienting and unfamiliar for some of us, and it may even bring us grief for recognizing how it should've been for us our whole lives. What does it mean to you to consider that you get to make rules for yourself about who your family is and what family is supposed to feel like for you?

LET'S TALK ABOUT PARENTING AS A SURVIVOR WITH TWO WONDERFUL SURVIVOR PARENTS

I have heard over the years from so many survivors that parenting is simultaneously healing and also immensely triggering. While I do not have children, I have two brilliant survivors who are parents to share their wisdom with all of us. Whether we want to have kids or not, it is likely that we will find ourselves in the lives of children, and I think their insights can be valuable to each of us in our own way.

The first is Lourdez Velasco, who is a brilliant artist and parent to a 13-year-old child who is a goofball just like them. Lourdez describes their child as "a wonderful, empathetic kid who feels his emotions loudly and big. We joke around a lot. He's a really great hang." The second is Alicia Sanchez Gill, a resource organizer and new parent to a 15-month-old precious baby.

Alicia shared that her child is currently very into dandelions, all kinds of music, and snack time. Same, kid, same.

IT'S NORMAL TO FIND ASPECTS
OF PARENTING RETRAUMATIZING

When I asked Alicia about the ways her trauma has resurfaced through becoming a parent, she said that the triggers began as early as when she and her wife began working on getting pregnant. "The process of going through intrauterine insemination (IUI) was more triggering than I expected and brought up really hard feelings of being out of control with my body."

Alicia shared with me that often when people are pregnant or attempting to get pregnant, there is a lot of deficit-based language. I've seen this lately a lot with friends who are trying to get pregnant and have to spend their time in medical offices being told what isn't "working right" in their bodies. I have already had so many triggering medical experiences that have made me feel like my body was wrong, and I appreciate how intensified those triggers may be when trying to have a child.

Lourdez said that when they first got pregnant at age 19, they were still in the process of understanding their own CSA survivorship. It wasn't until Lourdez started organizing with other survivors in the years after their son was born that they realized how retraumatizing becoming a parent had been for them.

Lourdez first started recognizing the trauma resurfacing through intense fears of what dangers could befall their baby. "Starting when he was a few months old, I found myself helicoptering over my child, worried that no one other than me could care for him. I don't want him to experience any harm, while also fearing that I may harm my child. What really helped me through that time was to talk with other CSA survivors who were parents too to recognize these fears were normal and that I wasn't alone in it."

WE SHOULD BE TEACHING KIDS
ABOUT CONSENT AT EVERY AGE!

Lourdez began parenting in a deeply intentional way to offer their child everything that Lourdez had needed when they were younger but had not received from adults. This included learning about consent, practicing apologizing, and having open lines of communication and trust. "I taught my child about consent throughout his childhood, evolving it as was age appropriate for him. I taught him about bodily autonomy, including what felt like a yes and a no in his body and what parts of his body are not okay for anyone to touch," they shared.

I've similarly learned from the work of The HEAL Project, a CSA-survivor-led organization that advocates for comprehensive holistic sexuality education, that ideas of consent and bodily autonomy can, and should, be taught throughout a person's life in different ways to be appropriate to the child's given age. We would talk to a three-year-old very differently than, say, an eight-year-old, but there are really smart people who have the expertise to help us understand what those lessons look like at all the stages of life.

Alicia showed me that parents can put these concepts into practice as soon as the baby is born by using correct language for body parts and practicing consent: "When I change my child's diaper, I tell them exactly what I am doing. I say, 'Mama is going to change your diaper now, Mama is going to gently touch you here,' and so on, so that I am checking in with my child and building the foundation that they should always be informed about what's happening to their body. I get to practice consent in a way that I never received it, and it is a beautiful and liberating gift." Alicia shared with me that their child has recently begun saying the word "body" during diaper changes because she always tells her baby, "This is your body—Mama has a body too."

WE CAN PRACTICE ACCOUNTABILITY AND OPEN COMMUNICATION IN OUR PARENTING IN A WAY WE MAY HAVE NEVER EXPERIENCED AS CHILDREN

Another important aspect of parenting in a way that was aligned with Lourdez's healing was to practice apologizing. Lourdez recalled a time when they got upset at their kid for something and he responded by crying and asking for space, which was something Lourdez had taught him was okay to need and ask for. When he was ready, he came back out and told Lourdez that the tone they had used with him hurt his feelings.

Lourdez replied by saying, "Thank you for sharing that with me. I wish I had used a different tone with you, and I want you to understand why I was upset." It was an opportunity for Lourdez to apologize and for their son to think about how his actions impacted his parent.

"I am learning to recognize that there are ways I respond sometimes to my son that are rooted in the way I was raised, as well as my own ego that shows up sometimes when thinking about apologizing to my child," shared Lourdez, "but I want him to know you can communicate about hurt and meaningfully apologize in all your relationships, and I acknowledge the power I have as a parent to teach him that."

I was so moved when Lourdez shared that example with me. Having been raised by my father, who never apologized and took responsibility for anything he ever did wrong, I felt overwhelmed when considering what simple apologies from a parent would have felt like as a kid. It is difficult for me to imagine what that would've been like, but I know that if I do become a parent, I really want to practice that.

In what ways is it important for children to experience their parents being accountable for their actions? What would it mean for you to model healthy accountability for the young people in your life?

Through my conversation with Lourdez, I saw so many ways that they were being intentional about offering their child love, safety, and support. Most of all, Lourdez and their son developed a relationship built on communication and trust: "As a young person myself, I could never give feedback to my parents; that was seen as culturally disrespectful. With my kid, I want to hear the feedback. I want us to be able to talk, even when it's hard." Lourdez recognizes that, as a parent, they have to make hard choices for their child's safety: "I am committed to being honest with him about why I need to make those choices and try to create space for him to express his feelings about it all."

When I heard Lourdez say that, it made me realize how radical and powerful it must be to allow children to express their feelings and show, through words and actions, that their feelings matter, even if parents need to make choices the children do not like. It is creating space for children to be full people.

Alicia has also been intentionally cultivating ways for her child to be their full selves, whomever they may grow up to be. She and her wife chose a gender-neutral name for their child and are raising the child in a way that will allow for them to understand the expansiveness of gender. They dress their kid in clothes traditionally deemed masculine and feminine and will continue to make decisions that minimize the binary of gender for the child. "We know the world will ultimately gender our child, but we want to give them the opportunity to express themselves and feel free and safe to tell us how they identify their gender in a way that my wife and I never had growing up. While the world may not be safe for them, especially as a Black child in a deeply anti-Black country, I want our home to be a safe space for them to explore their whole self."

It is so beautiful to hear how different survivor parents are finding ways to offer their children what they needed when they were younger but didn't receive. It is healing for me to expand my thinking of all the ways we can be in relation to the children of our lives, whether we are parents or not, by practicing our values with them.

PARENTING CAN BE TRIGGERING, ESPECIALLY
WHEN IT COMES TO OUR BODIES

Like all other survivors, Lourdez and Alicia still have to contend with the ongoing impact of their trauma and how it shows up in their parenting. Both shared with me that a lot of the triggers center around their bodies.

Alicia said that when she was breastfeeding her child, she was overwhelmed by constant demand from the baby for touch: "A baby needs so much and is so helpless, and my one job is to protect them. In order to do that, I had to, to an extent, suspend my own needs and disassociate from my body," she shared.

While the newborn phase was not enjoyable, Alicia said that her relationship to her trauma has shifted as her baby has gotten older. She is still working through layered feelings about her body and how it has changed through becoming a parent: "In surviving CSA, I always saw my body as wrong and a site of harm and violence, but now I also see my body as capable of carrying and birthing Black life. I am still understanding how my body is a place where bad things happened and also I am able to nurture this beautiful life through my body," Alicia said.

Lourdez also is working on healing parts of themselves and their body as it pertains to parenting. "As my son got older, I was afraid to be affectionate with him because I worried that he didn't want that affection. It would cause me to freeze and have a lot of grief around it. It can still be difficult for me to offer him hugs and kisses freely without that tension within myself," Lourdez told me.

I really appreciate having both that fear and the tremendous grief it must bring up within us to fear harming our own children, especially when seeing other parents who don't have trauma give affection without that same trigger response. Lourdez said that their son's father can offer affection with such ease, while they have to work so hard to separate their trauma experiences in their body from what is happening at the present moment with their child.

Lourdez shared with me that they've worked a lot on this physical affection piece of parenting in therapy: "I've been working on being okay with not offering hugs and kisses and that being okay in our relationship because I verbally tell him I love him and verbally express my love and support with such ease. But it's a continued healing effort for me to remember that offering him physical affection is not abuse. I know that in my relationship with my son, there are so many tools we've practiced together to build trust and safety, but there is still that fear in me of messing up, which means no physical touch. I am trying to heal those pieces of me." It was so helpful for me to be reminded that this healing work is ongoing for each of us and that it's okay if we aren't ever fully cooked—there are still opportunities for us to grow and continue to show up for the people we care about in the ways that matter to us.

HERE'S THE ADVICE LOURDEZ AND ALICIA HAVE FOR FELLOW SURVIVOR PARENTS

When I asked Lourdez what advice they'd offer other survivor parents, the first thing they recommended was for parents to practice compassion and patience with themselves: "Parenting with intention is so exhausting, especially if you don't have a blueprint for it. I am learning as I go, and learning as I grow. It's really hard. But building that self-awareness and practicing self-accountability is the power of healing."

Alicia told me that she is still working on the practice of self-compassion: "It is a practice to have grace with myself every single day around parenting." She shared that through working on her healing, she is confronting the impact of the CSA that left her feeling isolated, that she had to fend for herself and was unable to trust others, since she couldn't trust her family to keep her safe. "I used to move through the world like I was the only person who would defend me. I've learned from being in community with other survivors that it isn't true. A big way I move with self-compassion is asking for help and remembering that I am not alone in any of this."

I'VE BEEN WORKING ON HEALING MY FEARS
THAT I AM CONTAGIOUS TO CHILDREN

Alicia's and Lourdez's words made me feel like I had more space to be honest about my own fears that I've felt whenever I find myself around small children. I am often afraid that I am somehow contagious, like I am contaminated by my CSA and it isn't within my control to prevent it from spreading to someone else.

I think, for me, this feeling stems from my inability to understand how someone ever sexually abused me. While logically I know how harm happens and how common it is, when I think of my own story, I still can't believe that someone who said they loved me would do this to me. None of it makes any sense to me, so I can't understand how to ensure that I don't do it to anyone else.

Lourdez told me those fears are totally normal, and they know many other CSA parents who feel similarly: "Our abusers were people we trusted, and I couldn't understand why he would do this, and I'm learning now that actually what happened to me was very thought-out, but for a long time, when I couldn't understand it, it felt like the sexual abuse was contagious." They continued, "I know now that I will do everything in my will not to perpetuate this harm. While we may feel like all of this is irrational or beyond our power, the truth is that we can control ourselves, and we can prevent this from being passed down through us."

Truthfully, I don't think there are people less likely to harm a child than CSA survivor parents who have worked on their own healing. We are obsessed with autonomy, safety, and emotional health. We have created space to process our shit in a way that doesn't involve our accidently projecting that shit onto the children around us. We are interested in validating emotions, recognizing harm, and holding ourselves accountable when we fuck up. When we work on our healing, we develop skills that help us support children in all the ways they need. Most of all, we learn to be the adults that our child selves needed when we were younger and to be able to offer that to the kids in our lives.

A few months ago, I got a teeny tiny taste of what Lourdez had been talking about. I was sitting on a friend's patio catching up over a glass of wine as his two-year-old daughter played around us. She excitedly wanted to show off her new swing to me. We walked over to the little kiddie swing and I said, "Do you want to go in it?" and she smiled and lifted her arms up for me to pick her up and put her in the seat.

It was such an itty bitty moment that I didn't want to mention it, for fear of freaking my friend out over the smallest interaction with his child. But when I saw the little girl smile and lift up her arms, answering my question and giving me permission to touch her in order to get her into her chair, something unlocked in my chest.

Although I couldn't put words to it at the time, I now understand that I was full of both grief and hope at the same time. I felt so hopeful that I had such a positive experience with a small child where I could gently ask for consent, and in their own language, they offered it to me. The small interaction gave me a glimpse of how I could be as a parent.

But that relief brought such sadness with it, as I recognized that up until that moment, I had still been so afraid of myself. I didn't realize how scared I had been that my CSA was contagious, that I would contaminate a child, against my own will.

It was the smallest little thing, and I never mentioned it to anyone, but I think that day gave me the clarity I needed. Those fears are a part of me but only go so deep. Somewhere, much deeper in me, lay my truth, which is that for all the children of my life, I will be to them what I needed when I was younger. Because of what we've been through and what we know, we will have a unique understanding and calling to protect children in our lives, to make sure they are safe and revered.

STRATEGY: Remembering that when we are healing ourselves, we are healing our families, because we are a part of our families

The most powerful strategy for me is remembering that I am positively influencing family that has come before me and will follow after me.

I KNOW I AM NEVER ALONE—MY
ANCESTORS ARE HEALING ALONGSIDE ME

I did not grow up with a connection to spirits as a part of my religious practice. But in the past two years, something has shifted within me. In doing more intense healing work than ever before, I have felt a new level of connection to my ancestors who've come before me. I don't know how else to explain it except to say, plainly, that I feel them with me. It isn't anything I ever expected to feel, and it has been a surprising gift in my life at a time when I needed it the most. With that new experience has also come a new way of considering my family of origin, especially my father's family.

When I ended my relationship with my father, I accepted that it meant, for my particular situation, ending my ties with his family. I have not considered them my family for a long time, and knowing that has provided more of a sense of relief than grief for me.

The ancestors I have felt with me have not just been those that are a part of the lineage of my mother's side. I have also felt ancestors from my father's side. While part of me is resistant to say this because it is so beyond the tangible things I find comfort in, I have observed that as I do this healing work, I can feel some of the ancestors on my father's side of the family healing with me. When I heal myself, I offer healing to my family, because I am a part of my family.

Lourdez shared with me that an important component of their healing has been based in ancestral work, rooted in their tradition as a CHamoru person from Guåhan: "I totally believe the act of healing we are doing now is healing generations in the past and also in the future, and I think it's a very Indigenous framework that I have learned here on Turtle Island but also back home in Guåhan. I realized a lot of the grief I am moving through isn't just mine, it is generations of grief I know I come from, and some-times when I'm grieving, I can see that this isn't mine." I immediately un-derstood, in my own way, that feeling of grieving something beyond just my own lived experience.

I cannot make my living family members heal themselves. But by living my truth and protecting myself, I am allowing others to heal alongside me who never got the chance before. I may never know the names of all the people who came before me who went through what I went through as a child, but I feel them with me very often. They fortify me. They remind me that I am not alone in this work. They tell me that I am a good family member, that I am generously doing immense labor, not just for myself, but for them too.

Lourdez has taught me a lot about what deepening our connection to our ancestors can offer us in our healing. "This work is so hard, but when I feel alone, I turn to my ancestors. I felt so lonely being the only one who spoke out against what was happening in my family. I know that I am not the only CSA survivor in my family; there have been people from genera-tions I don't even know who have gone through this, and I practice turning to them for guidance, protection, and solace," said Lourdez.

WE ARE MODELING HEALING FOR OUR FAMILY MEMBERS, AND THAT IS A GIFT, WHETHER THEY SEE IT THAT WAY OR NOT

Whether connecting with ancestors is a part of your healing journey or not, when we work on our healing, we are positively impacting people beyond just ourselves. As Jude shares, "Both my parents were sexually assaulted, and neither ever addressed it. I feel like that through healing, I am saying, 'The buck stops with me.' I will not stay silent, and I will do everything I can to protect my future family from the abuse and suffering."

Often, our disclosures lead to other members of the family feeling safe enough to disclose too. When I went public about my story, I expected to hear from strangers that they could relate to what I had been through. What I hadn't been prepared for was to learn that I had been surrounded by other survivors my entire life. It was particularly wild to see how many of my friends' parents disclosed their own history of CSA to their adult children in those early months of my public work.

I don't know if that is happening in the family I do not speak with anymore. But by being honest about who we are and what we've been through, we are offering a gift to our families, a space without stigma. Carla has seen this for herself within her family: "I come from a family with a lot of mental illness that never knew how to have hard conversations about our demons. I've noticed now that I'm more open about my mental health in general, and my family is more open with me and each other."

Similarly, Nell has seen her own healing work inspire others around her: "Although it's incredibly challenging bringing to light the dark side of my family of origin, I feel like I have been given an opportunity to heal pieces of generational trauma and stop the cycle of dysfunction. I am currently witnessing other family members become empowered by my determination to heal to move forward on their own healing journeys."

Our families may never recognize this gift and may continue to reinforce the lie that we harm them with our disclosure. We cannot control their reactions or the pain those reactions cause, but you absolutely can know that our honesty offers healing.

Holy smokes, we made it—who wants a 'rita?

Wow, okay friendos, we got through the heaviest of heavy chapters. High-fives all around, margaritas are on me.

Before I start juicing limes and rimming glasses with salt, I want to leave you with this simple reminder: You get to decide how you define family. You decide what combination of words, experiences, bonds, and feelings makes someone or something your family. Anyone lucky enough to be your family gets to receive the gift of all your healing efforts. All that you have done, and all you continue to do, makes you a wonderful family member.

8

We Are Great at Spotting Abusive Workplaces

UNTRUE STORY
We are failures because our trauma is showing up in our work lives

BUT TRUTHFULLY
Our workplaces can replicate the dynamics of our abuse;
the responsibility to fix that is on the shoulders of people in power

'm going to start this chapter with a real spoiler. Skip ahead if you don't want to know: Even though *Game of Thrones* sets up Daenerys Targaryen to be the hero of the story, in the 11th hour, after thousands of real-life people have named their children after her, she becomes a murderous super-villain and is killed in the name of saving humanity. Never name your child after a TV character *before* the show ends.

Okay, fine, that is not the spoiler for this chapter.

The spoiler for this chapter is as follows:

No matter how many different ways you try to slice it, healing and capitalism are necessarily in direct conflict with one another. We can talk strategies, but until we have a radically different world where people's self-worth and ability to survive are not tied to their work, and where workplaces are not inherently patriarchal and exploitative, the way we work will continue to be in conflict with healing.

None of that is your fault! Even when the world lies to you and says it is! I lived for a while with the untrue story that I was a failure because my workplace was triggering me, and I am excited to share with you how I processed those feelings and came to understand my true story: it is a structural failure, not a personal shortcoming, that so many of us are retraumatized at work.

I used to fear that I was a failure for being triggered by my workplace

First let's go back to 2015, when everyone was singing "Can't Feel My Face" and slowly realizing it was a song about cocaine. About a year earlier, I had gotten my dream job at a small reproductive rights nonprofit that advocated for abortion access. My role was to travel around the world with the CEO putting on workshops to help legislators and other community leaders advocate for reproductive rights within their own countries. I had my own office with a window. I felt I couldn't be #girlbossing any harder.

Sure, there were some concerns, including that it was a women's rights organization led by a man who had his staff of almost entirely women terrified of his tantrums and outbursts. But having worked in the DC nonprofit world, I knew that no place was perfect—that often the nonprofits were bastions of hypocrisy, advocating for one thing and then failing to practice what they preached.

I had struggled really hard with disillusionment in my last two jobs, and I needed this one to be different. I had to prove to myself that I had a thick enough skin to be a successful professional.

When the shit hitteth the fan

As I narrowed in on my one-year anniversary on the job, I experienced the worst trigger of my adult life, with my father trying to reenter my life. On one extremely ill-fated trip to Kenya with my CEO boss, I received really triggering news about my dad just moments before losing cell and internet service for five days. I tried to stress to my boss why I needed to get internet service again, simply saying that I got a concerning message from my mom, but it was useless.

That trip was the hardest I've ever worked to fake being okay.

I spent five days alone in my trigger. I was in excruciating pain, staying up all night either physically ill with some sort of traveler's bug that gave me unstoppable vomiting and shitting or wide awake replaying the most abusive memories of my childhood on a loop.

Yet each morning I pulled it together to do what I was hired to do. My boss was visibly annoyed at my physical illness, especially when I had to bother him one evening to knock on his door and ask for some of his supply of bottled water because I risked severe dehydration, as though I had chosen to contract this bug as a personal inconvenience to him. What a cool and humane way to treat other people.

Despite all of that, I did damn well at my job, if I may say so. I'm not trying to brag to you all about how I crushed it at work, but I think it's important to challenge the misconception that those of us who are traumatized are somehow not very good at our jobs. We can be total emotional wrecks and simultaneously get shit done—in fact, I'd argue that there's no group of people better at that than us, considering we had to do it for our childhoods! We are, on the whole, actually too productive during emotional breakdowns and probably should be resting more than we are!

The line between my personal trauma and my professional trauma disappeared, and that confused the hell out of me

Back in DC, it was harder to separate the harm I was experiencing with my dad from what I saw at work with the CEO. The CEO talked about why "safe spaces" were ruining freedom of speech, said that "rape culture" wasn't a thing, and spewed transphobic and homophobic words. Whether I was at work or at home, I was still witnessing men abusing power and justifying themselves. It was all too much. I hoped a break would allow me to regain enough distance to stop being triggered at work.

Right before my time-off request, I heard the CEO yelling from down the hall again and realized that he was screaming at my supervisor. The

CEO told my supervisor that I hadn't been my bubbly self lately (complex trauma will do that to you). Can you imagine someone saying that about a male employee?

He was insisting that my supervisor disclose to him the reason I hadn't been cheery, even imploring, "What is it? Does her mother have cancer or something?" When my supervisor refused to disclose anything, both to protect me and also because she understands labor law and a bitch's right to privacy, the CEO gave his ultimatum. (What is it with abusive men and ultimatums?! God, if you love them so much, why don't you marry them?) He said that either my supervisor must tell him what was going on in my personal life, or he'd take it as a sign that I didn't care about my work and demote me.

To be super clear, the CEO's behavior was 100 percent unethical, and requiring the disclosure of irrelevant personal information creates a hostile work environment and is potentially harassment. The CEO of an organization that advocates for a woman's right to privacy was violating this woman's right to privacy. The irony was not lost on me.

Just like my father had with his ultimatum, the CEO determined that my emotions were not genuine and enthusiastic enough for his fragile ego. Once the CEO and my dad became so connected in my mind, I knew there was no amount of therapy, meditation, visualization, or yoga that could get me to feel safe in my workplace again.

After a waterworks of a conversation with my beloved supervisor, I made up my mind to exercise a financial privilege very few survivors have and quit my job without any plan. All survivors deserve a safety net that supports them leaving abusive environments, along with access to healing resources regardless of work status. But the reality is, most people have no option for leaving abusive and retraumatizing workplaces. That never ever is the fault of the survivor and never ever means they are complicit or not "objecting" to the abuse. It is the fault of the world we live in that so many have to rely on harmful workplaces for survival.

I had so many privileges: financial security, citizenship that kept me safe from deportation, access to private health insurance, and secure housing. I also felt like a complete failure. I knew my boss was disgusting and wrong, but I also knew that other colleagues had been able to tough it out for years under his reign. I couldn't even stomach staying long enough to find another job.

The guilt at being "sensitive" and "dramatic" was back. I spent the next weeks in a deep depression, replaying all the times I didn't smile, wondering if I could've given an ounce more to prevent this mess. I felt like a kid again, blaming myself for having thin skin.

In the following months, I discovered the truth: it is the fault of our workplaces built on white supremacy, patriarchy, and exploitation that I, as a survivor, could not safely do my job. The shame is not on me, but on the boss and his enablers.

There are lots of ways we can be triggered by our work

I'm not alone in feeling shame about being retraumatized by my workplace. When Sam chose an extremely competitive and fast-paced job and retraumatization occurred, she simply told herself, "I chose this profession and I have to adapt."

Sam said in retrospect, "What I failed to appreciate was that my past, my natural authentic self, was deeply misaligned to the values and principles of this workplace. The harder I tried to fit in, or disregard my discomfort, the worse I felt and performed." It led her to feeling worthless and incompetent, even though she, of course, wasn't. Sam now has more clarity about what she was experiencing: "Having recently discovered these triggers over the course of my healing, I am now much more appreciative of what my body and feelings are trying to tell me about my sense of self, worthiness, and safety."

Katrina shared, "I was retraumatized at work after being sexually assaulted by my boss, who had been twice my age and had the same name as my father. That was the year that the body memories of my father's abuse began to leak from my subconscious mind, causing cracks in the walls and warning of the unfathomable flood." This profound trauma challenged her previous notions about success and professionalism. "My work life was never the same; surviving each day became my new form of productivity and success."

Carla shared, "I used to work for a nonprofit organization that was understaffed and underresourced yet still managed to pay its president six figures. The staff was always expected to do whatever it took to get the job done and fulfill the organization's mission. This message often left me feeling used, unheard, unappreciated, and like my needs and experience did not matter. This invariably brought up many of the same feelings I felt in the wake of being abused."

Often, we receive messages that we should just "toughen up" or that this is just what it means to "be a professional." But the impacts of our trauma cannot be ignored or pushed aside.

Have you ever experienced your trauma showing up for you within your professional self, whether it's at work, in school, or in college? How did that make you feel? What has your experience trying to have healthy boundaries at work been like?

What are the origins of the bullshit?

Growing up in an elitist environment formed my ideas of success

I grew up in Bethesda, Maryland; the high school I went to was so intense that there was literally a book written about it called *The Overachievers*. Subtle.

Despite my mom's efforts to encourage me to have a healthy perspective on what actually mattered in life, I was conditioned by my peers and community that my self-worth was based on college, job, and achievement. I felt like a failure if I didn't live up to these elitist markers of success.

Sometimes perfectionism and overachieving tendencies are rooted in how we coped with our abuse

Capitalistic environments amplify survivors' tendencies to use perfectionism and achievement as coping mechanisms. Perfectionism can stem from a deep desire to exercise the control we lost as kids. As kids we might have thought that if we were perfect, it would protect us from more abuse.

I was the person who most often reinforced the untrue story that I had to "rise above" my trauma to be perfect. Perfectionism was part of an abusive relationship with myself. My shame led me to find new and unique ways to blame myself for things that were not my fault. I would set unrealistic expectations for myself and engage in unrelentingly cruel self-talk when I couldn't meet them.

This made me ripe for being exploited by capitalism. By trying to be overachieving in my own family, when I entered the workforce, I was primed to take on too much, to believe that things that weren't my problems to solve were my responsibility, to try to people-please, to be fearful of saying no and having boundaries. These things made me a desirable employee and a totally miserable person.

Some people's coping mechanisms get praised by the world around us, while others get judged

Not everyone's coping mechanisms are the same. Some young survivors appeared to be disengaged students, blamed for not paying attention in class or being "on top of things" when we were instead dissociating in order to keep ourselves as safe as we could. Do not judge our child-selves for how they survived. Our brains had to find ways to get us through insane amounts of pain, and we are here now, so our brains did what they needed to do to get us to adulthood. Have you thanked your brain today for that?

Self-compassion is difficult when the world rewards some people's coping mechanisms over others'. As my friend Amita Swadhin helped me understand, capitalism smiles upon survivors who happen to cope through overachievement and may punish those who cope in other ways.

This can lead some people to judge us and label some of us as "well-adjusted" for what we've been through. I've had experiences where people thought they were complimenting me when they said they couldn't believe a CSA survivor could be so "high functioning." Those comments reveal internalized stigma that survivors are supposed to be human disasters. In reality, we shouldn't be celebrated for coping mechanisms that are harmful or stigmatized for coping mechanisms that helped us survive.

What are the messages you received when you were young about what success meant or was supposed to look like?

Capitalism is the scam that keeps on scamming

The entire American Dream glorifies the idea that if we just work harder, we will achieve some fabled place of contentment and freedom. We literally condition people to think that working more will make us freer or happier. What a clever and effective way for those at the top of the food chain to persuade everyone else to work endlessly to make them more money. As I've learned from writers Aminatou Sow and Ann Friedman of the late, great *Call Your Girlfriend* podcast, capitalism is the biggest scam of them all.

There are so many factors in our capitalistic society that make people extremely dependent upon their jobs, not just for social identity, but also for health care, immigration status, ability to care for their own children, and access to safe housing. Perhaps you are reading this from another country and realizing that Americans literally have to stay at their jobs in order to have health care or afford childcare and see that this is extremely dumb. You are correct! It is dumb! And super harmful! And it leads to very exploitative power dynamics!

Until our country reckons with the very nature of our social fabric, there will always be an exploitative relationship between people and their employers, work will have an extremely outsized role in our lives, and folks will blame themselves for survival struggles they didn't cause. One of the biggest parts of the scam is that it makes people believe their issues with work are personal problems, when in reality it is a structural problem.

When it comes to our jobs, are we really consenting if we don't feel safe saying no?

We cannot meaningfully offer consent in a situation where saying no risks our safety. If we didn't feel safe saying no, then our yes isn't a real yes. Working conditions in the US will always be breeding grounds for exploitation unless workers have the opportunity to say no without risking their safety.

Jaden Fields shared with me, "I think more traditional work environments were really triggering for me because to say 'no' meant poverty, so it was a kind of 'yes' but to an environment where I was expected to martyr myself because I care so much about the cause. But I was expected to produce beyond my capacity to the point where my needs were not being met. My value was in what my body could do for someone else without my consent, and we aren't really consenting to something if we don't have a choice."

In what ways does the world around you make you feel like things are a personal problem when in reality they may be a structural or institutional problem?

Strategies

STRATEGY: For the love of all that is holy,
can we stop describing workplaces as families?

Raise a critical eyebrow when people in positions of power refer to a workplace as "a family." I have waited tables at more than one restaurant that described themselves as a family (not a family-run restaurant, though, to be clear). The family language was supposed to communicate that people were close and cared about one another more than in a regular work environment.

As Aminatou Sow and Ann Friedman discussed on their *Call Your Girlfriend* podcast, why would you want to base a workplace on family? Especially for those of us who've experienced how abusive families can be! Even in families without CSA, whose family is the model of healthy boundaries, respectful behavior, clear communication, and efficiency? No one's! Families are a terrible model for healthy work environments!

In workplaces self-described as families, work-life balance is often out of sync, people are guilted for having boundaries, and dysfunctional power dynamics run amok. Workplaces should not be families! They should be places where people come to do a series of predetermined tasks in exchange for fair and meaningful compensation.

STRATEGY: We can learn about institutional betrayal
to help us call out the bullshit when we see it

Institutional betrayal is a concept developed by the brilliant Dr. Jennifer
Freyd, a sexual violence researcher and the founder of the Center for Institutional Courage. It is a particular kind of psychological or emotional harm
that an institution, such as a college or workplace, causes someone who is
dependent upon it. When an entire organization prioritizes protecting the
status quo over protecting the injured person, it scales up from interpersonal to institutional.

An example would be a company that protects the boss instead of the
survivor when a sexual harassment complaint is filed. The survivor is hurt
not only by harassment but also by emotional and psychological hurt from
the institution they relied on.

I was hurt by the CEO of my organization, but the wound went deeper
when I reported him to his board of directors, and they chose to protect the
CEO and themselves and not hold him accountable. Interpersonal became
institutional when the reproductive rights movement leaders I trusted and
believed in knowingly allowed for this hypocrisy to stand.

What are some public examples of institutional betrayal that you can think
of; how have you seen survivors treated by their organizations in the media?

Dr. Freyd heard from survivors that institutional betrayal often hits
deeper than the initial abuse. "When someone says something was worse
than rape for them, and that their treatment from the institution was worse
than the interpersonal harm, we really need to study and understand it," she
shared. "We know this hurts people's minds and bodies because we've stud-
ied it in many ways. Even if you don't have material harm—for example,
you were not the person mistreated, but you witnessed a coworker being
mistreated—you can still feel the betrayal and be harmed."

INSTITUTIONAL BETRAYAL HELPS US UNDERSTAND WHY HARM
IN OUR FAMILIES AND OUR WORKPLACES CAN FEEL SO SIMILAR

Betrayal from institutions may remind you of your family; there's a good
reason for that. Dr. Freyd explained, "Yes, families can look a lot like institutions in terms of how they respond to violence and the harm they can

cause." Both workplaces/academic settings and families often respond to our harm with DARVO: Deny, Attack, and Reverse Victim/Offender, explained in detail in the last chapter.

An example of DARVO in an institutional setting:

- Deny that the harm happened (e.g., "You must've just misunderstood that person's behavior").
- Attack the credibility of those who are speaking out (e.g., "Oh, she's a disgruntled employee" or "She's trying to deflect because her performance has been poor").
- Reverse victim/offender (e.g., "Do you really want to ruin this person's career? Do you want to give fuel to our competitors/investors/customers to not support our business and to have our company go under?").

When I asked Dr. Freyd why so many organizations betray the people who depend on them, she said that this question was what inspired her to establish the Center for Institutional Courage to research fundamental questions around why institutions keep betraying people. Here are two of her theories:

- People are playing out dysfunctional family dynamics in the workplace.
- There is a misalignment of incentives, where people are incentivized at work for short-term benefits, such as covering up wrongdoing in order to protect their own reputation, that lead to betrayal.

Regardless of the reason, one thing is certain: it's not your fault. If an institution fails you, that's their fault. It's not your fault for asking for help or justice.

Are there ways that you've experienced or observed institutional betrayal, whether it was within your family, religious organization, school, or workplace? How does it feel to know that there is a well-researched term for this experience?

STRATEGY: We need to practice identifying
exactly where the responsibility lies

Too often, survivors are pressured to speak out against people who've harmed us. Others may even imply that we are somehow complicit in our mistreatment if we don't. While we have the right to speak out against harm we experience at work, it is not the responsibility of survivors to do so.

Survivors often have the most to risk when speaking out. People love to perpetuate the lie that ending abuse is the job of survivors, a lie that shifts the responsibility and blame to the people with the least amount of power in a situation. Rather, responsibility must be allocated to the people who have power and can actually do something to change the situation.

WE CAN USE OUR BULLSHIT GOGGLES TO PUSH BACK
AGAINST ANY MISPLACED SENSE OF RESPONSIBILITY

We, as survivors, are incredible bullshit detectors. We can smell it from miles away. We've navigated so many dysfunctional power structures, and we can see through power-based deception, gaslighting, and manipulation. I'm not trying to silver-line our trauma, but rather, acknowledge that these are real and important professional skills that we have! A great opportunity for us to use our bullshit-detecting skills is when people in power try to misplace blame and responsibility in workplaces.

For example, when I was working at a restaurant, management said it was our responsibility to get our shifts covered when we were sick. I used bullshit goggles to see management dodge responsibility that was actually theirs. By making us find coverage, they made us feel guilty for taking (unpaid!) time off. This encouraged us to come to work when sick, endangering customers. It is the manager's job to make sure the restaurant is staffed. It is not the job of a low-level employee.

My bullshit googles helped me resist their guilt trip.

In your workplace, do you see people in positions of power wrongly trying to assign responsibility to people in positions of lesser power? Remember, this behavior is a scam!

THE DECISION OF WHETHER TO TAKE ACTION IS
ONE THAT IS DEEPLY PERSONAL FOR EACH OF US

I'm not urging you toward one path or another if your workplace is abusive. I chose to speak out at the nonprofit because I calculated the risks, and due to my privilege, taking action was a low-risk endeavor for me. I wasn't worried about burning professional bridges because I knew I was switching fields. Colleagues of mine who also had been mistreated did not want to speak up because they either needed the job or needed to maintain good relationships and references to find another job. Their decision was not invalid, but rather, just different from mine. Speaking out was in alignment with my own healing needs.

Dr. Freyd says, "I know I've had so much personal healing coming through my activism, but I also know that a lone individual who is not in a position of power going up against a powerful institution is likely to get demolished." If you are considering taking action, Dr. Freyd recommends solidarity among several people to push powerful change. "Sometimes it takes one person to get the ball rolling to find other people to build a coalition of people who want their environment to be better to work in solidarity together to confront power."

STRATEGY: We can deepen our understanding
of inherent ableism in our workplaces

Identify the ableism in your academic and work settings. "Ableism prioritizes labor and the idea that we have to be doing something and producing something and moving things or we are worthless," explains Jaden.

Ableism is foundational to workplaces. Workplaces are designed for people without mental health struggles or disability, and for people who do not ever get sick or even contract the common cold! Many US workplaces do not offer paid sick leave and have no way to support people when they step away due to health needs. Employees are made to feel simultaneously irreplaceable (if we don't do this task when we are sick, then no one will, and everything will be our fault!) and completely disposable (we could lose our jobs at any point, and advocating for our basic needs can lead to our being replaced—just look at how companies treat employees who try to unionize).

Do you see the ways that ableism impacts your studies or work? Can you see that if your workplace doesn't accommodate you, it is not you that is the problem? Learn about your country's rights for workers with disabilities, and see if exercising some of those rights may be supportive. In the US, there's the Americans with Disabilities Act (ADA), a federal law that protects people with disabilities and covers post-traumatic stress disorder as well as clinical depression.

Reader, you can insert your own corny joke here about how reading the work chapter was a lot of work

Phew! You made it this far and you're doing great. And you look amazing. Like, really great. Trauma is such a cute look on all of us—gives us that extra-dewy glow, ya know?

My wish for all of us is to continue divorcing our sense of self-worth from our jobs. This is very tough because we live in a world that tells us our job is who we are. I live in Washington, DC, where people ask me, "What do you do?" before asking me how I am. We are going against a lot of forces in society when we decouple our sense of value from our jobs, which is why it feels so difficult to do! But you are not what you produce.

As Jaden Fields said to me, "Maybe you don't want to create. Maybe you just want to be cute. Maybe you just want spaciousness to adjust and have your needs met and still be cute." Explore where your self-worth lies and where we can place it so that we feel most fulfilled. And most cute.

Being retraumatized is never something we should blame ourselves for. You are doing your absolute best to care for yourself through this tricky and triggering world.

So let's get ourselves some food and a lovely beverage, and maybe go feel the earth under our feet. When you're ready for more, I'll be here.

9

We Are the Experts in Our Safety

UNTRUE STORY
We are complicit if we do not report our abuse

BUT TRUTHFULLY
We are never to blame for our abuse, and we need to make decisions around justice and accountability based on what's best for ourselves

Welcome back, friends. Hope you've hydrated and got a good snack by your side, and bonus points if you are in a cozy position. This chapter is going to dive into ideas of forgiveness, accountability, and justice. I'm sure you can see the frozen piña coladas and hear the groove of party music getting louder because these topics are nothing if not a merry good time.

When it comes to healing, there is no one right way to do it. We will discuss reporting, not reporting, forgiving, not forgiving, and everything in between. I have no idea what is best for you in your situation: I trust that you are the expert in your own safety and healing, and I am not here to judge your steps. Listen to your own inner expert.

There is so much pressure on survivors to take certain actions as regards reporting and healing. We should do what's best for us, not what people think we *should* do.

See? It's a party.

It is an untrue story that we are complicit in our harm if we do not report our abuse. This untrue story is total bullshit. You are never responsible in any way for abuse you've endured, ever. There are a lot of people who are complicit in our abuse, and we will get into that in a beat! But just real quick, I need you to know that this untrue story is Victim Blaming 101, and it sucks.

I'm in this with you, and I have felt a lot of pressure to take steps with accountability that weren't actually right for me

Over the past seven years since I became public about my CSA, one of the most common questions from people, including many fellow survivors, is "What happened when you confronted your father about your abuse?" The first couple of times I got asked that, I brushed it off, but when it kept happening over and over again, I had to stop and take a pause.

I always wanted to respond with the question, "What makes you think I ever did that?" Instead, I gently explain that I never had that conversation with my abuser, and doing so would have been in conflict with my healing and safety needs.

Why was everyone making this assumption? All of us, including survivors, live in a world that has conditioned us to believe that sexual violence survivors have only two options:

- ► Option A: We stay silent and suffer in isolation.
- ► Option B: We shout what happened to us from the rooftops and we do *the most*. I'd define *the most* as confronting the person who harmed us, telling everyone we know, and reporting to some authority system, like the police.

I also like to call Option B the Lifetime Movie-of-the-Week Option. In this scenario, we are screaming (in the rain, always) at the person who abused us, "*I know what you did to me!*" Our abuser looks shocked and guilty. From there, either we go to the police and our abuser goes to prison and justice *is served*, or our abuser begs us for forgiveness while the *Grey's Anatomy* season two soundtrack plays in the background. Or, we reluctantly decide that forgiveness is best for the soul, and we are all better and healed.

By now, we've talked a lot about all-or-nothing thinking and identifying false binaries, common thought patterns for those of us who've experienced abuse. Here's another false binary on our hands to deconstruct! The reality is, the space between these two polar options is nearly infinite. But when finding the middle path, we contend with other people's ideas about what we are "supposed" to do. For a while, I felt like I was letting people down and failing their idea of what an unashamed survivor does. It made me wonder if I wasn't as courageous as I thought I was.

During really bad moments, I feared people might be implying that I hadn't done enough to stop him. People spoke to me as though I were Luke Skywalker (to be clear, I'm Admiral Akbar, or, as I like to call him, General FishHead, whose one line is iconically shouting, *"It's a trap!"* Hell yes, hypervigilant Queen!), and if I didn't stand up to my abusive father, then I'd have done nothing to stop the evil Darth Vader before he struck again!

It's so fucking easy for people who aren't us to look at our lives in fictional terms of heroes and villains and imply that we haven't done enough to stop bad guys from doing more bad-guy shit. It's so fucking hard to not internalize that misplaced sense of responsibility. But it is not the survivors' responsibility to end the violence that other people cause.

I, of course, have imagined how this confrontation would go

So much about my life has changed since I first cut my father out of my life. I've stood on stages across the country and told my story. People from all over the world have read my words. But my thoughts about how the hypothetical confrontation would go remain pretty unchanged. When I imagine it, all I can see is me being triggered and emotionally reverting to a harmed child.

I have decades of experience with my abuser letting me know how harmfully he would react to confrontation. There is no indication that he has engaged in any healing work and has rather indicated that he is unready and unable to hold himself accountable for harm. I've never doubted what was best for me. It's only been a question of whether I can accept the misalignment between my needs and others' expectations. Sometimes that's hard. Still, I have let go of the idea that enduring a confrontation is necessary to prove how healed I am.

Maybe having a conversation with the person who abused you is right for you. I know survivors who have asked the people who harmed them for accountability; I know others who don't even know the identity of who abused them. The decision is personal. Only we know our specific safety concerns, needs, and hopes. My hope is that we can remove other people's projections, pressures, and comparisons off our lists of considerations.

When have you felt pressure or expectations around speaking out about your abuse? Have you ever felt that you were somehow complicit in your harm or not a real victim if you didn't report it? What feelings come up for you when you consider what justice would mean to you? It's okay if those emotions are murky or conflicting!

These are all big, hard questions. You do not need to know the answers; I just hope you can peel back the layers of self-blame and misplaced responsibility.

What are the origins of the bullshit?

People's completely unrealistic and harmful expectations for us

What causes this pressure and guilt around reporting? I see two diametrically opposing reactions that people give survivors:

- ▶ The "Do more!" people: These are the people who judge us for not speaking up more or, in their minds, not taking enough action (reminder, just continuing to survive and exist is more than enough action!).
- ▶ The "Do less!" people: These are people who pressure us to stay silent because of real and perceived risks to our families and communities.

Let's talk about the "Do more!" folks and laugh at their absurdity, even though it isn't funny

The "Do more!" people in my life asked me variations of the question, "Why didn't you say anything when it was happening?"

Can we all just laugh for a second over the chutzpah of a person asking a survivor why their abused child-selves didn't take a certain action while they were being abused? It places the burden on the child to have protected themselves, as if we were to blame for what we suffered because we didn't speak up.

Perhaps the funniest part of being asked, "Why didn't you say something sooner?" is that the answer is, "Because of terrible questions like that one." Irony.

The idea that I could've said something earlier about my abuse is hilariously outlandish to me. Like some of you, I didn't understand that I was sexually abused until I was an adult and had memories resurface. I couldn't tell them what was happening because I didn't know or understand what was happening.

But in my own way, I had reported. A lot of us, in our own ways that kept us as safe as possible, communicated that something wrong was happening.

I may not have had the words to say, "Hello, responsible adult! Child here, and I'd like to report to you that I am the lead choreographer for my friends' dances to Spice Girls songs, I intend to marry Zach Morris in the future, and also my father is abusing me. In the enclosed binder you will see all of my documented evidence. Thank you for your consideration, and please take action accordingly."

But I'd have emotional meltdowns and make enormous efforts to prevent myself from being near my father. Child-me was actually communicating a lot. But at some point, young Future Mrs. Zach Morris was getting implicit and explicit information that my attempts at disclosure would be received with denial and minimization. Were there times that you received information that a disclosure would not or did not result in safe and loving support for you?

If you don't have a memory of communicating that something was wrong, like I do, that's okay! To me, that just means that younger-you assessed the situation and determined it wasn't safe to indicate that anything wrong was happening. We don't judge what our younger selves had to do to try to keep ourselves as safe as possible through these nightmares!

If you've ever found yourself judging your own past decisions around speaking out, what would it take for you to feel ready to release that self-judgment, while knowing that it isn't your fault that you feel that way?

Okay, now it's only fair that we talk about the "Do less!" people

Conversations about what happens after violence do not adequately acknowledge the literally impossible situation that so many survivors navigate. We are navigating not only our own safety and well-being but also that of our families and communities. We may have so much pressure to stay silent from people speaking from a place of fear.

"We do not take into consideration the collateral damage of a survivor coming forward, depending on age, circumstances, and conditions, and it can be excruciating for survivors for a variety of reasons," Tashmica Torok, the founder of the Firecracker Foundation, an organization in Lansing, Michigan, that supports kids and teens who've experienced CSA, shared with me. Tashmica said that some of the physical safety concerns for survivors include "losing their home; their families being pulled apart by Child Protective Services; if they or their family members are undocumented, it could risk their immigration status; they may experience financial abuse if the family is monetarily dependent on the abuser; and they may have to navigate the risk that disclosure may out them or someone they love's sexuality or gender identity."

Survivors may be making high-risk calculations about how to protect parents, siblings, and perhaps also the people who've abused them. "Many children do not want to see someone go to jail or have something violent happen to their abuser," Tashmica shared.

Survivors may also have to contend with people who are wrongly prioritizing their own comfort and desires over the safety and well-being of the survivor. Families may discourage a survivor from coming forward for a whole host of reasons, including that:

- ▸ they do not want to emotionally face the truth of loving someone who was abusive,
- ▸ they are overwhelmed by the stigma of CSA and fear judgment from others, or
- ▸ they want to protect the reputation of their family or community over the safety of the survivor.

Jaden Fields, the codirector of Mirror Memoirs, experienced this pressure himself as a child disclosing to his mother: "When I tried to tell my mom what was happening to me, she didn't believe me. I grew up in an environment where her belief was children were seen and not heard, so it didn't matter what I said."

Have you had to take into consideration not just your safety, but also the safety of people you love, when thinking about speaking out and what comes next? Those responsibilities and pressures should never have been placed on your shoulders.

The media are still getting their coverage of survivors wrong

In 2017, we all experienced the resurgence of the #MeToo Movement, founded by Tarana Burke. For over a year, the internet was flooded with survivors speaking up about violence.

I am in admiration of Tarana's work and am grateful for her leadership. She has worked so hard to try to recenter the pop culture dialogue around #MeToo on survivors' actual needs and healing. While Tarana's vision for the work had always been a commitment to young Black survivors, the most high-profile of these stories centered white women being harmed by famous and powerful men.

Since that time, I've noticed a shift in the messages I receive from survivors. Survivors now deal with an undercurrent of pressure to speak publicly. The pressure seems related to the way the media exalted public survivors, myself included, by framing us as heroic and courageous martyrs, wrongly devaluing those who stayed private.

Being a CSA survivor and just continuing to live your life in this world is courageous. If you determine it is best for your healing to not come forward in some public way, then that is just as courageous as deciding you want to shout your truth from the rooftops.

I do not speak out publicly "for the greater good." I am not a fucking martyr. Remember, martyrdom isn't a cute look on any of us. I decided to become public about my abuse, including using my full name all over the internet, because it made me feel safer than being private.

So many people, over the years, had tried to get me to stay silent and not "make a mess" about things. It was suffocating. I felt that if my full name and truth were all over the internet, no one could ever try to manipulate me into silence again.

No one else could've made that decision for me, and only I could know what I needed at that time. And who knows? Maybe in a few years I'll feel totally different and not want to talk about any of this shit anymore—try to scrub myself from the internet or get a cool pseudonym like Meryl Street, Ina Garten, or Sarah Jessica Hawker. I'm allowed to change my mind, just like you are too. Nothing is more important than you doing what your inner healing expert tells you is best for you.

Have you noticed the ways mainstream media portray public survivors influencing your ideas? Perhaps these impacts are positive and have offered us validation and affirmation, or perhaps they bring complicated or hard feelings about what we think a survivor is supposed to do. Make space for all the feelings and layers.

Coming back to our old friend the Dick Wolf effect, because our lives are not a TV show

The Dick Wolf effect is the term I coined to talk about the cultural impact that shows like *Law & Order* have on the way we think about victimhood, reporting, and accountability. Jaden shared, "I blame things like *Law & Order SVU* for giving people a false idea of what a survivor process is like, and it is so false because what it depicts doesn't even have anything to do with what healing might be for a survivor." The shows act like you just have to get the abuser arrested and the survivor out of the house. "But these systems aren't actually able to respond to the need for healing, and these fictional depictions completely ignore what kids may think their needs are in that moment."

For people encouraging us to report, they may have watched way too many hours of *SVU* and think that if we go to the police, Mariska Hargitay will be awaiting us at the station with a coffee in hand, wearing the hell out of a power suit, and she will instantly validate our abuse and fight the good fight to get the bad guys behind bars.

But no matter how many times I hear those *dun-duns* in the background, *Law & Order* is not real life. As Tashmica said, "People love to cling to the idea that if abuse happens, then the logical next thing happens, like the person who caused harm goes to prison or stops causing harm." But that is simply not how the system works for most survivors.

When choosing to report, survivors have to undergo steps that are often retraumatizing for them. Survivors have to heal not only from the abuse, but also from the harm caused them by the criminal legal system. Of sexual violence survivors who do involve the criminal legal system, more than half report that the experience with the criminal legal system was "harmful, unsatisfactory, unfair, and in some cases, more harmful than the assault itself.[1,2,3] Survivors may risk further sexual violence, as police sexual misconduct is the second-most commonly reported form of misconduct, after misuse of force.[4]

I am not encouraging or discouraging anyone from engaging in the criminal legal system—I do not know what is best for you. It's just important to understand that the people encouraging or insisting that we engage in the criminal legal system often have deeply unrealistic ideas about the experience.

Mandatory reporting is a mess, and we have to talk about it

In all 50 states of the US, laws require certain people who work with children, like child therapists, teachers, some health care providers, and coaches, to report any disclosure of child abuse to the state. Children may think they are confiding in a safe adult, only to learn that the adult is legally required to report to the state. That reporting may result in nothing, or it may involve agents of the state removing the child from the home, arresting family members, and taking other life-changing actions.

Mandatory reporting laws perpetuate the idea that others, especially the state, know what is best for a child who has experienced sexual abuse. In accordance with Michigan law, some members of the Firecracker Foundation staff are mandated reporters. Tashmica Torok has seen first-hand the harm these policies can cause: "The thing that frustrates me the most about mandatory reporting is it is yet another place where the state is saying that they know what is best for a child's safety and well-being and that there is a one-size-fits-all solution to violence." Mandatory reporting laws specifically erase any autonomy a child may have and do not take into account what survivors may need for their own safety and healing, like wanting an abusive parent to move out but not go to jail, or wanting an apology from their abuser, or needing access to healing resources.

My friend Amita Swadhin, founder of Mirror Memoirs, is the child of two immigrants from India and had to contend with mandatory reporting in their childhood. Amita recalled, "I was 13 when I disclosed, for the second time, to my mom about my dad raping me. This was nine years after my first disclosure, one year after the sexual violence had ended, and this time she was finally ready to take action. Her first instinct was to send me to a therapist to get help, but my mom didn't know about mandatory reporting. The therapist was a licensed agent of the state, and so she was mandated to call the New Jersey Division of Youth and Family Services."

In Michigan, the law states mandatory reporters have to report abuse immediately. People may have only a few hours to help prepare the survivor and loved ones for what comes next. During those brief precious hours, Tashmica and the other advocates of her organization work vigorously to safety-plan with the survivor and their family: "We spend that time trying to be strategic about resolving what we can before we have to make that call, like an immigration situation we need to navigate, how this may impact the survivor and their family's housing, what the medical implications may be. All our work is centered around how we can minimize the harm to the survivor and their loved ones that comes from the state's involvement," Tashmica explained.

These brief windows of time do not allow for the survivor to process what they've gone through, determine what they want, and prepare for what comes next. This is reflected in Amita's personal experience. Amita recalled, "Before I had an opportunity to have proper support from my own community, I had white cisgender strangers in my living room who had state authority to take me and my sister away and to incarcerate me and my mother if they deemed it the 'right thing to do.' And they had the power to make that decision after only meeting us once or twice."

Once the state was involved in their home, Amita said, they had to make impossible calculations as a 13-year-old about their safety and the safety of their family: "I had to navigate how to get help and not experience more harm, particularly for my mother, who had been such a victim of my father's abuse. My mom also needed help and support, but instead the state said they were considering prosecuting her for being complicit in my abuse."

Like all other aspects of our criminal legal system, mandatory reporting disproportionately harms families of color. Tashmica explained, "CPS (Child Protective Services) targets Black and brown parents, and we know that there is a foster care to adoption pipeline that harms families of color." To see an example of this on a massive scale, we can look at the history of the US and Canadian governments forcibly removing Native children from their homes and communities to be adopted by white families and/or sent to residential schools where the children endured sexual and physical abuse and the cultural genocide of Native people. Interventions like these, including sending children to foster homes or group homes, are done in the name of "violence prevention," yet they can result in children actually being further exposed to abuse. In contrast, there is a long history of white families successfully evading or minimizing the harm of state intervention.

Amita said the system forced silence: "In a moment when I was ready to be honest, I was denied the safety to speak my truth. Being honest could've resulted in me and my sister having to go to a white foster family and risking further abuse, as there is a long history of white foster parents adopting children of color and sexually abusing them." Mandatory reporting was in direct conflict with Amita's desires for healing and stability.

If you've experienced painful challenges with mandatory reporting, please know you are not alone in your pain. When I asked Amita what they would say to their younger self, they said, "I think about the fact that my younger self didn't have the support to be protected and cared for. I feel even worse knowing what I know now, which is that my experience was not unique, even though it should be exceptional. The hardest part is that what I went through is actually a really common way to grow up."

Strategies

STRATEGY: We can practice asking,
"Who is responsible here?"

We may choose to engage in some form of an accountability process with our abuser, but it is never our responsibility to do so. To push back on those pressures we may feel, we can practice asking the question, "Well, who actually is responsible for addressing and preventing this abuse?"

The first people we have to consider responsible are the people who've abused us. They are responsible. Typing this out seems so simple, but the simplicity is the point. It's so easy to say, but so difficult for us to feel and fully internalize that truly. What feelings come up for you when you consider that responsibility lies with the person who abused you?

Adults in our lives who had a level of power similar to or greater than that of the people abusing us also hold responsibility. These adults might have failed to protect us or advocate for our safety and healing in the aftermath. What does it feel like to look at your own story and consider these adults? It may bring up a whole host of challenging feelings to think about the people who loved us but who failed to protect or support us.

I am not encouraging a blame game. There are a lot of complicated reasons why the people we love may have failed us in this way. I have no intention of vilifying them or telling you how you should feel about any of them. It is just helpful to take a step back and remind ourselves that we were children. It is not a child's job to keep themselves safe, nor is it a child's job to address abuse and violence. So many of us have been treated like adults since we were very young, so it can be easy for us to forget that.

LET'S USE OUR IMAGINATION!

Leaders of the movement for abolition, like Mariame Kaba and adrienne maree brown, teach us to use imagination in the fight for liberation. We can't fight for a future we can't see. I invite you to tap into your imagination.

Think about one thing that you would've wished the adults in your life had listened to you about. That thing could be as big or small as feels right to you.

Now imagine an alternative reality where the adults around you protected you in a way that prioritized your safety and well-being, whatever that may have entailed.

Get really creative! It could be that you are on a different planet or plane than this one, or life conditions were just different. In this alternate reality, maybe your parents had plenty of money or a different immigration status, or kids could make decisions without adults being allowed to shame them. Let your imagination be free of reality's restrictions.

Sometimes this imaginative prompt makes me very sad and angry for the younger, unprotected version of me. Often, it helps me to understand that CSA is a problem so much bigger than the victim and abuser. It is a community problem, and there should've been so many adults in my community fighting to keep me safe and support me in healing. None of that responsibility should have been laid upon my shoulders. As Tashmica said, "Until we reckon that CSA happens within the community and accountability has to happen within the community, then we aren't going to be in a place where we can address it honestly."

How does it feel for you to imagine another way it all could have gone, or another world where all children's safety is all adults' primary priority?

STRATEGY: We can create space
for all our hard feelings

Transformative justice leaders teach us to be honest about the strong, sometimes conflicting, emotions that abuse causes. For those of you unfamiliar with transformative justice (TJ), it is a political framework and approach to responding to violence created by and for communities of color and other communities that are targeted and oppressed by the state. Mia Mingus, a CSA survivor and leader within the transformative justice movement, explains on TransformHarm.org that TJ responses to and intervention in violence neither rely on the state nor reinforce or perpetuate violence, but rather, they "actively cultivate the things we know prevent violence such as healing, accountability, resilience, and safety for all involved."[5]

I used to think that since I didn't want my father harmed in prison, it meant that I didn't really hold him responsible for what he did. But TJ practitioners have taught me that we can both recognize the humanity in the people who abused us and also still hold them responsible for the harm they caused us.

Aishah Shahidah Simmons explains, "You can have compassion if you understand the conditions that led them to cause the harm or for people who stood by and allowed it to happen, but you don't have to allow them into your lives, or you can decide how you want to engage with them again if at all. It's just about holding space for their humanity while protecting yourself simultaneously."

Tashmica shared about her feelings, "My father sexually abused me since I was very small and died when I was eight; I was a very young child when those acts occurred and I *still* have good memories of my dad. Something happened and I thought, 'Oh, my dad would love this.' There is space for anger and rage and hatred, and all of these feelings that come with someone violating you, and that are valid and real and very necessary to feel and move through, along with mourning and grief."

I am not saying you have to love the person who harmed you, sweet dear God no, but I do want to show you that it's okay to feel however you feel about them, and it's okay if those emotions also are in flux and change over your healing journey. The biggest help for me has been my survivor friends being open with me about their feelings, and my goal is to offer you that experience too.

I LOVE TALKING ABOUT BEAUTIFUL, POWERFUL, RIGHTEOUS RAGE

Now we will talk about one of my favorite of all the emotions: anger. Of course we can't discuss anger without contextualizing race and gender; harmful stereotypes literally make the world less safe for some people to express anger. Jaden Fields shared, "As a female-assigned Black person, I'm not supposed to be angry for a lot of reasons. Anger is not what girls are supposed to do, and as a Black man, Black men's anger can get us killed."

I hadn't felt safe enough to really feel my anger until I was 27. I remember when I started feeling rage at the time that I was going through some accountability conversations with members of my family. It was like a faucet had been turned open, and suddenly anger poured out of every fiber of my being. It scared me because I didn't know how to make sense of an emotion that felt so unfamiliar.

I decided to learn how to box, and boxing helped me fall in love with my anger. These feelings no longer felt dangerous to me, because I had a safe space to express them. Each day, as I wrapped my hands in preparation for my workout, I would invite my rage in, welcoming it back to me.

Anger was a stage of my healing: not a liability, a much-needed source of power. "I really believe what Audre Lorde said in the uses of anger: 'Anger is like a mirror.' I feel like it really gets to the core of the needs sometimes," shared Jaden.

To this day, when I am working with a survivor and they tell me that they are dealing with unprecedented levels of rage, I get excited for them. Yes, I know being furious can feel so awful, but hear me out:

To be enraged is to know, deep down, that what happened to us was wrong and that we shouldn't feel shame or blame for our pain. Our anger is evidence that we are releasing the lie that our abuse is our fault. Rage puts responsibility for abuse where it belongs.

This kind of anger is often accompanied by deep grief. We grieve what our younger selves had to endure, we grieve the childhoods we should have had, and we grieve the ways the people we loved didn't protect us. This grief is so painful, even physically. I am not trying to sugarcoat it or diminish how awful it feels. The grief comes when we really know, deep down, that what happened to us never should have happened, and we are not to blame.

REVENGE FANTASIES CAN BE A POWERFUL TOOL FOR US

Jaden says, "Revenge fantasies allow us space to flourish and for the rage to expand, which is important, but for many survivors there isn't enough value and space for them to name and explore their rage."

While revenge fantasies may, on the surface, appear to be in conflict with wanting humane ways of addressing harm, I've learned that's not the case. Elisabeth Long, a community organizer rooted in anti-carceral feminism, wrote an essay in the anthology *Beyond Survival* called "Vent Diagrams as Healing Practice."[6] In it she writes, "Honoring survivor contradictions makes transformative justice possible. Revenge fantasies and transformative justice are not mutually exclusive."

In her essay, Elisabeth draws a Venn diagram with one side saying, "I want the person who raped me to have the community love and support needed to heal, transform, and have the liberated relationships we all deserve." On the other circle of the diagram it reads, "I wish my rapist were dead." I found her visual depiction so helpful, and it encapsulated my own torn feelings.

Elisabeth shared in her essay that she found it liberatory to express her revenge fantasies. It felt so refreshing to see revenge fantasies as an active part of my healing, as opposed to some dark thoughts that I should feel shame over. Jaden Fields is a firm believer in the power of revenge fantasies as a tool for healing: "It can help to visualize and rewrite the narrative of the violence we experienced and to reimagine these experiences with access to power and control in those moments."

In her essay, Elisabeth offers up some tips for any of us interested in exploring our own revenge fantasies. Her recommendations include writing out the revenge fantasy as many times and ways as we want, punching/stabbing a pillow, vocalizing our fantasies to trusted people with their consent, some sort of combative exercise, and my personal favorite: listening to "Goodbye Earl" 20 times a day.

It may be uncomfortable for you to consider tapping into your anger in such a direct way. There were times in my life when I was too afraid to tap into my rage because I feared it was uncontrollable and I would harm other people. But I've learned that I don't have to be afraid or ashamed of my feelings. The more honest and direct I can be about it, the less threatened I feel by my own rage.

STRATEGY: We get to create our own rules around forgiveness

I get very angry when I hear people say that we have to forgive in order to heal. Please raise your hand if you've been personally victimized by this bullshit glorification of forgiveness.

Forgiveness has to be deeply personal to each of us. The way we feel about the idea of forgiveness may be so different from one survivor to another, but also it may be different within ourselves from one day to the next.

I've had relative strangers, who are not survivors, ask me if I ever forgave my father. This question is truly wild to me. At no point did those people ask me if my father ever apologized, ever admitted what he did.

RELIGION CAN PUSH FORGIVENESS STUFF ONTO ALL OF US

I trace these kinds of questions back to religious traditions that emphasize forgiveness over accountability.

In the United States, we live in a Christian hegemony, where Christian beliefs dominate all aspects of our society, and I especially observe this within the conversations around forgiveness. All over movies, in popular culture, and in the news I see how someone's capacity to forgive is viewed as a morally valuable and necessary thing for a good and merciful person.

This larger social pressure to forgive is in conflict with my Jewish upbringing. As Rabbi David J. Blumenthal explains in his article "Is Forgiveness Necessary?," in Judaism, we are taught that those of us who are harmed are not expected to even consider forgiving someone unless they have stopped all abusive behavior, reformed their character, and actually asked us for forgiveness several times.[7] Even when all those conditions are met, we are never required to offer our forgiveness.

It is funny for me to think about how literally not a single one of the stipulated conditions have been met for me to seriously consider forgiveness, yet so many people expect me to depart from my own faith's forgiveness traditions.

Christianity certainly isn't the only religion that presses the concept of forgiveness upon people. Aishah Shahidah Simmons shared, "I was raised Sufi Muslim, my grandparents were Christians, and I am a practicing Buddhist. In all these religious traditions, I've seen forgiveness weaponized. At various points in my life, people have asked me, 'What would Buddha do? What would Jesus say?' in imploring me to forgive. But it is a way to deny rage, trauma, and harm, and to obfuscate accountability. It is dangerous.

If forgiveness happens, it has to come from within. That's it. If it doesn't come from within, and it is forced upon or coerced onto someone, that is a form of violence, frankly."

Writing today, I do not have an interest in the concept of forgiveness. But you may, and that is 100 percent valid! Forgiveness doesn't feel applicable right now because I am still busy trying to remind myself that my abuse wasn't my own fault. Right now, I need to practice holding my father responsible for the harm he caused. I am open to being curious about forgiveness in the future.

Aishah also believes forgiveness is so personal to each survivor: "If they don't want to forgive the harm-doer or the bystanders, then they don't have to, and that should never be a required part of anyone's healing process. It is something that is almost always asked of survivors, often by those who caused the harm through their actions or by bystander inaction."

It's important to acknowledge that it is okay if some things are never forgivable to us. It isn't a limit of our compassion or our hearts; it can just be an accurate reflection of life if we determine that some things, including our CSA, are simply not forgivable.

THERE ARE PARTS OF MYSELF I'D LIKE TO FORGIVE

I do think there is a role for forgiveness to play in my healing, and it has to do with cultivating more self-compassion.

I am still exploring the ways I've judged myself for how I've survived and coped with immense pain. I want to have more compassion for younger-me and offer her forgiveness for doing her best when her best was super messy. I want to work on forgiving myself for the hurt I've caused people who have forgiven me.

Are there ways that the practice of forgiveness can contribute to your healing? If not, let's honor that too.

Let's honor and validate whatever feelings we may have in this moment, and then how about we go lie down for a bit?

Justice and accountability are super complicated and mean different things to each of us. For some, justice and healing can be conflicting aspirations. I say that not to encourage or discourage any choices you make, but because I want each of us to be so gentle and loving and understanding toward ourselves when dealing with this really heavy shit.

The judgment of others on how we choose to explore, or not explore, ideas of accountability, justice, and forgiveness has no place in our hearts. While it's so hard not to internalize those judgments, I hope we've inched closer to intellectually accepting that the only person whose opinion matters in all of this is you. Everyone else's judgment can, kindly, get fucked.

It is the most natural thing in the world for any of us to wish to have, at a minimum, an acknowledgment or admission of harm from the people who abused us. Wishing for this is such an exceedingly reasonable thing. It isn't even the bare minimum of what we deserve; it's below that bar. Yet, that shit is totally out of our hands.

I will never tell you to stop wanting that. However, we cannot allow for that person's admission, or lack thereof, to dictate the validity of our harm. It is our own reality that matters. We cannot allow for someone else, especially the people who abused us, to determine our reality.

How about we go give our bodies some much-needed rest and practice centering ourselves? I want us to feel nourished going into our final chapter because it is my absolute favorite and, in my opinion, a goddamn delight. So, let's do what we need to do to care for ourselves and finish this baby feeling strong and well-cared-for!

10

We Always Deserve Healing

UNTRUE STORY
Healing is about transforming from a survivor to a thriver

BUT TRUTHFULLY
*Healing is a messy but beautiful nonlinear journey
that requires rest, deep care, and celebration*

Hot diggity dog, my friends. We made it to the last chapter. Or, we skipped to the last chapter. Either way, we are here, and I, for one, am thrilled.

I never, ever want anyone to describe this book as a guide to help you transform from a "survivor to a thriver." Does this sound like a very niche concern? For sure.

But my experience as a public survivor sharing my story in the media quickly taught me a few things:

- ► The words *survive* and *thrive* rhyme.
- ► Almost every person I've worked with in media thinks they are the first to realize those two words rhyme.

Which causes me to scream into the void, "It isn't even that clever of a rhyme!" and then face-plant onto my desk.

It bothers me not just because it is a cliché, but because I think the whole idea behind it rings so untrue to how I understand healing. You've heard me lament over false binaries and the importance of pushing back against all-or-nothing thinking. Well, we saved my absolute favorite false binary for this chapter.

While healing, necessarily, means different things to each of us, I am confident to say that we are never all broken and fucked or all fixed and free of trauma forever. None of us has some trauma light switch where we are living in absolute opaque darkness, and if we work hard enough at our healing, we muster the strength to flip the switch on, and the darkness disappears and we are all light, all the time.

Even if we could be all light all the time, doesn't that sound exhausting? I could not handle being around that person, and they definitely would have zero sense of humor. They aren't funny because they never had to be. Hard pass.

I'm in this with you, and I, too, have wished there were a finish line for healing

To tell you how this untrue story of "survivor to thriver" has impacted me, I want to take you back to the first time I asked my therapist Susan for a gold star. I was not interested in some metaphoric pat on the back for all my hard work. I wanted a literal gold star, preferably on some sort of paper certificate, but something with a sticky adhesive back would also suffice. The overachieving student in me was showing up week after week to sit on an office couch, and I needed to have earned something.

Reader, Susan did not give me said gold star. She laughed, which was a fitting response. Her reaction didn't deter me from asking for more gold stars each week. I wanted anything I could point to that showed me that all the pain I was going through to deal with my trauma amounted to something.

The work of healing, at the time, meant having excruciating conversations with my closest family members about accountability, going to therapy regularly, boxing out my homicidal rage, figuring out the right meds for me, and refusing to ask myself to hide my truth anymore. It was exhausting.

It was hard to see the fruits of my enormous labor. Instead, all I could see were the ways I was struggling so much: daytimes full of triggers and evenings full of nightmares. I felt like I was in a tunnel, and not only could I not see the light at the end of it, but I didn't even have enough lumination to know whether I was moving forward or just walking in circles.

Here comes the forest metaphor

It was around that time that my therapist suggested maybe I wasn't actually in a tunnel, despite how it seemed to me.

Instead, she asked me if maybe I was in a forest. At this point, I was like, okay lady, we are heavy on the metaphors, and maybe I'm on the goddamn moon. Who knows? But we stuck with the forest for a beat. And she suggested that there were two paths in the woods, very Robert Frost energy.

THE FIRST PATH IN THE WOODS IS WELL-WORN
AND FAMILIAR, BUT FULL OF SELF-BLAME AND SHAME

The first path in the woods was the one I had previously been on my whole life: well-worn. A fancy professionally cared-for trail without spiderwebs, rocks, or branches blocking the way. But it wasn't the path I wanted anymore. This trail has signs posted that say my abuse is my fault, I should feel shame, and I can't believe the truth in my bones. It is a path that gaslights me.

THE SECOND, NEWER PATH IS FULL OF SELF-COMPASSION
AND VALIDATION, BUT IT'S ALSO OVERGROWN

Then there is this other path. It's brand-new. It looks overrun with branches and weeds and rocks because no one has tread it yet. It requires a machete in hand to clear the way, one smash at a time. While it is gnarly and labor-intensive, this trail has signs of validation and affirmation posted.

On this path, I no longer lie to myself and others about what I need and no longer feel responsibility and blame for harm that isn't my fault. It is a route that leads me to be accepting and self-compassionate about the way the trauma impacts me, without stigma and shame.

BE PROUD OF BUILDING YOUR NEW PATH

My therapist's forest metaphor is a realistic representation of the neuroplasticity of our brains. While familiar thoughts are easier to travel along, we can build new pathways of thought, new muscle memories for our brains.

Building the new trail was messy and intensely exhausting—just look at all those branches I had to clear out with my machete! No wonder I felt like I was in darkness! I could not see the road before me, since I was literally clearing it with each step.

It was then that I realized two things that brought me tremendous comfort:

▶ Just because it felt so hard and uncomfortable didn't mean I was doing something wrong or on the wrong path for myself.

▶ The new trail wouldn't always be hard to traverse; the more often I opted for it and spent time on it, the greater ease I would feel.

OUR CUTE PATH-IN-THE-WOODS METAPHOR IS
IN CONFLICT WITH THE LIE THAT WE TRANSFORM
FROM A SURVIVOR TO A THRIVER

Even when we walk the new path, the old path still exists. There's no going from a survivor who struggles with trauma symptoms to a thriver who shits out rainbows, has all the answers, and speaks in self-care platitudes. Trauma doesn't disappear.

When I experience triggers, my muscle memory leads me back onto the old path, feeling shame and self-blame. It isn't fair or realistic to ask myself to never visit that old path again, and I don't want to feel like a failure each time I end up on it. But it gets easier as I rewire my brain: I can now quickly recognize when I'm on the wrong trail and take steps to gently bring myself back to the one I want to be on.

After all these years, the new path has become much more comfortable! I've built some nice benches for rest, I have friends of both the furry and human variety that join me, and I never run out of good snacks. It feels less scary and more inviting than ever before. My muscle memory is adjusting.

It's not like I destroyed the past: there is no movie-worthy radical transformation of a thriving phoenix rising from the ashes. I frankly don't want any ashes on my path anyway; no forest fires, please! I just keep making small choices each day to make my new path feel more like home.

Healing means something different to each of us, and I think that's very cool

Here are some other survivors' definitions of healing, which I sought out after being inspired by Amita Swadhin's work interviewing survivors through the Mirror Memoirs audio archive project. Elizabeth shared, "In the past, I would have said that I'll know when I'm healed because I'll be able to have sex without getting triggered and upsetting my partner," but that has changed for her over the years: "Now I've been able to find things I want just for me. I want to feel like I am alone in my body. I want to be able to look at myself in the bath and feel like I'm the only person seeing me." Elizabeth put into words something I've felt but previously been unable to express: I want the only voices I hear in my head to be my own and to release the shame that others imposed.

Robby shared with me that his definition of healing has also changed a lot in recent years: "I have grown to realize that trauma is not actually a mountain we're climbing. This isn't something I eventually get over or conquer or put fully behind me. Trauma is more like rocks that are added to my life-backpack, and as I go further I get stronger, and they impact me less and less, but they are still present." I love how Robby's definition of healing allows for space and understanding that the impacts of the abuse may continue to be with us, and that doesn't mean we aren't healing.

Similarly, Mike told me that he used to think that if he worked hard enough and tried to "tackle each and every impact of the abuse," then he'd eventually "get over it." But that has changed for him over the years. Mike imagines trauma as a circle and healing as a box that sits inside that circle, touching the border of the circle. With that visual, the circle seems to have an outsized presence, but that changes as we work on our healing. "As we keep at our healing work, whatever that looks like for each of us, the box keeps getting bigger, expanding beyond the confines of the circle, with us having more space to be present in our lives and find more joy and connection, but hopefully the circle of trauma stays the same size." Healing is not an effort to shrink our trauma until we can't see it any longer, but rather an effort to expand the whole of ourselves and feel fully alive.

For some of us, we may feel like we've just begun our healing journey and do not yet have the words to talk about it, and that is totally normal too! M.R. told me, "I am not sure what healing means to me just yet, as I have just begun at age 43. It is hard to let myself feel what I have been avoiding for years. Right now, I guess that healing for me would be for me to be able to truly understand that what happened to me was abuse and that it was not my fault."

Healing means so many things. What ways has your definition of healing changed over time? We decide what healing means.

What are the origins of the bullshit?

The people around us struggle to understand the nonlinear nature of living with trauma

A lot of people wrongly assume trauma is some kind of ailment that, with treatment, dulls or disappears. So people say really shitty things like "Can we just leave the past in the past?" or imply that we may be overreacting, overly dramatic, or in love with our victimhood when we are simply just trying to live. But we can go through years of feeling okay-ish and then, seemingly out of nowhere, get smacked right in our gorgeous sexy faces with trauma symptoms.

What are some of the things people have said that contribute to your untrue stories around what healing is supposed to look like?

The funniest, most disastrous online competition ever

A few years ago, I answered a call that a writer from an internet media company put out to talk with CSA survivors who had online communities. When the writer and I spoke, she told me the media outlet was publishing what can only be described as a competition for the CSA survivor who had most overcome their trauma. Obviously, the title of the competition had "survivor to thriver" in it.

I shit you not, the writer wanted me to send in a blurb about my personal story and Healing Honestly, and then people would vote online for their favorite survivor story and the winner would win a prize. A prize for being the most popular survivor-to-thriver on the internet.

It was a hilariously horrible idea.

I wrote a strongly worded email explaining why I wouldn't participate. I outlined all the ways that content like this competition contributed to rape culture and quite literally encouraged us to judge survivors and their coping mechanisms to determine some as more sympathetic and "better" than others. It was a competition of who could best uphold the myth of the perfect victim, and it was deeply fucked.

While this is a perfectly awful/awfully perfect example to offer you, I do think it hits on a larger trend that we see of cherry-picking certain survivors and lifting them up as role models, saying that they are doing it the "right" way because they are refusing to allow their trauma to "win." Gross.

How much do we love the self-improvement montage in movies?

In movies, we often witness the perfect victim hitting "rock bottom" after a clear, linear descent, which is captured in one profound moment. After rock bottom, we get an emotional montage of "self-care" and healing, which includes her doing yoga, going to therapy, and forgiving everyone for everything ever.

This was confusing. I repeatedly "hit rock bottom," and when I climbed out of another dark hole of pain, I couldn't understand how a trigger could throw me right back down into it. I did my self-care montage many times!

Where was my happiness? All these stories made me feel like I was doing it all wrong.

One of the reasons why Michaela Coel's 2020 TV miniseries *I May Destroy You* was such a revelation was because she offered a realistic portrayal of healing as being immensely messy, involving flawed, human people. In the show, the main character is unsure of what healing would mean for her and has so many real, honest, and conflicting feelings, though I give a content warning for sexual trauma processing. If we had more realistic survivor representations like this in media, maybe people would be more compassionate.

Does this sound like a "thriver" to you?

I have to tell you something:

I woke up at noon today. I found out that instead of taking my two meds for C-PTSD the past week, I was taking a double dose of one of them. I picked a full-blown fight where I threatened divorce with my loving husband because he took the leftovers I was planning on having for lunch. The only way I can live in my beautiful apartment and have the life I do is because of inherited wealth. I slept through my most recent therapy appointment and lied and told my therapist that I thought she had gotten the time wrong.

Although I am not totally sure what it means to thrive, I feel confident that whatever it means, I am not thriving, and frankly, as I am writing this during the COVID-19 pandemic, I don't think anyone but dogs is thriving. I don't say any of this to be falsely self-effacing, as I have always suffered from high self-esteem, but rather, to be honest with you.

While I am not thriving and I haven't had a single green juice in months, I'm also not a fucking caricature of a sad, useless disastrous victim. I am doing work I believe in that I know will help other people like me. I have never been better at caring for myself, establishing and maintaining boundaries, calling bullshit on myself when I notice self-shame and self-blame, and holding myself accountable for when I fuck up. I feel all the feelings, in full Technicolor, and I've come to believe that's more than enough for me. I embrace the messiness.

In what ways are you not "thriving"? What are some of the many reasons why that is totally okay and actually more than enough?

Strategies

STRATEGY: It's important that we try to
honor the nonlinear nature of healing

Some of us may find it freeing to reject the story that we are supposed to go from victims to superhero thrivers. On the other hand, some of us may be really struggling to accept that our trauma may always play some role in our lives. I understand that deeply.

While trauma stays with us, it does not remain stagnant and unchanged. We are able to grow and evolve our relationships to our trauma so that we can live full and vibrant lives.

WHAT DO WE MEAN WHEN WE SAY "NONLINEAR"?

Often, when we talk about something in life being nonlinear, we think about it as being bad days and good days. But with trauma, it can be bad years and easier years, and any amount of time in between.

It is also common for us to be doing okay and then have a major life-changing event, like moving, someone dying, or having a child, that triggers us in a new and profound way. I want you to know that if that is happening to you, you are in such good company, and I promise you haven't done anything wrong.

Since healing is nonlinear, it means there is no timeline, even if we really want one. I can try to collect as many gold stars as possible, but I cannot rush through a checklist of healing shit to be fully cooked and done. It has to take the time it has to take. There is no way to rush ahead, but also, there is no way we've fallen behind.

I talk with survivors who are in their 60s and 70s, for whom their trauma was at bay for the majority of their lives, but now they are suddenly facing a difficult time that requires a lot of space and energy for their healing. That is normal.

DON'T WORRY, WE AREN'T ACTUALLY EVER "BACKSLIDING"

The bullshit binary of survivor/thriver can make us fear that we've reverted from thriver back to lowly survivor with each trigger. But that's simply not true.

When triggers make us feel like our healing work has disappeared, we can give ourselves this reminder: "What is happening to me is a completely normal experience of living with trauma. My new path that I've worked so hard to clear hasn't disappeared; I just am not on it for a little while because I am going through something difficult. It feels hard, not because I am doing anything wrong, but because living with this trauma is super hard! I experienced something so incredibly horrible at the most vulnerable moments of my life, and that still impacts me."

My pain may feel the same, but the way I am approaching it isn't the same, and rather, it is evolving with me. For example, I may have the same terrible nightmare about my abuser that I've been having for 10 years that leaves me feeling fully wrecked in the morning. It may feel like nothing has changed; the dream is identical to a decade ago. But the way I talk to myself when I wake up is completely different.

In the past, I would've tried to bury down my pain and fake a smile and just power through my pain, and not tell anyone. And I would've found a way to blame myself for the trigger, like beating myself up for watching a TV show that upset me. Now, when I wake up, I take extra time to be as gentle as possible with myself. I try to cancel things, expect less out of myself that day, and ask for help. I tell myself, as many times as I need, that I did nothing to cause this pain and that my trauma is not my fault.

Our new trail never disappears, even if we have to spend a lot of time on that old triggering and painful one. I promise.

What are some messages you can offer yourself when you hear those bullshit voices saying you are backsliding?

I KNOW IT SUCKS, BUT SOMETIMES MOVING FORWARD IN OUR HEALING WORK CAN ACTUALLY MAKE US FEEL WORSE BEFORE IT MAKES US FEEL BETTER

Sometimes going deeper into our healing causes our trauma symptoms to be even more present in our lives. Aishah Shahidah Simmons likens it to unlocking doors within ourselves. The more doors we unlock, the more new doors we find. New doorways can reveal new depths of harm and hurt. They can make us feel like we are reverting away from our healing, when in reality we are exploring something new and important, previously unavailable.

There have been times when my trauma symptoms were very intense, but that was because I was processing new, deeper aspects of the abuse. I was peeling back layers of the onion, and that onion was making me cry, like, all the time.

It's frustrating. Robby shared, "The most sinister part of trauma is how it needles its way into seemingly random things. Just when we think we've discovered all of the ways we've been affected, we catch a whiff of something or hear someone's voice, and the trauma viscerally rises up out of nowhere to slap us down again." Ugh, I know.

But this is why we have to be immensely patient and tender with ourselves. Elizabeth's advice for these moments felt perfect to me: "There are a lot of days we just have to hang on and get through. Just do nothing except rest to make it to another day. It may feel like in those moments we aren't improving, but it is only because on those days it's too hard to see it. We just need to hang on."

STRATEGY: What would it feel like for us
to treat healing as real work?

Treating healing as real work has helped me and so many survivors create space within ourselves for patience and self-compassion. While we aren't getting paid for it, and our capitalistic society doesn't recognize it as labor, healing is actual work. It feels hard and exhausting because it is hard and exhausting.

Yes, I've worked hard at various jobs over the years. If you, too, have ever been a server during a boozy brunch in a DC restaurant, then you know I've worked hard before. But nothing, and I mean nothing, has been as difficult as processing my CSA. Slinging mimosas for unruly drunk patrons is a walk in the park compared with learning how to soothe myself through enormous triggers, having conversations with people about boundaries, and going to bed knowing that nightmares may be waiting for me.

What would it be like for you to treat your healing work as the hardest labor you do?

Now, I know you might be thinking that it's hard to treat something as labor when we still have to do all the labor to take care of our families, keep our jobs, make money, etc., and I agree with you! While it would be super great if we could change the world to acknowledge that our healing efforts are real labor and should be treated accordingly, we, unfortunately, do not have control over that.

What is within our control is the stories we tell ourselves about our healing work. After a difficult memory or nightmare, which of these are we saying to ourselves?

> ▶ Option A: "Wow, that was super fucking hard. Now is the time to ask less of myself and clue in the people around me that maybe they need to step up while I take that time. Now is the time to be more indulgent and tender with myself."
> ▶ Option B: "I have to keep it all together, even though everything feels like it's on fire and I may burst into flames. I must not be trying hard enough, and that's why I'm so drained and don't feel like myself."

Can you tell from my extremely leading examples that I want Option A for all of us?

It's totally understandable if you hear Option B more often than Option A! We've received a lifetime of messages from everyone. It is not your fault if you can't shake them off. But now is an opportunity for us to offer ourselves messaging that is based in self-compassion and the truth.

STRATEGY: I love to embrace the humor
and absurdity in living with trauma

Of all the crazy shit I've ever written (and good grief I have written a lot of crazy shit), nothing has gotten me as much negative feedback as when I use humor to talk about survivorship. Humor isn't the right coping strategy for everyone, but it's been important for me to see the absurdity of living as a CSA survivor. Trying to heal from trauma is fucking hilarious except when it isn't. The late, great Carrie Fisher said it best: "If my life wasn't funny it would just be true, and that's unacceptable."

Making jokes helps it be less scary and more approachable to talk about CSA. Even better, laughing helps me feel like an actual human being at times when my trauma makes me feel like I am just a bag of damaged bones and hurt feelings.

Robby reflected, "Learning to embrace humor and absurdity in healing goes hand-in-hand with learning to forgive yourself over and over again. Humor is truly just letting yourself laugh at things that may be painful, even painfully true, and forgiving yourself for the ways you've had to respond to your trauma." Humor can help us tap into our own self-compassion.

Yet, I've seen humor really challenge people's idea of what healing is supposed to look like, including other survivors telling me I had to remove jokes from my writing before they'd be willing to amplify my work.

My humor gets backlash because it isn't part of the perfect-victim stereotype. I refuse to be a very serious thriving survivor who only speaks in Instagram platitudes. Speaking about my trauma in the same manner that I speak about anything else allows me to integrate it into my life and find the balance I need. For example, right now I am writing about all this trauma stuff while wearing a sweatshirt that reads, "Dumb Bitch University." Balance.

MY PEOPLE HAVE ALWAYS FOUND HUMOR IN THE SUFFERING

I come from an amazing lineage of Jewish people who have taught me that humor is an invaluable source of resiliency in the face of unimaginable suffering. My family are the funniest people I know, and laughing to cope with pain is literally in my DNA.

As a Jewish person, I know I am not alone in coming from a tradition of humor being a source of comfort and power through pain, and I have met so many Black Americans and Irish people who say the same thing about their communities. Many oppressed groups have their own style of humor to process the suffering. Aishah Shahidah Simmons shared with me, "Laughter feeds our spirits because so much is so heavy, and yet, life still goes on."

IT'S SO FUNNY TO ME WHEN PEOPLE ASSUME THAT
SURVIVOR FRIENDSHIPS ARE A STONE-COLD BUMMER

Survivors find comfort and solidarity in laughing together. Survivor humor can help us point out the scam of rape culture and how ridiculous it is that we are blamed for our own abuse. Sometimes the kindest, most honest and human response a survivor friend can offer me when I'm deep in the shit is to laugh with me at how fucked up it is that we have to go through this self-blaming nonsense.

If it feels good to you, embrace the absurdity of living with trauma. Because this shit is ridiculous. What could be more absurd than living your life one way for decades, to be hit with a ton of bricks, out of nowhere, that cause you to suddenly and involuntarily time-travel back to previously unknown moments of tremendous harm? As Aishah put it, "Laughter can help us look at the madness of it all."

But you make the rules. You decide just how funny this all is and isn't to you. Just know that, at least in my book, it's okay to laugh.

STRATEGY: Let's celebrate the good, baby!

This is my favorite strategy of all the strategies in all of this book. I saved the best for last for you beautiful people.

Healing is hard work and can take so much out of us, so it's natural for us to focus on the difficult parts. But these past couple of years I've been trying to create intentional space to reflect on all the beautiful and good things that my healing efforts have brought me.

There are big moments that feel epic and obvious to me to celebrate, like the first time I got my first email from a survivor, all the way from India, in response to launching HealingHonestly.com! That was enormous for me. But even more important than a big milestone are the everyday moments when we can see that all our healing efforts are showing up for us. How can we shine a beautiful disco ball of sparkly light onto those moments?

A few times a week, I journal for just, like, three minutes at the beginning of my workday. I write out my to-do list. Then I take a couple of moments worthy of celebration. Writing them down forces me to pay attention and honor the good stuff.

HERE'S THE KIND OF STUFF I CELEBRATE

I honor the moments when I found my self-compassion. Some examples of healing choices I celebrate:

- ► The trauma is really tough, and instead of powering through, I give myself space to feel my feelings.
- ► I am triggered and hear voices of self-blame, and instead of believing that they are fact, I write in my journal, speak to myself in the mirror, or ask a trusted person to repeat to me that what happened to me isn't my fault, that what happened to me is real, and that I am not to blame for my abuse.
- ► I have a decision to make, and I make the choice that my inner expert told me I needed to do for my well-being.
- ► I create or maintain a boundary with someone that feels really hard but necessary for my safety and well-being.
- ► I advocate for my own needs, even if it's awkward or uncomfortable.
- ► I take a risk and share with someone, and that leads to strengthening my connections to other people.
- ► I explicitly ask for help from the people around me and tell them exactly what I need or want.
- ► I feel compelled to apologize for my emotions, and then I catch myself and don't apologize for them.

What kinds of moments do you want to honor and celebrate in your healing? Is there some sort of ritual or practice that you want to experiment with incorporating into your day?

THE MOMENTS WE WANT TO CELEBRATE WILL BE SO PERSONAL TO EACH OF US

Here are some other survivors' examples of healing times. Elizabeth told me, "One day I had a moment where I was able to think about my parents and the pain they might be feeling and be separate from it. In that moment, I knew I wasn't responsible for their pain, and it wouldn't kill me or force me to do anything. It was fleeting, but I'm looking forward to more moments like that."

Mike told me that it's the moments when he feels really present, like when playing with his grandchildren or talking with a friend, that help him to see that he's healing. For Robby, it's been the moments when he feels free to talk about what he experienced on his own terms and in his own words.

When I asked Aishah how she knew she was healing, she told me that she sees it in the way she shows up in her relationship with her partner, Sheila: "It feels like one of the first times where I feel grounded enough to find my most authentic voice in a relationship with another person. I can articulate my voice, and I know Sheila will meet me there and believe me and hear me."

Our little disco ball sparkles of evidence of our healing work will be specific to each of us. What's coming to mind for you?

It's okay if celebrating the good moments in healing feels uncomfortable. It is a practice and can take time to . . . well, practice. Our trauma conditioned us to have a bias toward seeing all the things we haven't done perfectly. This bias we were given is something we can push back against and actually shift over time. Feel proud of yourself in a way that feels right for you.

CELEBRATING IS SUPER SWEET WHEN
WE GET TO INCLUDE OTHERS IN IT

It can be easier for me to process the happy stuff and lower the volume on the voices of toxic perfectionism and self-blame when someone else is happy for me. I know this can be true for other survivors too. One of my favorite welcoming questions I use when facilitating my group coaching sessions is to ask people, "What's something from your week that we can all cheer for you about?"

The first week I ask this question, people are always a little reluctant about how to answer. But without fail, after a few weeks, people's relationship to that prompt completely shifts! Everyone is so excited to share about a new boundary they enforced that week or a way they treated themselves with self-compassion while facing a trigger. It is so thrilling to see.

Sometimes the people we are sharing with are not survivors and perhaps don't understand why our accomplishments are a big deal. So I just let them know what is a big deal—for example, "This really triggering song came on in the coffee shop, and I was able to stay and breathe through it and stay in my body for the first time while hearing it. It was a big step for me. I know I need to celebrate this even though it may sound small!"

How does it feel to consider including trusted people in your moments of celebration? Would it help or would you rather stay private? Do what feels best for you.

My darling friends, we have made it to the end

Here we are, together at the end of this book. How are you feeling? Elated? Energized? Exhausted? Or perhaps a different feeling that doesn't start with the letter *E*?

However you feel, I want you to know I am here. This book will always be here for you. You may take a break from trauma-related exploration for months, or for years, and eventually come back to revisit. That is totally normal. When you find you need more, come back, pick this puppy up, and read whichever parts provide you support and affirmation.

As for me, I am done waiting around for that old shame-filled path full of untrue stories in the woods to disappear. It may always show up during the hard, vulnerable, and triggering moments of my life, as a remnant of decades of abuse. But I am ready and eager to keep tending to my new trail, where my true stories lie. Over time, the path of self-compassion gets easier to find. I trust that I know how to care for myself on my healing journey. I trust that you know how to do the same for you too.

And so, as we prepare to say goodbye for now, I want to leave you with a little wish: Stay connected with your own innate trust in yourself. My wish is that, even when it's super hard, you trust yourself to listen to your needs and be your own best advocate. It's okay for things to be messy, beautiful, painful, and fulfilling all at once. When it gets disorienting, you can come back to your truth: you deserve infinite compassion, support, and love.

You can do this. I know you can, because look at you—you already are.

Until you need me again, I'll be here cheering you on, every step of the way.

Notes

Preface

1. D. Finkelhor, G. Hotaling, I. A. Lewis, C. Smith, "Sexual Abuse in a National Survey of Adult Men and Women: Prevalence, Characteristics, and Risk Factors," *Child Abuse & Neglect* 14, issue 1 (1990): 19–28.

2. adrienne maree brown, *Pleasure Activism: The Politics of Feeling Good* (Chico, CA: AK Press, 2019).

Chapter 1

1. D. Finkelhor et al., "Sexual Abuse in a National Survey of Adult Men and Women."

2. Andrea L. Roberts et al., "Childhood Gender Nonconformity: A Risk Indicator for Childhood Abuse and Posttraumatic Stress in Youth," *Pediatrics* 129, no. 3 (2012): 410–17.

3. Emily M. Lund and Jessica E. Vaughn-Jensen, "Victimisation of Children with Disabilities," *The Lancet* 380, no. 9845 (2012): 867–69, https://doi.org/10.1016/s0140-6736(12)61071-x.

Chapter 2

1. Katie Heaney, "The Memory War," *The Cut*, January 6, 2021, https://www.thecut.com/article/false-memory-syndrome-controversy.html.

2. Judith Lewis Herman, MD, *Trauma and Recovery: The Aftermath of Violence—from Domestic Abuse to Political Terror* (New York, NY: Basic Books, 2015).

3. Herman, *Trauma and Recovery*.

4. Mike Stanton, "U-Turn on Memory Lane," *Columbia Journalism Review* 36, no. 2 (July/Aug 1997): 44.

5. Herman, *Trauma and Recovery*.

6. Katherine Beckett, "Culture and the Politics of Signification: The Case of Child Sexual Abuse," *Social Problems* 43, no. 1 (February 1996): 57–76.

7. Heaney, "The Memory War."

8. Bessel van der Kolk, MD, *The Body Keeps the Score: Brain, Mind, and Body in the Healing of Trauma* (New York, NY: Penguin Books, 2015).

9. Van der Kolk, *The Body Keeps the Score*.

10. Liz Kowalczyk, "Allegations of Employee Mistreatment Roil Renowned Brookline Trauma Center," *Boston Globe*, March 7, 2018, https://www .bostonglobe.com/metro/2018/03/07/allegations-employee-mistreatment-roil -renowned-trauma-center/sWW13agQDY9B9A1rt9eqnK/story.html.

11. Herman, *Trauma and Recovery*.

12. Van der Kolk, *The Body Keeps the Score*.

13. Van der Kolk.

14. Jennifer J. Freyd, *Betrayal Trauma: The Logic of Forgetting Childhood Abuse* (Cambridge, MA: Harvard University Press, 1996).

15. Herman, *Trauma and Recovery*.

16. Van der Kolk, *The Body Keeps the Score*.

17. Van der Kolk.

18. Jennifer Freyd, PhD, interview with the author, January 22, 2020.

19. Jody Messler Davies and Mary Gail Frawley, *Treating the Adult Survivor of Childhood Sexual Abuse: A Psychoanalytic Perspective* (New York, NY: Basic Books, 1994).

Chapter 3

1. H. R. Harris et al., "Early Life Abuse and Risk of Endometriosis," *Human Reproduction* 33, issue 9 (September 2018): 1657–68, doi:10.1093/humrep /dey248.

2. Herman, *Trauma and Recovery*.

3. Herman.

4. Stephanie Foo, *What My Bones Know: A Memoir of Healing from Complex Trauma* (New York, NY: Ballantine Books, 2022), 78.

5. L. Irish, I. Kobayashi, D. L. Delahanty, "Long-Term Physical Health Consequences of Childhood Sexual Abuse: A Meta-analytic Review," *Journal of Pediatric Psychology* 35, issue 5 (June 2010): 450–61, doi:10.1093/jpepsy/jsp118.

6. S. R. Jaffee, "Child Maltreatment and Risk for Psychopathology in Childhood and Adulthood," *Annual Review of Clinical Psychology* 13 (May 2017): 525–51, doi:10.1146/annurev-clinpsy-032816-045005.

7. Ana T. D. D'Elia et al., "Childhood Sexual Abuse and Indicators of Immune Activity: A Systematic Review," *Frontiers in Psychiatry* 9, article 354 (August 6, 2018), doi:10.3389/fpsyt.2018.00354.

8. Paulyne Lee et al., "Racial and Ethnic Disparities in the Management of Acute Pain in US Emergency Departments: Meta-Analysis and Systematic Review," *American Journal of Emergency Medicine* 37, no. 9 (2019): 1770–77, https://doi .org/10.1016/j.ajem.2019.06.014.

Chapter 4

1. Christine Miserandino, "The Spoon Theory," ButYouDontLookSick.com, April 26, 2013, https://butyoudontlooksick.com/articles/written-by-christine/the-spoon-theory/.

Chapter 5

1. National Center on Violence Against Women in the Black Community, https://ujimacommunity.org/wp-content/uploads/2018/12/Ujima-Womens-Violence-Stats-v7.4-1.pdf.
2. brown, *Pleasure Activism*.
3. brown.

Chapter 6

1. https://www.akpress.org/love-with-accountability.html
2. Prentis Hemphill @prentishemphill, Instagram, posted April 5, 2021, https://www.instagram.com/p/CNSzFO1A21C/?hl=en.
3. From *The Mindy Project*, season 1, episode 13, "Harry & Sally."

Chapter 7

1. "Child Sexual Abuse," RAINN, https://www.rainn.org/articles/child-sexual-abuse.
2. Emily Guarnotta, PsyD, "Emotional Incest: Definition, Signs, & Effects in Adulthood," *Choosing Therapy*, September 11, 2021, https://www.choosingtherapy.com/emotional-incest/.
3. Sarah J. Harsey and Jennifer J. Freyd, "Defamation and DARVO," *Journal of Trauma & Dissociation* 23, issue 5 (2022): 481–89, DOI: https://doi.org/10.1080/15299732.2022.2111510.

Chapter 9

1. R. Campbell et al., "Preventing the 'Second Rape': Rape Survivors' Experiences with Community Service Providers," *Journal of Interpersonal Violence* 16, no. 12 (December 2001): 1239–59.
2. P. A. Frazier and B. Haney, "Sexual Assault Cases in the Legal System: Police, Prosecutor, and Victim Perspectives," *Law and Human Behavior* 20, no. 6 (1996): 607–28.
3. Uli Orth, "Secondary Victimization of Crime Victims by Criminal Proceedings," *Social Justice Research* 15, issue 4 (December 2002): 313–25.
4. "The Cato Institute's National Police Misconduct Reporting Project," *2010 Annual Report*, Cato Institute, 2010.
5. Mia Mingus, "Transformative Justice: A Brief Description," TransformHarm.org, March 1, 2021, https://transformharm.org/transformative-justice-a-brief-description/.

6. Elisabeth Long, "Vent Diagrams as a Healing Practice," in *Beyond Survival: Strategies and Stories from the Transformative Justice Movement*, eds. Ejeris Dixon and Leah Lakshmi Piepzna-Samarasinha (Chico, CA: AK Press, 2020).

7. David J. Blumenthal, "Is Forgiveness Necessary?" My Jewish Learning, https://www.myjewishlearning.com/article/is-forgiveness-necessary/, accessed May 1, 2022.

Resources

Experts Included in the Book

In order of appearance:

Jaden Fields, he/him
Mirror Memoirs Project
mirrormemoirs.com

Jennifer Freyd, PhD, she/her
Center for Institutional Courage
institutionalcourage.org

Amita Swadhin, they/them
Mirror Memoirs Project
mirrormemoirs.com

Anna Holtzman, LMHC, she/her
annaholtzman.com

Ignacio Rivera, they/them
The HEAL Project
heal2end.org@heal2end

Aishah Shahidah Simmons, she/her
Author, *Love WITH Accountability: Digging Up the Roots of
Child Sex Abuse*
Filmmaker, *NO! The Rape Documentary*
@afrolez

Lourdez Velasco, they/them
Trans Women of Color Solidarity Network
tendervirgo.com

Alicia Sanchez Gill, she/her
aliciasanchezgill.com

Tashmica Torok, she/her
The Firecracker Foundation
thefirecrackerfoundation.org

For More Reading

The following are books that have helped support me in my healing. While I do not have specific content warnings for each of them, many of them contain descriptions of sexual violence. If you choose to read on, I encourage you to do so in a way that prioritizes your safety and well-being. As always, read what is right for you and skip what isn't! As always, you are the expert in your own healing.

brown, adrienne maree. *Pleasure Activism: The Politics of Feeling Good.* Chico, CA: AK Press, 2019.

Dixon, Ejeris, and Leah Lakshmi Piepzna-Samarasinha, eds. *Beyond Survival: Strategies and Stories from the Transformative Justice Movement.* Chico, CA: AK Press, 2020.

Factora-Borchers, Lisa, ed. *Dear Sister: Letters from Survivors of Sexual Violence.* Chico, CA: AK Press, 2014.

Foo, Stephanie. *What My Bones Know: A Memoir of Healing from Complex Trauma.* New York, NY: Ballantine Books, 2022.

Herman, Judith, MD. *Trauma and Recovery: The Aftermath of Violence—from Domestic Abuse to Political Terror.* New York, NY: Basic Books, 2015.

Patterson, Jennifer, ed. *Queering Sexual Violence: Radical Voices from Within the Anti-Violence Movement.* Riverdale, NY: Riverdale Avenue Books, 2016.

Simmons, Aishah Shahidah, ed. *Love WITH Accountability: Digging Up the Roots of Child Sexual Abuse.* Chico, CA: AK Press, 2019.

Taylor, Sonya Renee. *The Body Is Not an Apology: The Power of Radical Self Love,* 2nd ed. Oakland, CA: Berrett-Koehler Publishers, 2021.

Tovar, Virgie. *You Have the Right to Remain Fat.* New York, NY: The Feminist Press at CUNY, 2018.

Acknowledgments

First and foremost, I want to thank each and every survivor who shared their words with me to be included in this book. It means more to me than I can say that you trusted me with your experiences and wisdom to be shared in this way, and I know that this book and my life are so much richer for having your voice as a part of it. I am forever so grateful for you.

While this is the only book I've written, I know that what we've gone through to bring it to life is remarkable. To Charlotte Ashlock, my editor, you believed in me and this project before I ever did and always helped me stay true to myself. You are incredible at your job. To Danielle Chiotti, my literary agent, every single day you championed me and centered my well-being, no matter what that needed to look like. You are the absolute tits.

The three of us created an extraordinary and transformative team to get this book into the world. I am so proud of the work we've done and even more proud of the way we did it. We brought our immense talents, vision, and personal stakes to share with each other on this long journey. I know this process was hard for each of us and required us to navigate countless triggers while doing the work we love. I am forever grateful for the ways you each ferociously advocated for this book and for me. I love what we've built together.

Thank you to the entire Berrett-Koehler team, including Ashley Ingram and Sarah Nelson, for supporting my baby and helping bring it into the world. Thank you to my reviewers Dani Wilson and Luna Merbruja for your invaluable feedback.

Thank you to Amita Swadhin, Ignacio Rivera, and Aishah Shahidah Simmons for being my favorite teachers and such wonderful friends. This project would not exist if not for the work you all have done for years to support survivors and create space for our truth. It's really great becoming friends with the people you most admire. I can't recommend it enough.

Thank you to my friends who have loved me for me and cheered me on every single step of the way: #Hamwarmedup and the G-House for always having my back. Sarah, Aaron, and Clive for accepting me exactly as I am and wanting me to come out with you even though you know I will cry in public. Anthony and Meghan for their constant encouragement and early readings of my writing. Jason Wasser for making my website baby. Danny for being an amazing cheerleader and the first to open my newsletter every Friday. Nelly for teaching me brain things and having a really good couch to cry on. Michelle for helping me read medical studies and also being my personal concierge doctor. Devonne for helping me be my strongest. Rebecca Grant for guidance and support. Mariah Miranda for your gorgeous photography.

To Kate, who changed my life by standing beside me in the darkness and seeing me so clearly even when light was nowhere to be found: you are my favorite thought partner, my ultimate style inspiration, and I am so grateful for all you've done to help me be here today.

To all my survivor friends who showed me the transformative power of being ourselves, together. To Dani, Dani, Sydney, and Brooke for our building something so beautiful together.

Thank you to my therapists past and present, Sandy, Susan, and Connie, for being wonderful therapeutic partners in healing.

To my family: my Chazie and Pops, Naomi for being my all-things-Jewish confidante, and our whole Katzman family, who are still the funniest people I've ever met. Thank you for teaching me how to tell a good story and loving me so fiercely.

To my chosen father, John Quale, for providing me love, support, and safety. Your love reverberates through every day of my life.

To Holmes for teaching me the healing power of the river and supporting me in every imaginable way.

To my sister, Rachel, and brother-in-law, Carlos, there are no people I love more or who make me laugh harder.

To my mom, thank God you already know how I feel about you or we'd be here forever. You have modeled for me how to love deeply, live boldly, and fight for what is important. Thank you for all you have done to support me in my healing and in taking on this project, emotionally, physically, financially, and beyond.

To Franklin Coy Zipursky, my dog, my miracle child, and Healing Honestly's most-improved (and only) employee, thank you for helping me manage all of the triggers and dissociation and reminding me that being present here with you is exactly where I want to be.

And lastly, to Charlie. You never once doubted that I could do this, even though I doubted it so many times. You never let a milestone pass without celebration, a trigger pass without deep love and endless compassion, or a hard day pass without telling me that rest is part of writing too. Thank you for all the cups of tea, all the reminders to take my meds, and all the hours spent watching *The Golden Girls* with me, and for doing every single thing you could possibly think of to help me get to this moment. I would wolf all the teamster subs for you. I love you.

Index

brain, and neurobiology of trauma,
30–32
brown, adrienne maree, xiii, 110, 196
Burke, Tarana, 21, 191
ButYouDontLookSick.com, 81

C

Call Your Girlfriend (podcast), 178,
179
capitalism in conflict with healing,
77, 171, 176–177, 178
celebration, moments of, 218–221
celibacy, as healing strategy, 107
Center for Institutional Courage,
24, 181
Child Protective Services (CPS), 195
Christianity and forgiveness, 201
chronic illness, 55–56, 81
Coel, Michaela, 212
communication
as a parent, 161–163
in relationships, 128–131
community-level denial, 147–148
compassion, 15–16, 198
confrontations with abusers,
186–188
consent
teaching children about, 160–161
in work environments, 178–179
cortisol, 56–57
court system, 28–29
covert/emotional incest, 141–142
C-PTSD (complex post-traumatic
stress disorder), 54–55, 81.
See also PTSD (post-traumatic
stress disorder)
craniosacral therapy, 65
criminal legal system, 28–29, 195

D

data collection to track triggers,
37–39
dating. *See* romantic relationships
Davies, Jody Messler, 41
denial
on community level, 147–148
on family level, 153–157
Deny, Attack and Reverse Victim
and Offender (DARVO), 144–
145, 181
Dick Wolf effect, 28–29, 192–193
disability community, 12, 77–78.
See also ableism
disclosing our stories, 123–127
diseases and conditions, 55–56, 81

E

EDMR (Eye Movement
Desensitization and
Reprocessing), 23
emotional/covert incest, 141–142
energy levels and spoon theory,
80–83

F

False Memory Syndrome
Foundation (FMSF), 24–27
false narratives. *See* untrue stories
family building, 158–159
family level denial, 153–157
family level healing, 167–169
family loyalty, 148–149
family reactions, 119–120
fantasy and role-playing, 98–99
fat liberation, 64
Fields, Jaden, 11–12, 77–78, 85,
98–99, 123, 132, 134–136, 179,
184, 191, 198–199

pleasure, 109–111. *See also* sexuality
Pleasure Activism (brown, editor),
    xiii, 110
popular culture, 122
psychiatrists. *See* Therapists
PTSD (post-traumatic stress
    disorder), 77. *See also* C-PTSD
    (complex post-traumatic stress
    disorder)
purity culture, 95–96

R
rage, 198–200
rape culture, 93
rape fantasies, 98–99
religion and forgiveness, 201–202
reparenting ourselves, 158
reporting, guilt surrounding,
    188–191
repression of trauma, 30–31, 76
responsibility, allocation of, 182–183,
    196–197
revenge fantasies, 199–200
Rivera, Ignacio, 68, 97, 98, 108, 110,
    111, 158
Rivera, Sylvia, 71
role-playing and fantasy, 98–99
romantic relationships
    and accountability, 131–133
    and communication, 128–131
    and disclosure conversations,
        123–127
    qualities to seek in partners,
        136–137
    and untrue stories, 113–122
rom-coms, 122

S
safety plans, 67, 130
self-advocacy, 67–69
self-blame, 121, 143
self-compassion, 15–16, 177, 202,
    218–219
self-criticism, 61
self-doubt, 40–42
self-knowledge, 35–37
self-responsibility, 134
sensorimotor psychotherapy, 65
sexism, 94
sexuality
    all-or-nothing thinking, 108–109
    body wisdom, 100–101
    fluctuating levels of desire, 104
    lack of desire for sex, 102–107
    sexual healing, 91, 98–99
    and shame, 92–95, 97–98
Simmons, Aishah Shahidah, 86, 120,
    123, 128, 131–133, 136, 145,
    151–152, 158, 198, 201–202, 214,
    217–218, 220
slut-shaming, 92–93, 100–101
Somatic Experiencing, 65
somatic therapy, 65
Sow, Aminatou, 178, 179
spoon theory, 80–83
Stanton, Mike, 26
storytelling, in third person, 39–40
support teams and networks of care,
    85
suppression of emotions, 62–63
survival behaviors, 60–62
Swadhin, Amita, 55, 93, 148, 158, 177,
    194–196, 209

About the Author

© Mariah Miranda

Alisa Zipursky is a storyteller, writer, facilitator, and child sexual abuse survivor. She is the founder of HealingHonestly.com, where she offers survivor-to-survivor support in healing from sexual trauma. She has written for publications including *Allure* and *Teen Vogue*. When she isn't writing, Alisa travels around the country giving talks and facilitating workshops to support other young survivors in their communities. Alisa lives in Washington, DC.

You can find additional resources and learn more about working with Alisa at HealingHonestly.com.

Dear reader,

Thank you for picking up this book and welcome to the worldwide BK community! You're joining a special group of people who have come together to create positive change in their lives, organizations, and communities.

What's BK all about?

Our mission is to connect people and ideas to create a world that works for all.

Why? Our communities, organizations, and lives get bogged down by old paradigms of self-interest, exclusion, hierarchy, and privilege. But we believe that can change. That's why we seek the leading experts on these challenges—and share their actionable ideas with you.

A welcome gift

To help you get started, we'd like to offer you a **free copy** of one of our bestselling ebooks:

www.bkconnection.com/welcome

When you claim your **free ebook**, you'll also be subscribed to our blog.

Our freshest insights

Access the best new tools and ideas for leaders at all levels on our blog at ideas.bkconnection.com.

Sincerely,

Your friends at Berrett-Koehler

Certified

Corporation